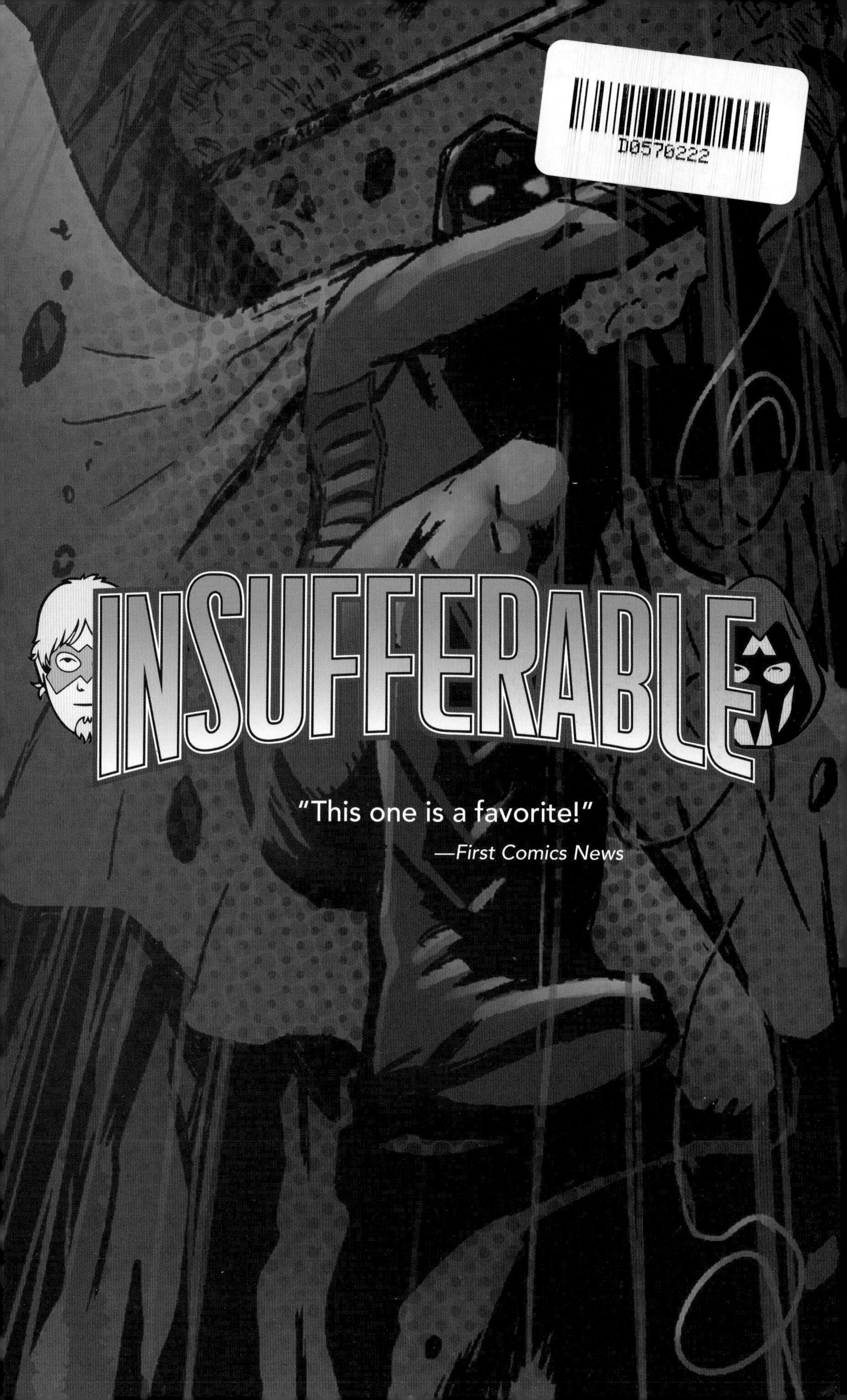

INSUFFERABLE

"This one is a favorite!"

—*First Comics News*

IDW

You Tube

A *THRILLBENT* Publication.

Become our fan on Facebook **facebook.com/idwpublishing**
Follow us on Twitter **@idwpublishing**
Subscribe to us on YouTube **youtube.com/idwpublishing**
See what's new on Tumblr **tumblr.idwpublishing.com**
Check us out on Instagram **instagram.com/idwpublishing**

ISBN: 978-1-63140-609-6   19 18 17 16   1 2 3 4

COVER ART BY
PETER KRAUSE

COLLECTION EDITS BY
JUSTIN EISINGER
AND ALONZO SIMON

PUBLISHER
TED ADAMS

COLLECTION DESIGN BY
GILBERTO LAZCANO

INSUFFERABLE, VOLUME 2. MAY 2016. FIRST PRINTING.
Insufferable® is a registered trademark, © 2016 Mark Waid and
Peter Krause, all rights reserved. The stories, characters, and
incidents featured in this publication are entirely fictional. © 2016
Idea and Design Works, LLC. The IDW logo is registered in the
U.S. Patent and Trademark Office. IDW Publishing, a division of
Idea and Design Works, LLC. Editorial offices: 2765 Truxtun Road,
San Diego, CA 92106. Any similarities to persons living or dead
are purely coincidental. With the exception of artwork used for
review purposes, none of the contents of this publication may be
reprinted without the permission of Idea and Design Works, LLC.
Printed in Korea.

IDW Publishing does not read or accept unsolicited submissions
of ideas, stories, or artwork.

Originally published as INSUFFERABLE #5–8.

Ted Adams, CEO & Publisher
Greg Goldstein, President & COO
Robbie Robbins, EVP/Sr. Graphic Artist
Chris Ryall, Chief Creative Officer/Editor-in-Chief
Matthew Ruzicka, CPA, Chief Financial Officer
Dirk Wood, VP of Marketing
Lorelei Bunjes, VP of Digital Services
Jeff Webber, VP of Digital Publishing & Business Development
Jerry Bennington, VP of New Product Development

For international rights, please contact
licensing@idwpublishing.com

INSUFFERABLE CREATED BY
MARK WAID AND PETER KRAUSE

WRITER / STORYTELLERS / ARTIST
MARK WAID
& PETER KRAUSE

COLORIST
NOLAN WOODARD

LETTERER
TROY PETERI

SERIES EDITOR
MICHAEL BENEDETTO

CHAPTER FIVE

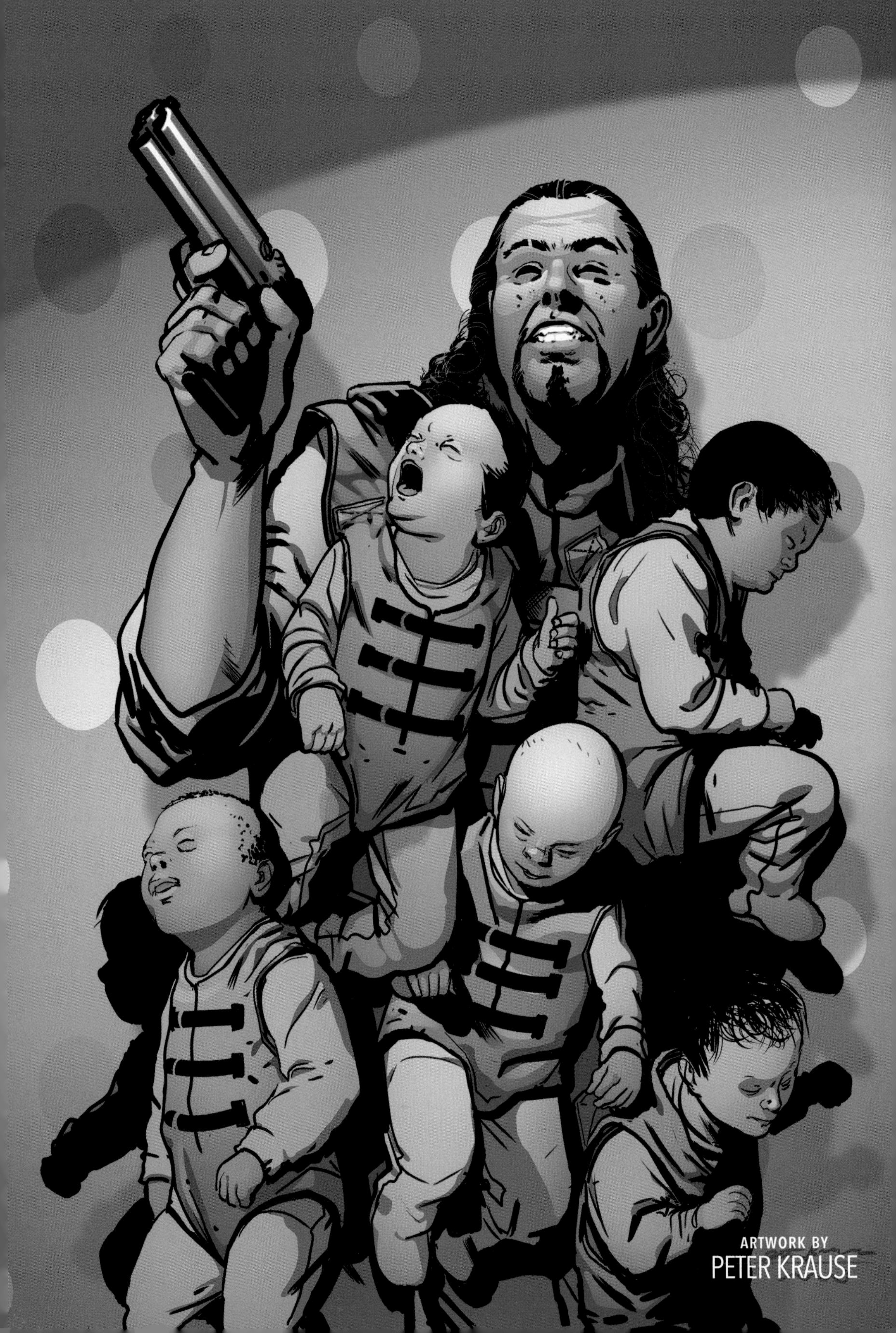

ARTWORK BY
PETER KRAUSE

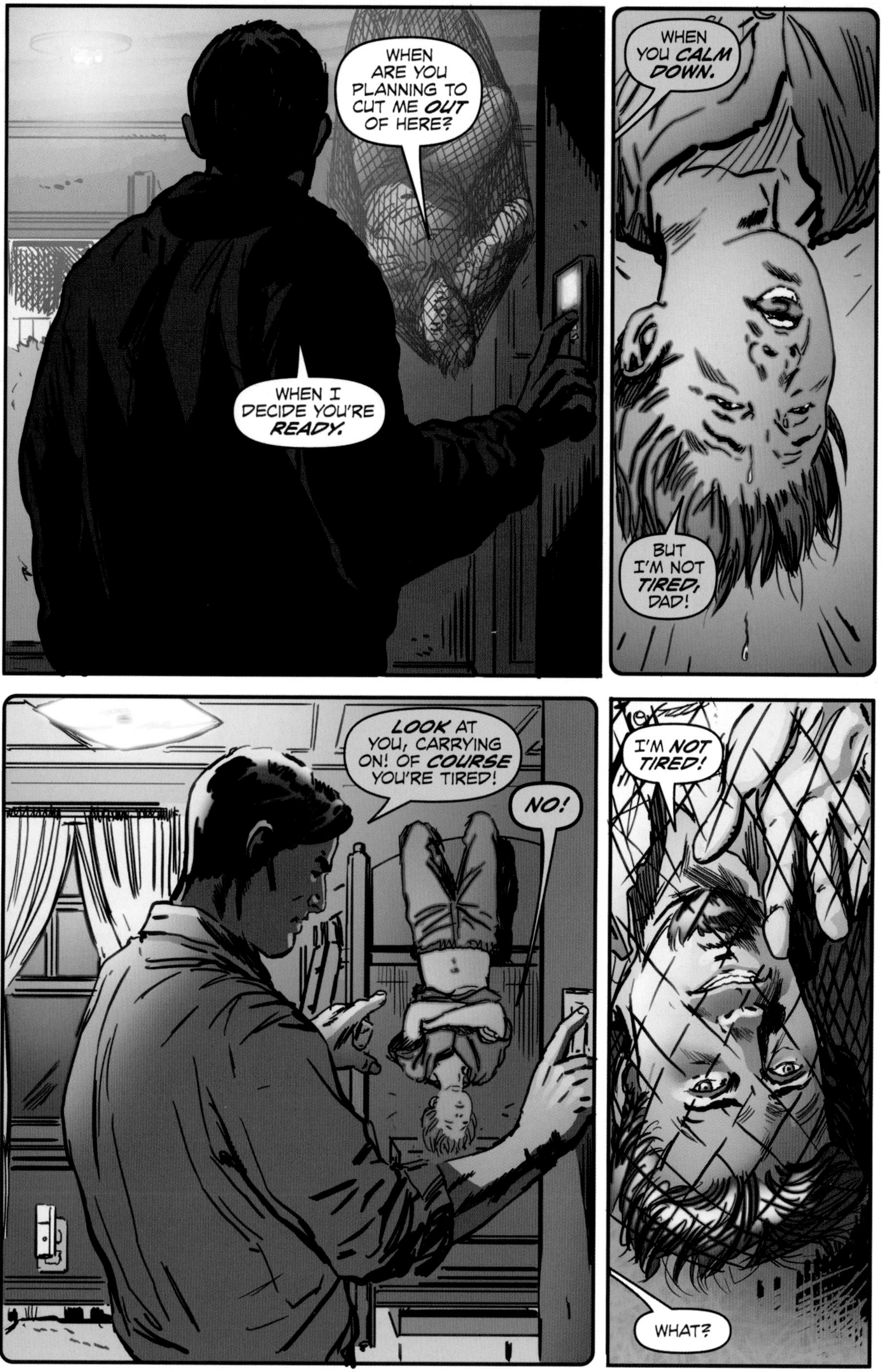
WHEN ARE YOU PLANNING TO CUT ME OUT OF HERE?
WHEN I DECIDE YOU'RE READY.
WHEN YOU CALM DOWN.
BUT I'M NOT TIRED, DAD!
LOOK AT YOU, CARRYING ON! OF COURSE YOU'RE TIRED!
NO!
I'M NOT TIRED!
WHAT?

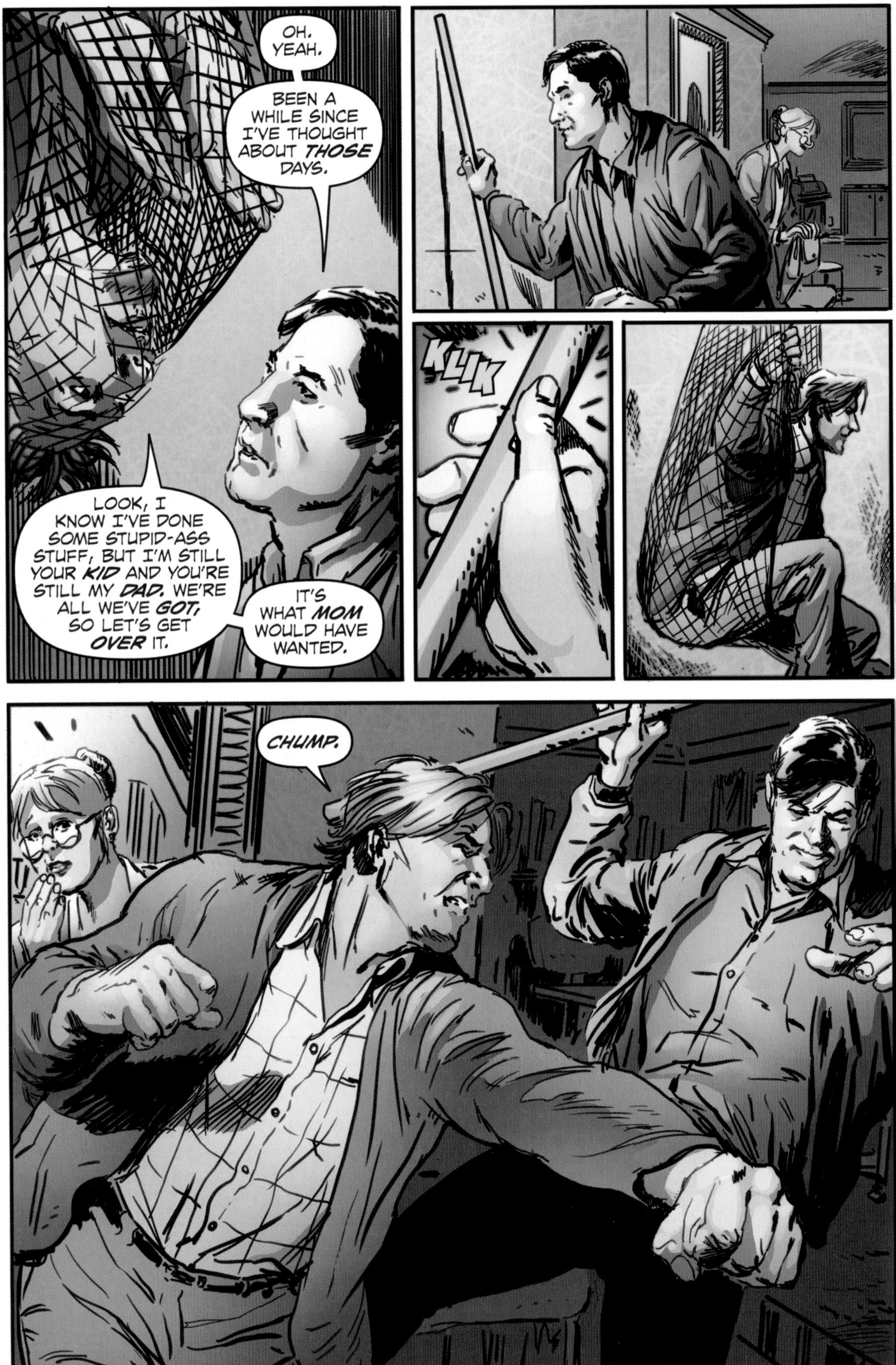
OH. YEAH.
BEEN A WHILE SINCE I'VE THOUGHT ABOUT THOSE DAYS.
LOOK, I KNOW I'VE DONE SOME STUPID-ASS STUFF, BUT I'M STILL YOUR KID AND YOU'RE STILL MY DAD. WE'RE ALL WE'VE GOT, SO LET'S GET OVER IT.
IT'S WHAT MOM WOULD HAVE WANTED.
KLIK
CHUMP.

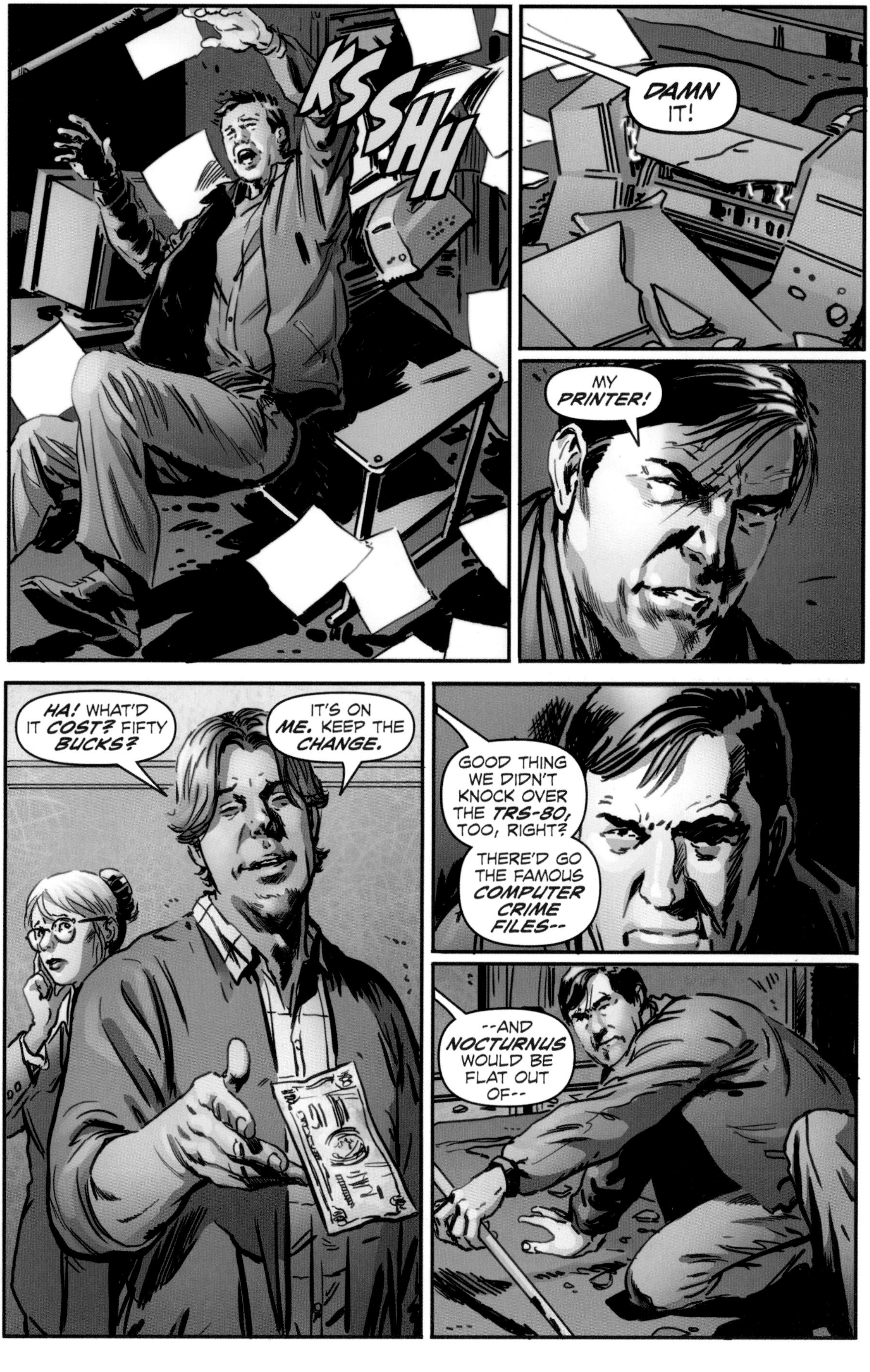
KSSHH
DAMN IT!
MY PRINTER!
HA! WHAT'D IT COST? FIFTY BUCKS?
IT'S ON ME. KEEP THE CHANGE.
GOOD THING WE DIDN'T KNOCK OVER THE TRS-80, TOO, RIGHT?
THERE'D GO THE FAMOUS COMPUTER CRIME FILES--
--AND NOCTURNUS WOULD BE FLAT OUT OF--

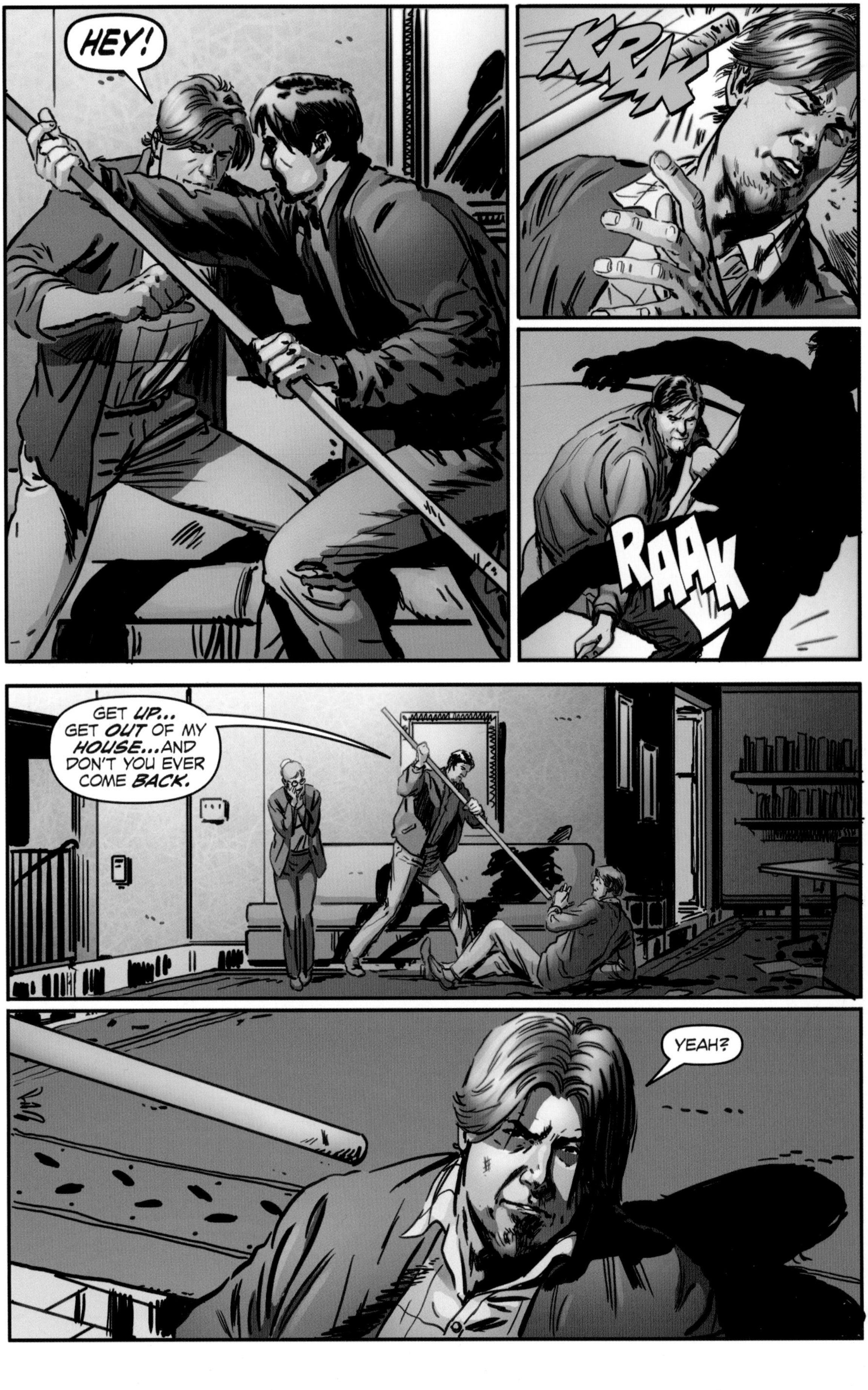
HEY!
KRAK
RAAK
GET UP... GET OUT OF MY HOUSE...AND DON'T YOU EVER COME BACK.
YEAH?

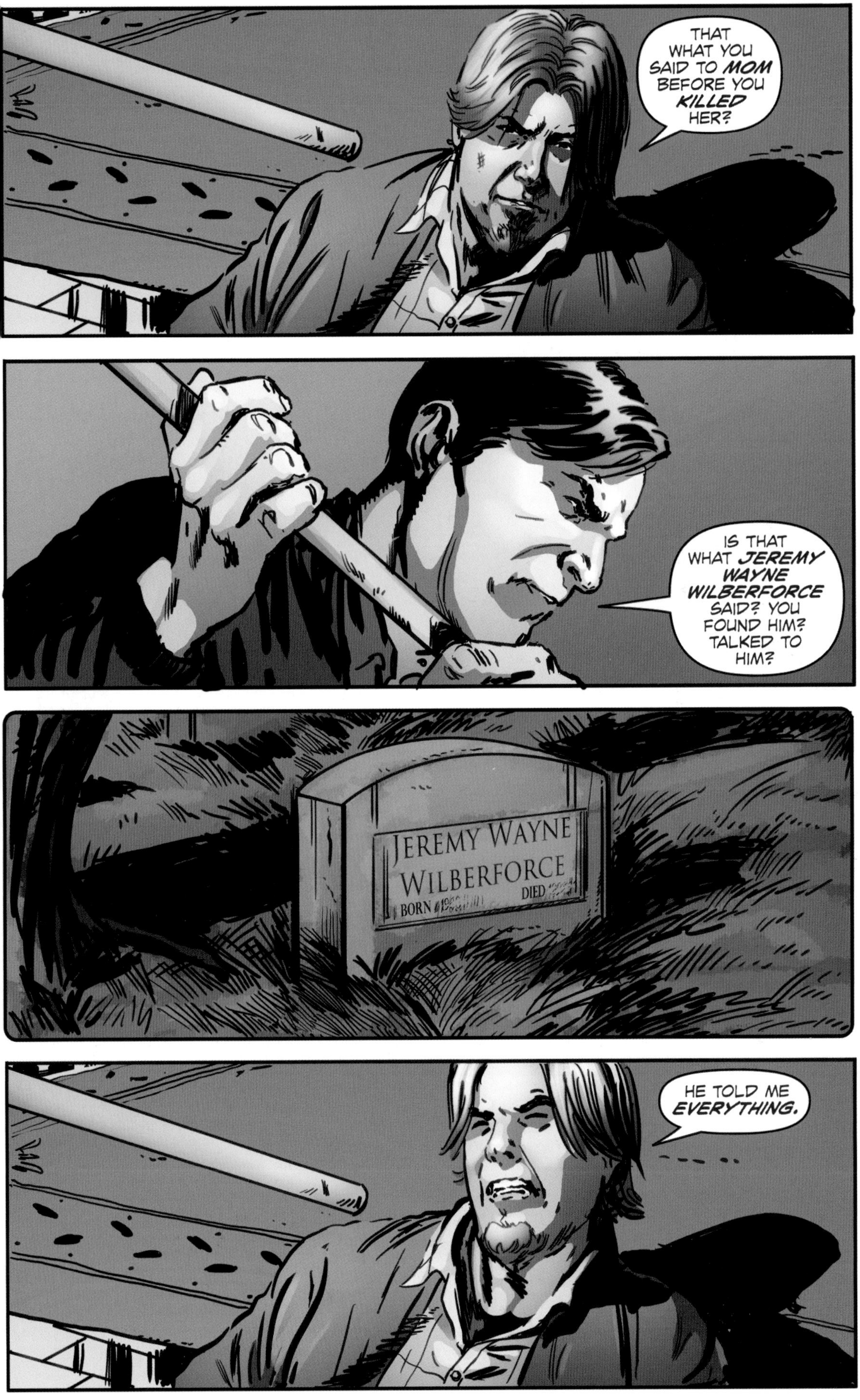
THAT WHAT YOU SAID TO MOM BEFORE YOU KILLED HER?
IS THAT WHAT JEREMY WAYNE WILBERFORCE SAID? YOU FOUND HIM? TALKED TO HIM?
JEREMY WAYNE
WILBERFORCE
BORN
DIED
HE TOLD ME EVERYTHING.

WRONG ANSWER.

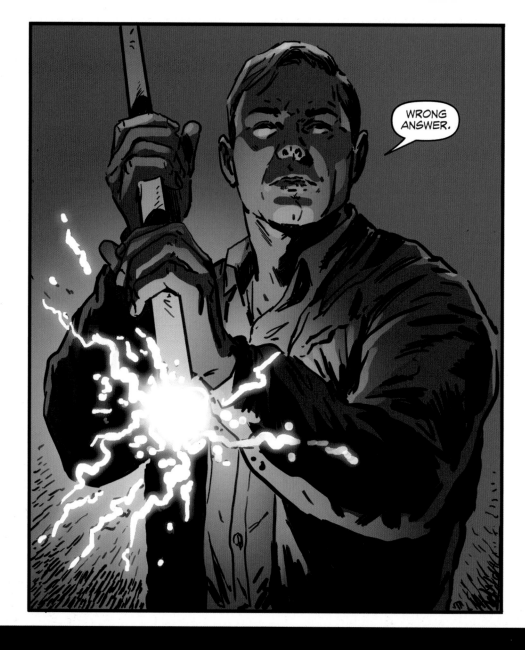

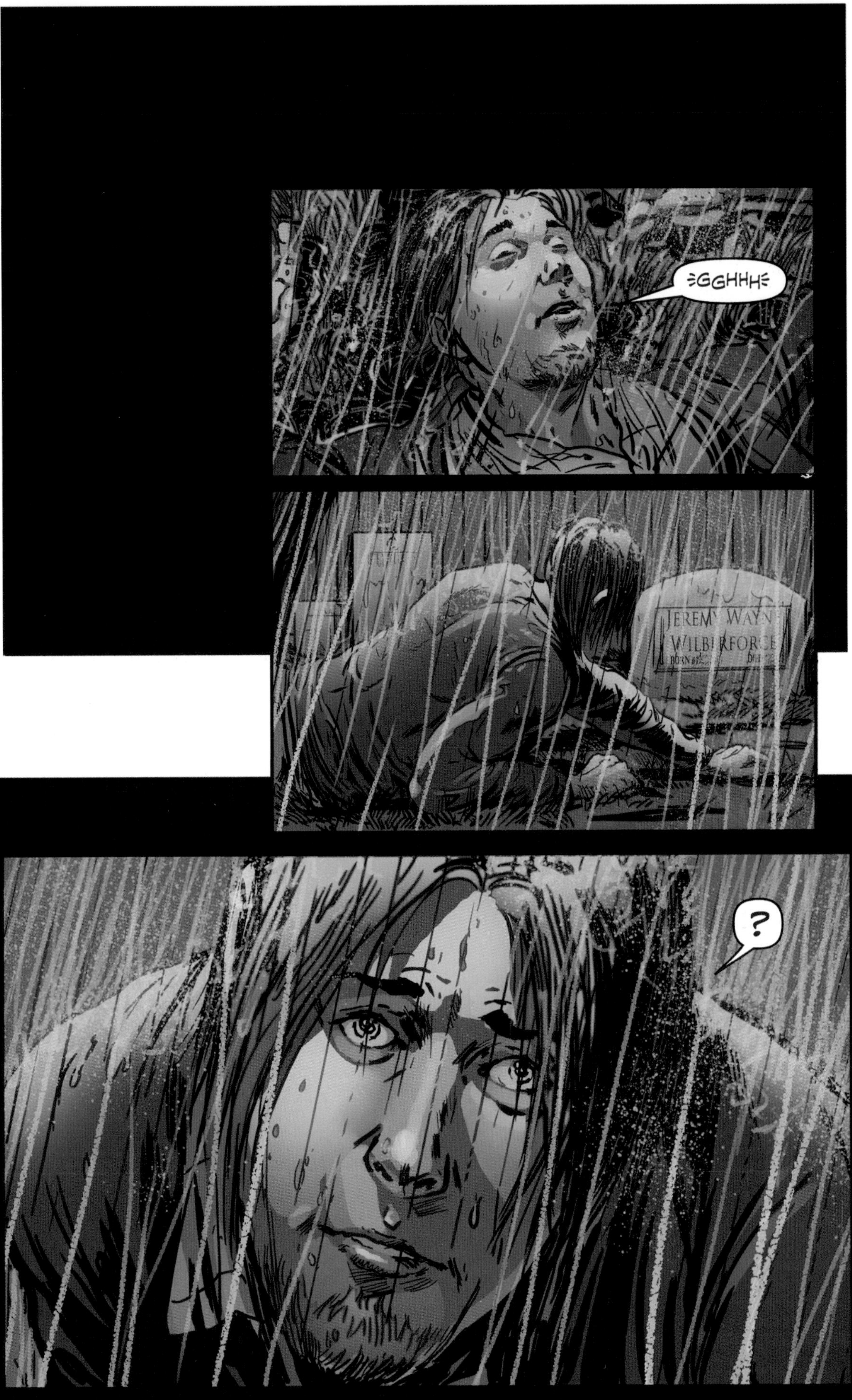
GGHHH
JEREMY WAYN
WILBERFORCE
?

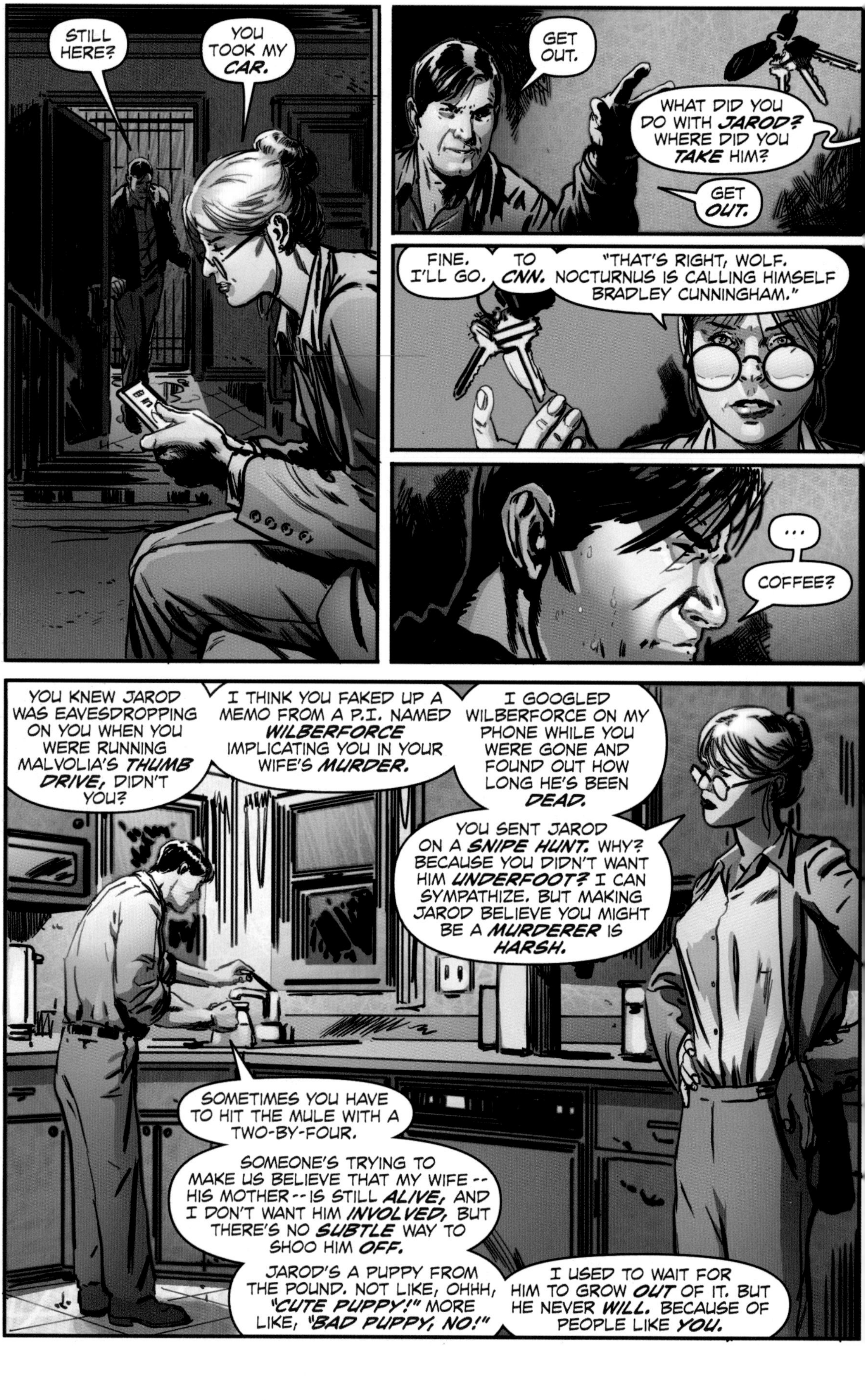
STILL HERE?
YOU TOOK MY CAR.
GET OUT.
WHAT DID YOU DO WITH JAROD? WHERE DID YOU TAKE HIM?
GET OUT.
FINE. I'LL GO.
TO CNN.
"THAT'S RIGHT, WOLF. NOCTURNUS IS CALLING HIMSELF BRADLEY CUNNINGHAM."
...
COFFEE?
YOU KNEW JAROD WAS EAVESDROPPING ON YOU WHEN YOU WERE RUNNING MALVOLIA'S THUMB DRIVE, DIDN'T YOU?
I THINK YOU FAKED UP A MEMO FROM A P.I. NAMED WILBERFORCE IMPLICATING YOU IN YOUR WIFE'S MURDER.
I GOOGLED WILBERFORCE ON MY PHONE WHILE YOU WERE GONE AND FOUND OUT HOW LONG HE'S BEEN DEAD.
YOU SENT JAROD ON A SNIPE HUNT. WHY? BECAUSE YOU DIDN'T WANT HIM UNDERFOOT? I CAN SYMPATHIZE. BUT MAKING JAROD BELIEVE YOU MIGHT BE A MURDERER IS HARSH.
SOMETIMES YOU HAVE TO HIT THE MULE WITH A TWO-BY-FOUR.
SOMEONE'S TRYING TO MAKE US BELIEVE THAT MY WIFE -- HIS MOTHER -- IS STILL ALIVE, AND I DON'T WANT HIM INVOLVED, BUT THERE'S NO SUBTLE WAY TO SHOO HIM OFF.
JAROD'S A PUPPY FROM THE POUND. NOT LIKE, OHHH, "CUTE PUPPY!" MORE LIKE, "BAD PUPPY, NO!"
I USED TO WAIT FOR HIM TO GROW OUT OF IT. BUT HE NEVER WILL. BECAUSE OF PEOPLE LIKE YOU.

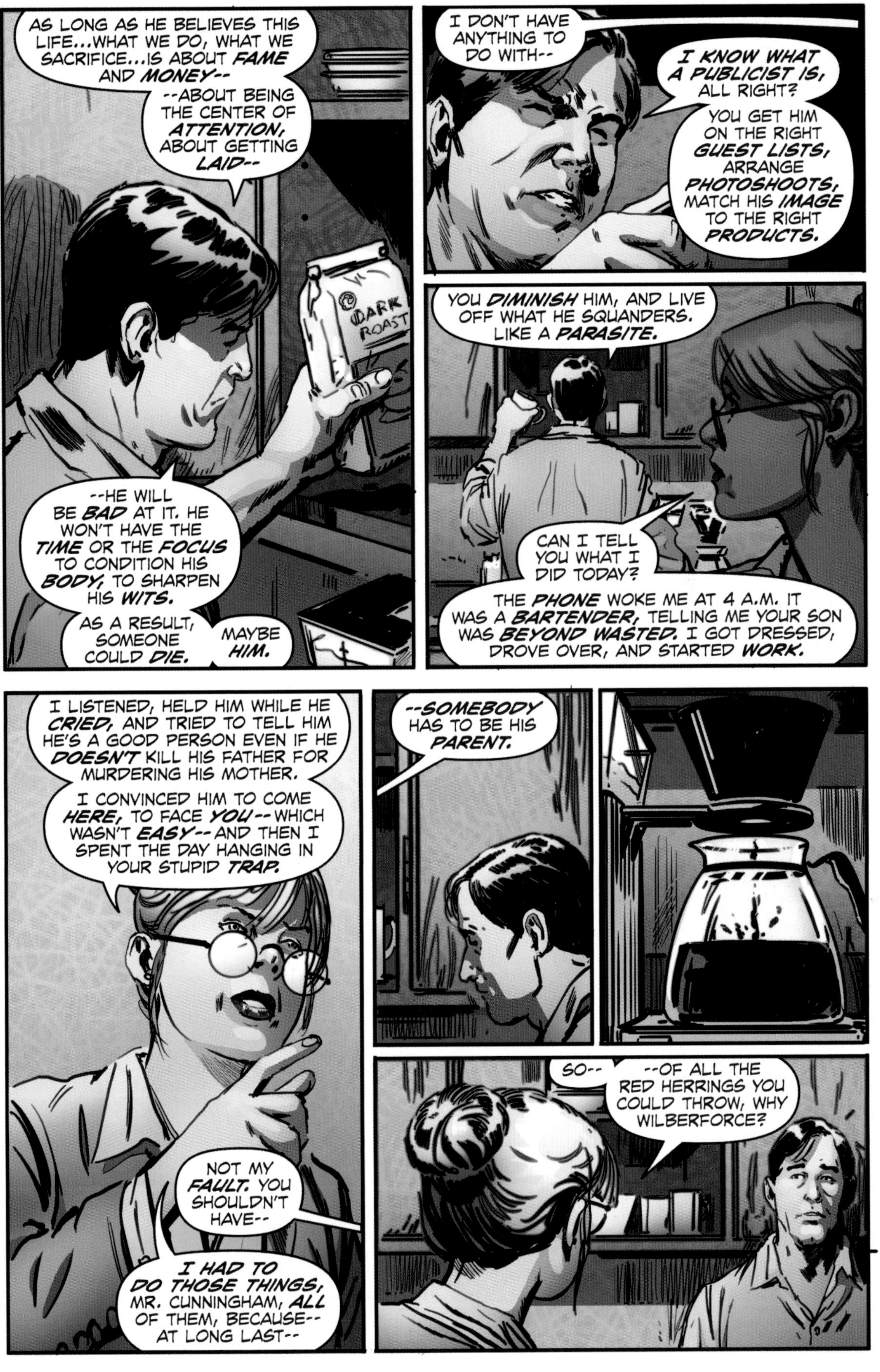
AS LONG AS HE BELIEVES THIS LIFE...WHAT WE DO, WHAT WE SACRIFICE...IS ABOUT FAME AND MONEY--
--ABOUT BEING THE CENTER OF ATTENTION, ABOUT GETTING LAID--
DARK ROAST
--HE WILL BE BAD AT IT. HE WON'T HAVE THE TIME OR THE FOCUS TO CONDITION HIS BODY, TO SHARPEN HIS WITS.
AS A RESULT, SOMEONE COULD DIE.
MAYBE HIM.
I DON'T HAVE ANYTHING TO DO WITH--
I KNOW WHAT A PUBLICIST IS, ALL RIGHT?
YOU GET HIM ON THE RIGHT GUEST LISTS, ARRANGE PHOTOSHOOTS, MATCH HIS IMAGE TO THE RIGHT PRODUCTS.
YOU DIMINISH HIM, AND LIVE OFF WHAT HE SQUANDERS. LIKE A PARASITE.
CAN I TELL YOU WHAT I DID TODAY?
THE PHONE WOKE ME AT 4 A.M. IT WAS A BARTENDER, TELLING ME YOUR SON WAS BEYOND WASTED. I GOT DRESSED, DROVE OVER, AND STARTED WORK.
I LISTENED, HELD HIM WHILE HE CRIED, AND TRIED TO TELL HIM HE'S A GOOD PERSON EVEN IF HE DOESN'T KILL HIS FATHER FOR MURDERING HIS MOTHER.
I CONVINCED HIM TO COME HERE, TO FACE YOU--WHICH WASN'T EASY--AND THEN I SPENT THE DAY HANGING IN YOUR STUPID TRAP.
NOT MY FAULT. YOU SHOULDN'T HAVE--
I HAD TO DO THOSE THINGS, MR. CUNNINGHAM, ALL OF THEM, BECAUSE--AT LONG LAST--
--SOMEBODY HAS TO BE HIS PARENT.
SO--
--OF ALL THE RED HERRINGS YOU COULD THROW, WHY WILBERFORCE?

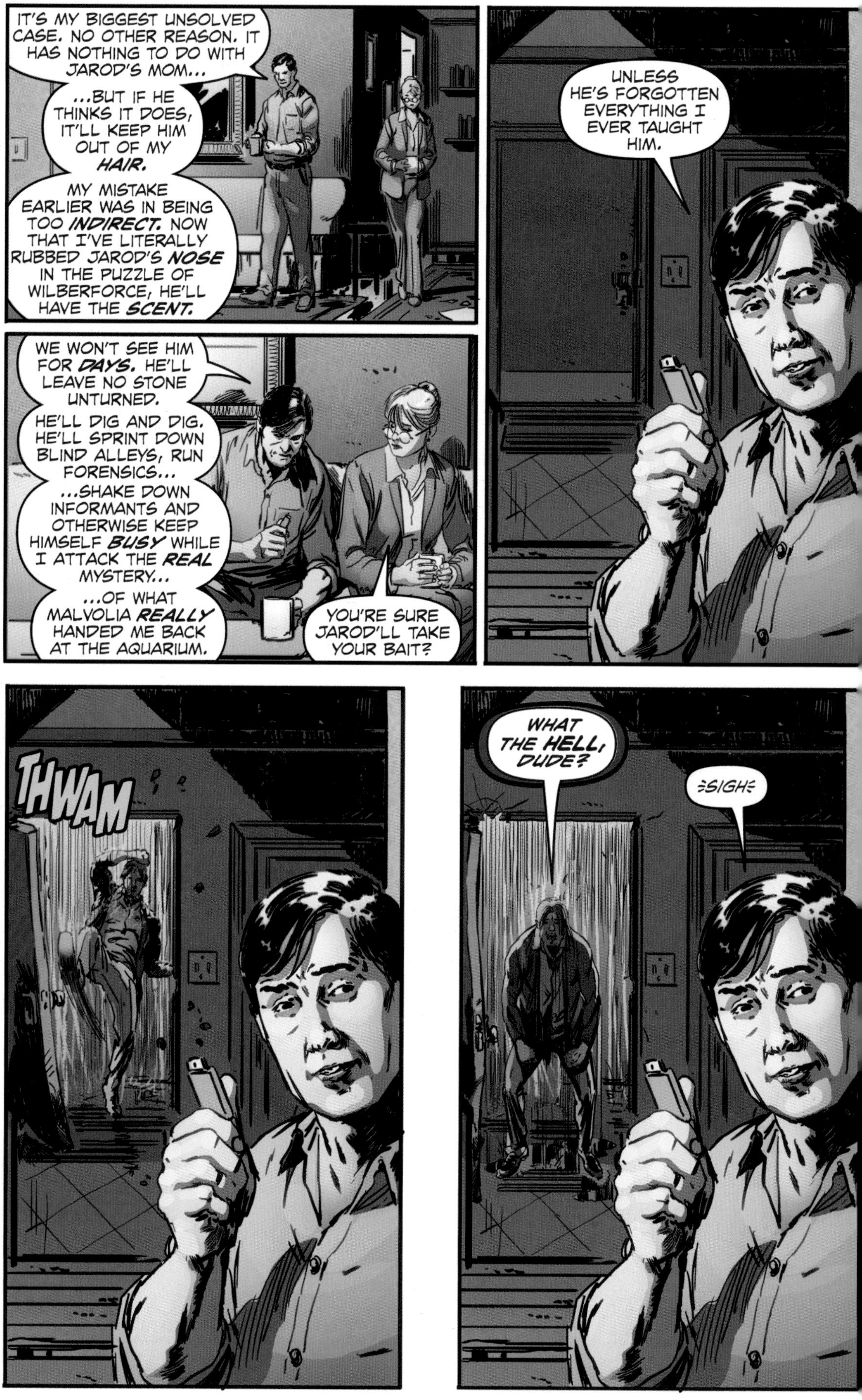
IT'S MY BIGGEST UNSOLVED CASE. NO OTHER REASON. IT HAS NOTHING TO DO WITH JAROD'S MOM...
...BUT IF HE THINKS IT DOES, IT'LL KEEP HIM OUT OF MY HAIR.
MY MISTAKE EARLIER WAS IN BEING TOO INDIRECT. NOW THAT I'VE LITERALLY RUBBED JAROD'S NOSE IN THE PUZZLE OF WILBERFORCE, HE'LL HAVE THE SCENT.
WE WON'T SEE HIM FOR DAYS. HE'LL LEAVE NO STONE UNTURNED.
HE'LL DIG AND DIG. HE'LL SPRINT DOWN BLIND ALLEYS, RUN FORENSICS...
...SHAKE DOWN INFORMANTS AND OTHERWISE KEEP HIMSELF BUSY WHILE I ATTACK THE REAL MYSTERY...
...OF WHAT MALVOLIA REALLY HANDED ME BACK AT THE AQUARIUM.
YOU'RE SURE JAROD'LL TAKE YOUR BAIT?
UNLESS HE'S FORGOTTEN EVERYTHING I EVER TAUGHT HIM.
THWAM
WHAT THE HELL, DUDE?
SIGH

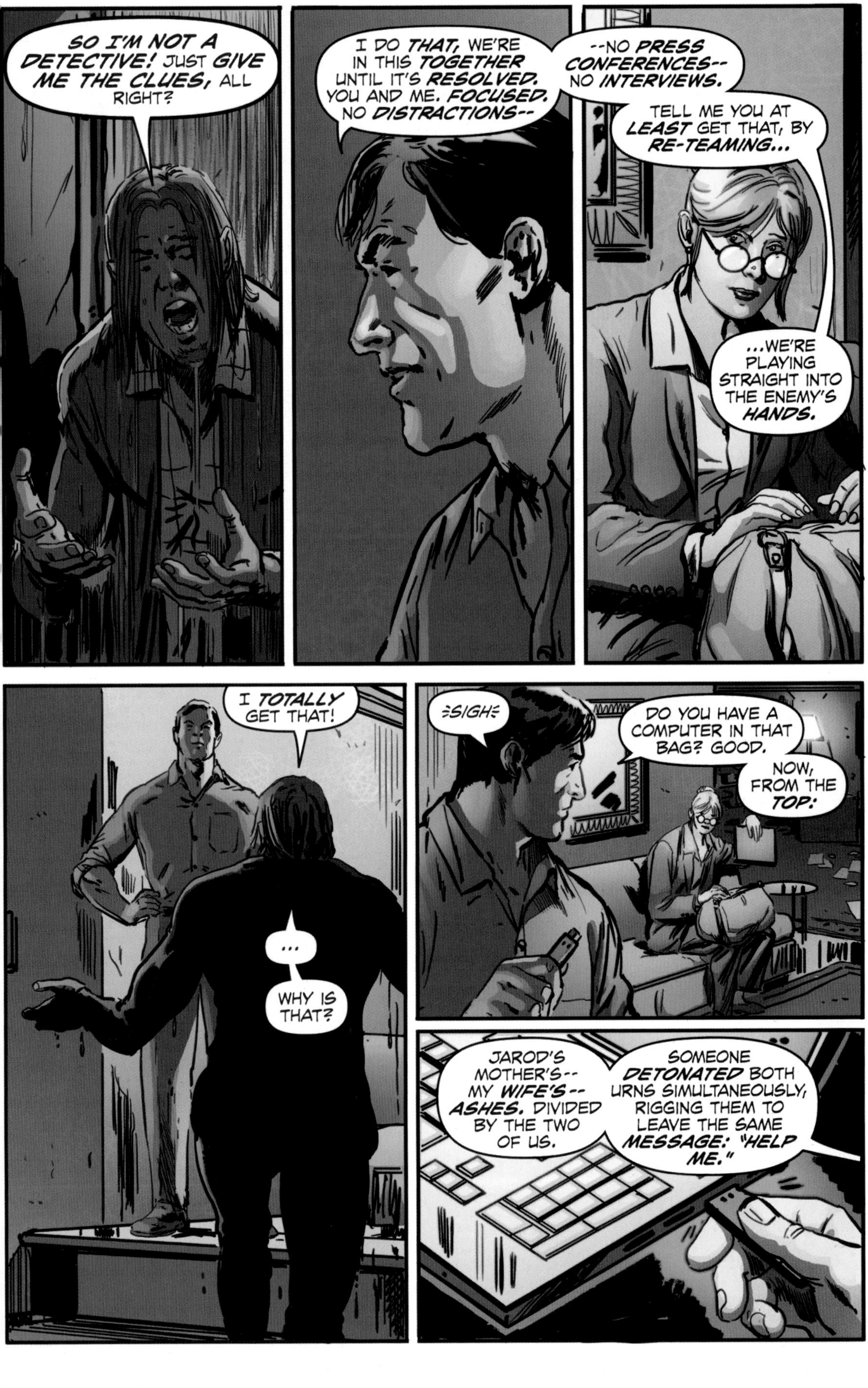
SO I'M NOT A DETECTIVE! JUST GIVE ME THE CLUES, ALL RIGHT?
I DO THAT, WE'RE IN THIS TOGETHER UNTIL IT'S RESOLVED. YOU AND ME. FOCUSED. NO DISTRACTIONS--
--NO PRESS CONFERENCES-- NO INTERVIEWS.
TELL ME YOU AT LEAST GET THAT, BY RE-TEAMING...
...WE'RE PLAYING STRAIGHT INTO THE ENEMY'S HANDS.
I TOTALLY GET THAT!
...
WHY IS THAT?
SIGH
DO YOU HAVE A COMPUTER IN THAT BAG? GOOD.
NOW, FROM THE TOP:
JAROD'S MOTHER'S-- MY WIFE'S-- ASHES. DIVIDED BY THE TWO OF US.
SOMEONE DETONATED BOTH URNS SIMULTANEOUSLY, RIGGING THEM TO LEAVE THE SAME MESSAGE: "HELP ME."

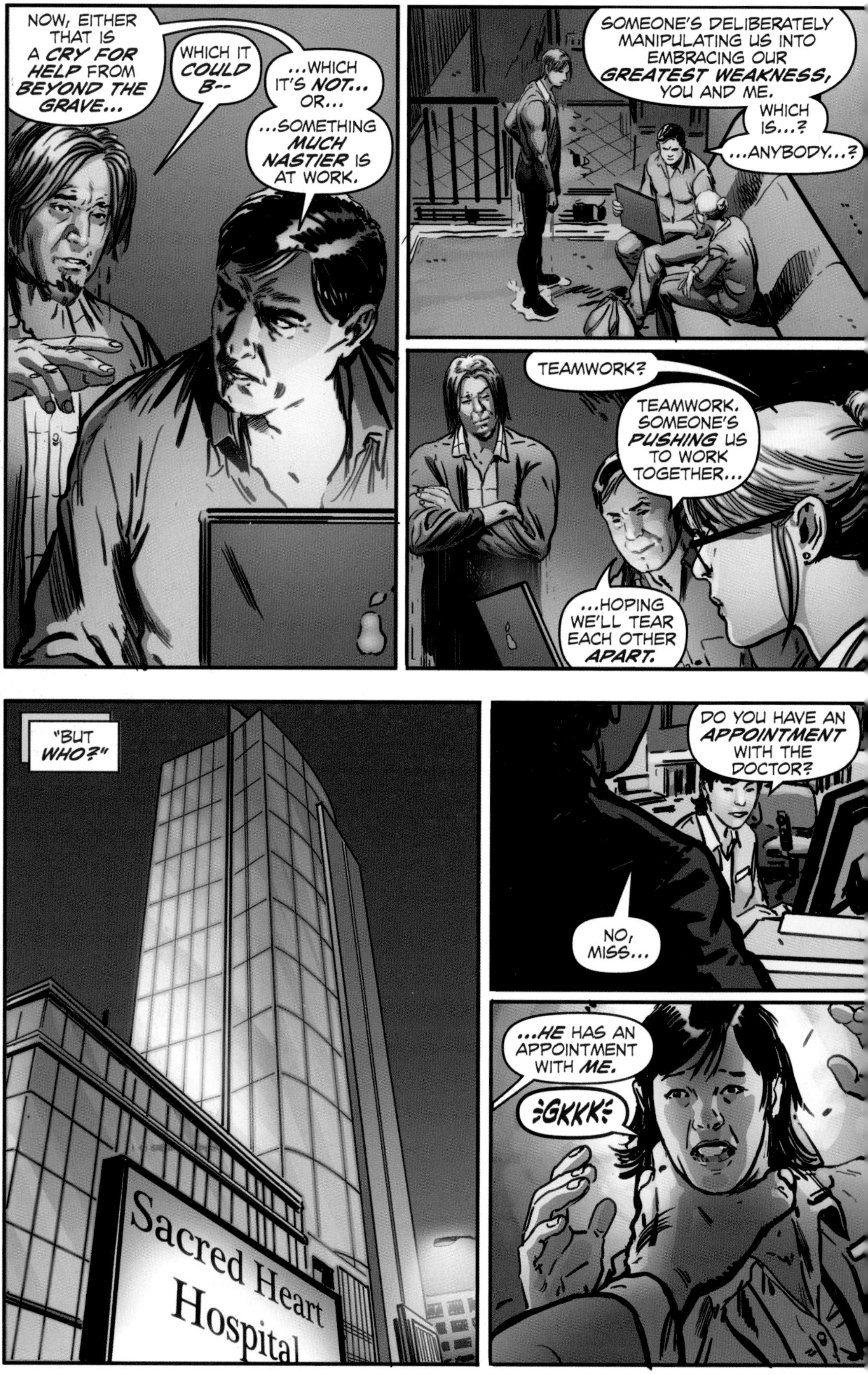
NOW, EITHER THAT IS A CRY FOR HELP FROM BEYOND THE GRAVE...
WHICH IT COULD B--
...WHICH IT'S NOT... OR...
...SOMETHING MUCH NASTIER IS AT WORK.
SOMEONE'S DELIBERATELY MANIPULATING US INTO EMBRACING OUR GREATEST WEAKNESS, YOU AND ME.
WHICH IS...?
...ANYBODY...?
TEAMWORK?
TEAMWORK. SOMEONE'S PUSHING US TO WORK TOGETHER...
...HOPING WE'LL TEAR EACH OTHER APART.
"BUT WHO?"
Sacred Heart Hospital
DO YOU HAVE AN APPOINTMENT WITH THE DOCTOR?
NO, MISS...
...HE HAS AN APPOINTMENT WITH ME.
GKKK

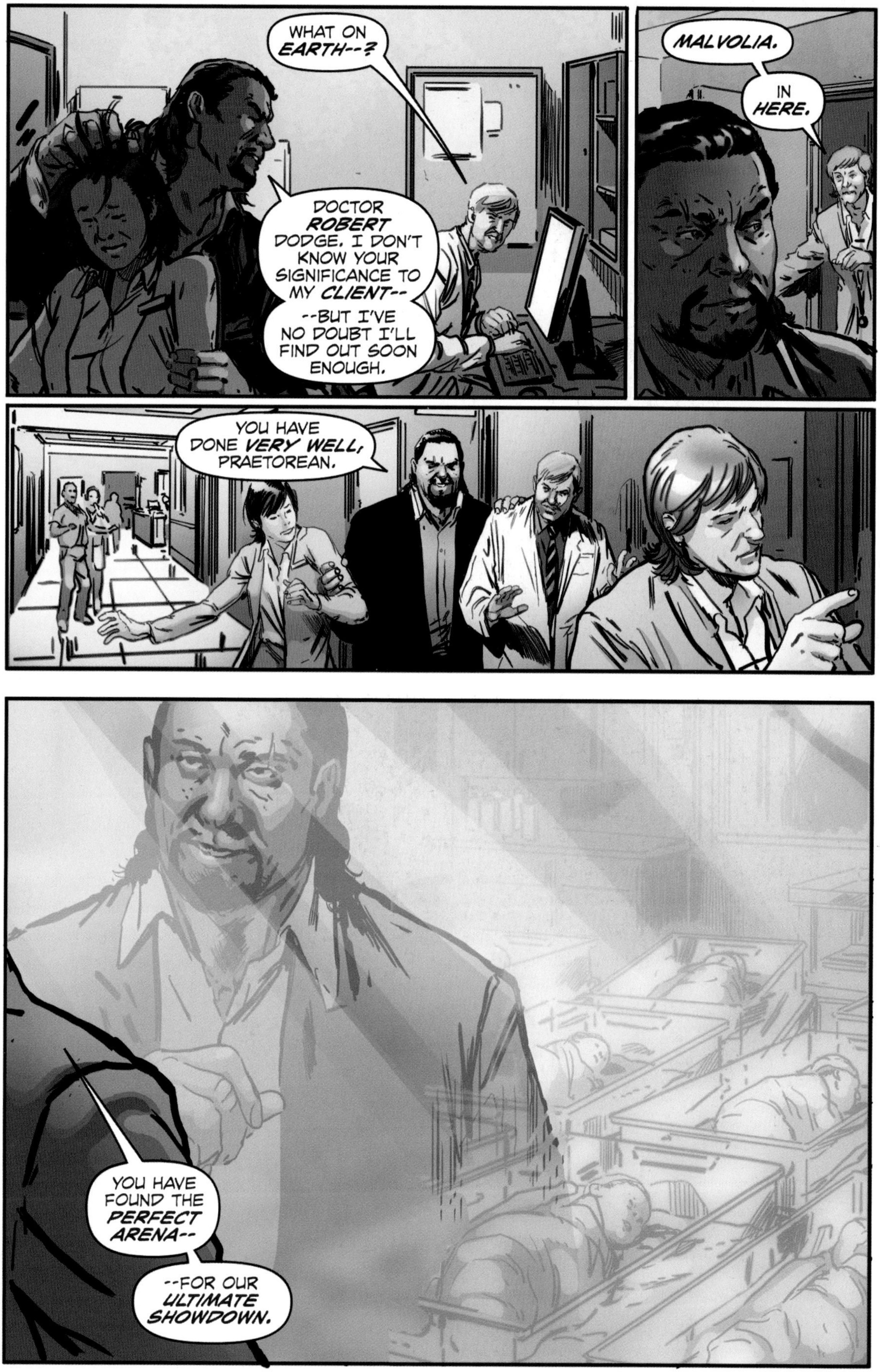

WHAT ON EARTH--?
DOCTOR ROBERT DODGE. I DON'T KNOW YOUR SIGNIFICANCE TO MY CLIENT--
--BUT I'VE NO DOUBT I'LL FIND OUT SOON ENOUGH.
MALVOLIA.
IN HERE.
YOU HAVE DONE VERY WELL, PRAETOREAN.
YOU HAVE FOUND THE PERFECT ARENA--
--FOR OUR ULTIMATE SHOWDOWN.

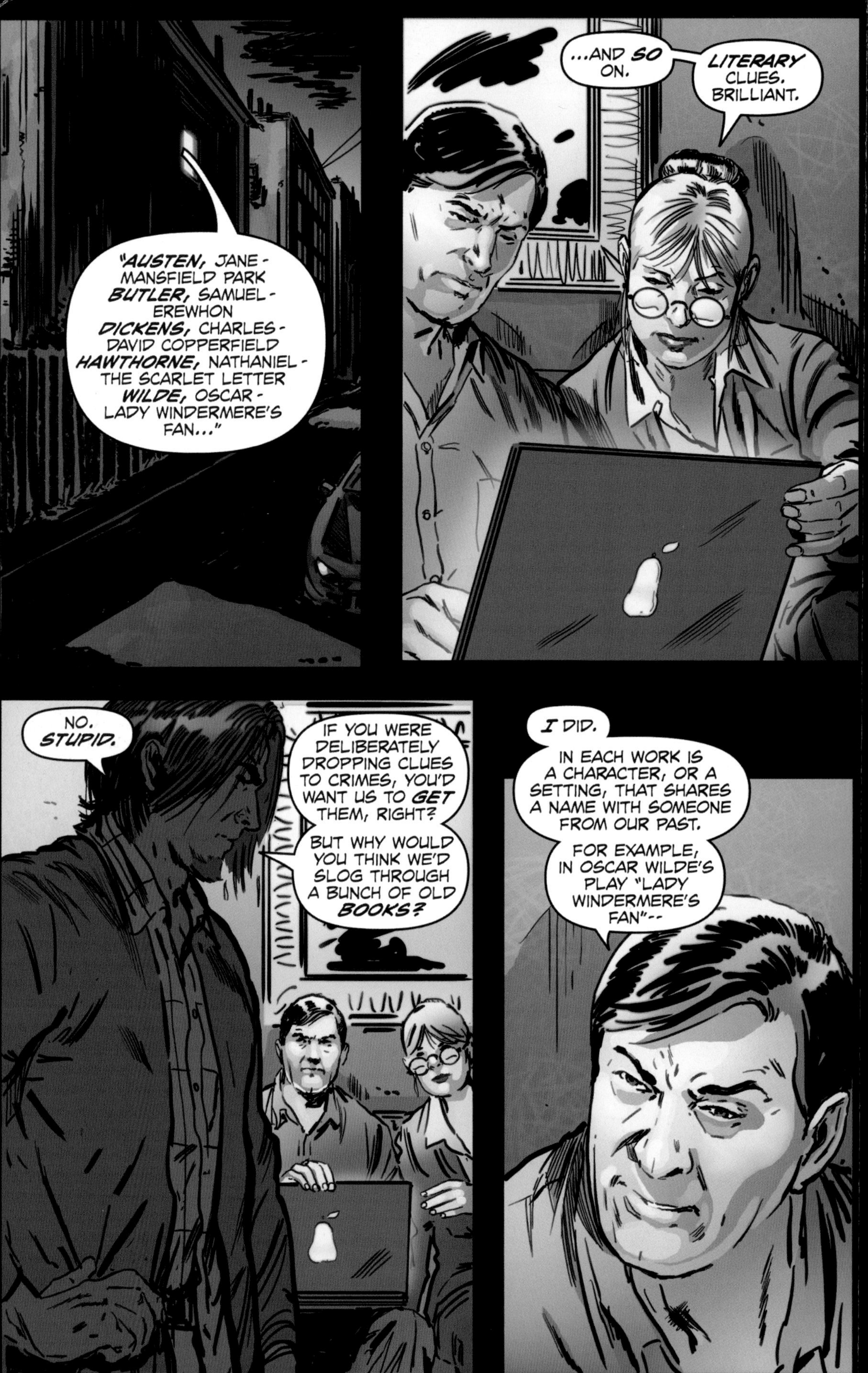
"AUSTEN, JANE - MANSFIELD PARK BUTLER, SAMUEL - EREWHON DICKENS, CHARLES - DAVID COPPERFIELD HAWTHORNE, NATHANIEL - THE SCARLET LETTER WILDE, OSCAR - LADY WINDERMERE'S FAN..."
...AND SO ON.
LITERARY CLUES. BRILLIANT.
NO. STUPID.
IF YOU WERE DELIBERATELY DROPPING CLUES TO CRIMES, YOU'D WANT US TO GET THEM, RIGHT?
BUT WHY WOULD YOU THINK WE'D SLOG THROUGH A BUNCH OF OLD BOOKS?
I DID.
IN EACH WORK IS A CHARACTER, OR A SETTING, THAT SHARES A NAME WITH SOMEONE FROM OUR PAST.
FOR EXAMPLE, IN OSCAR WILDE'S PLAY "LADY WINDERMERE'S FAN"--

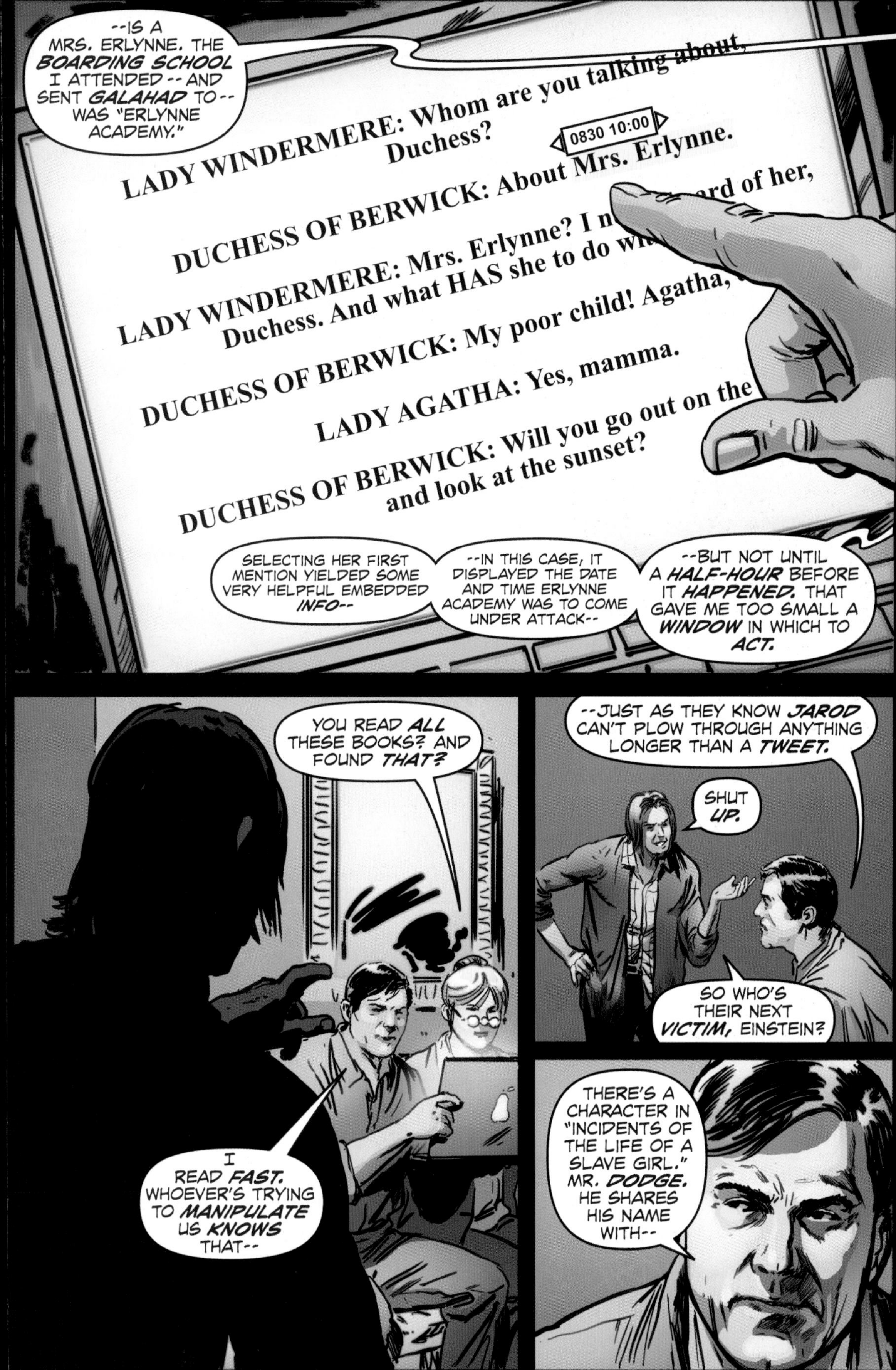
--IS A MRS. ERLYNNE. THE BOARDING SCHOOL I ATTENDED -- AND SENT GALAHAD TO-- WAS "ERLYNNE ACADEMY."
LADY WINDERMERE: Whom are you talking about, Duchess?
0830 10:00
DUCHESS OF BERWICK: About Mrs. Erlynne.
DUCHESS OF BERWICK:
LADY WINDERMERE: Mrs. Erlynne? I n
Duchess. And what HAS she to do wi
DUCHESS OF BERWICK: My poor child! Agatha,
LADY AGATHA: Yes, mamma.
DUCHESS OF BERWICK: Will you go out on the
and look at the sunset?
SELECTING HER FIRST MENTION YIELDED SOME VERY HELPFUL EMBEDDED INFO--
--IN THIS CASE, IT DISPLAYED THE DATE AND TIME ERLYNNE ACADEMY WAS TO COME UNDER ATTACK--
--BUT NOT UNTIL A HALF-HOUR BEFORE IT HAPPENED. THAT GAVE ME TOO SMALL A WINDOW IN WHICH TO ACT.
YOU READ ALL THESE BOOKS? AND FOUND THAT?
I READ FAST. WHOEVER'S TRYING TO MANIPULATE US KNOWS THAT--
--JUST AS THEY KNOW JAROD CAN'T PLOW THROUGH ANYTHING LONGER THAN A TWEET.
SHUT UP.
SO WHO'S THEIR NEXT VICTIM, EINSTEIN?
THERE'S A CHARACTER IN "INCIDENTS OF THE LIFE OF A SLAVE GIRL." MR. DODGE. HE SHARES HIS NAME WITH--

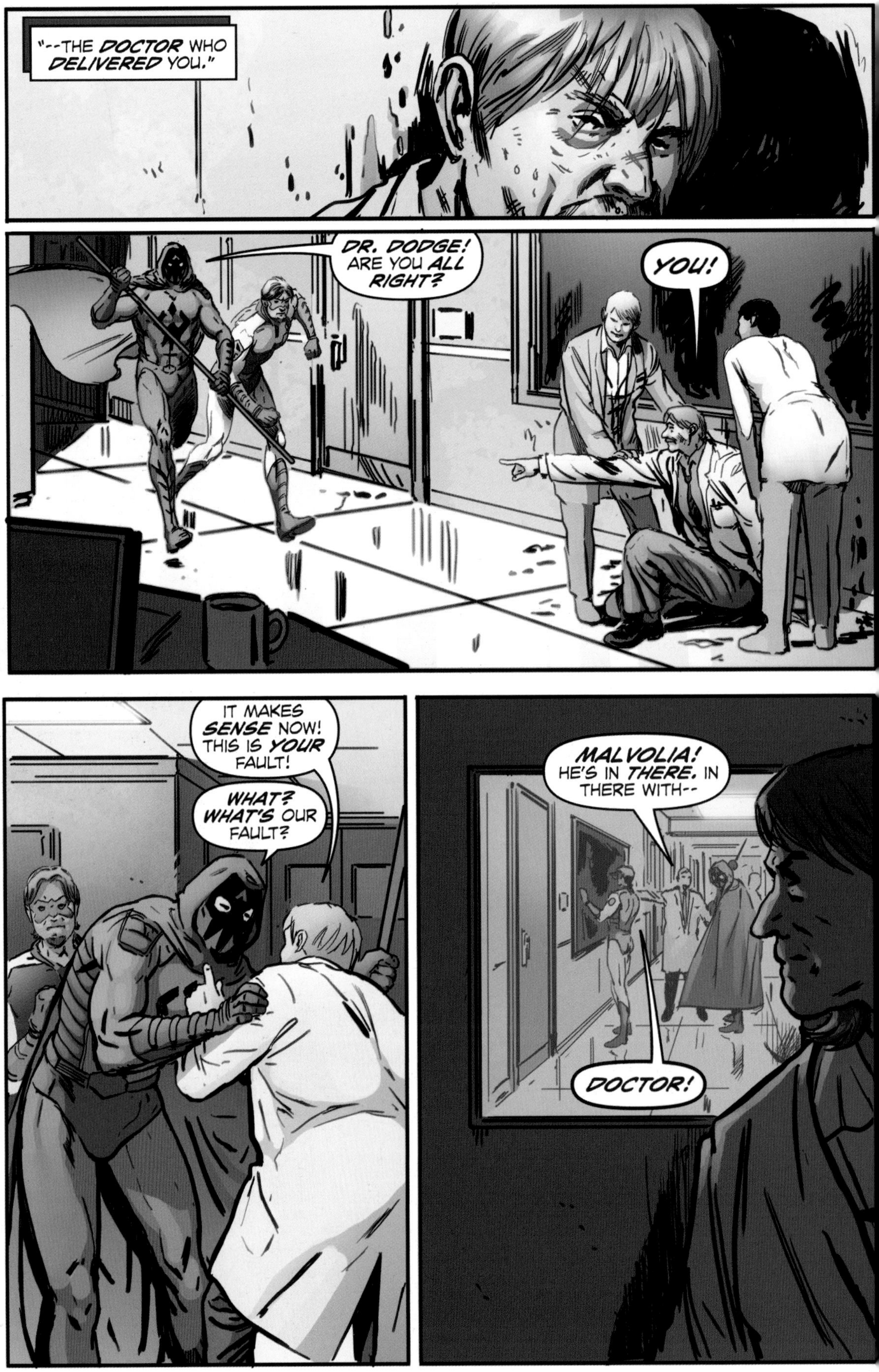
"--THE DOCTOR WHO DELIVERED YOU."
DR. DODGE! ARE YOU ALL RIGHT?
YOU!
IT MAKES SENSE NOW! THIS IS YOUR FAULT!
WHAT? WHAT'S OUR FAULT?
MALVOLIA! HE'S IN THERE. IN THERE WITH--
DOCTOR!

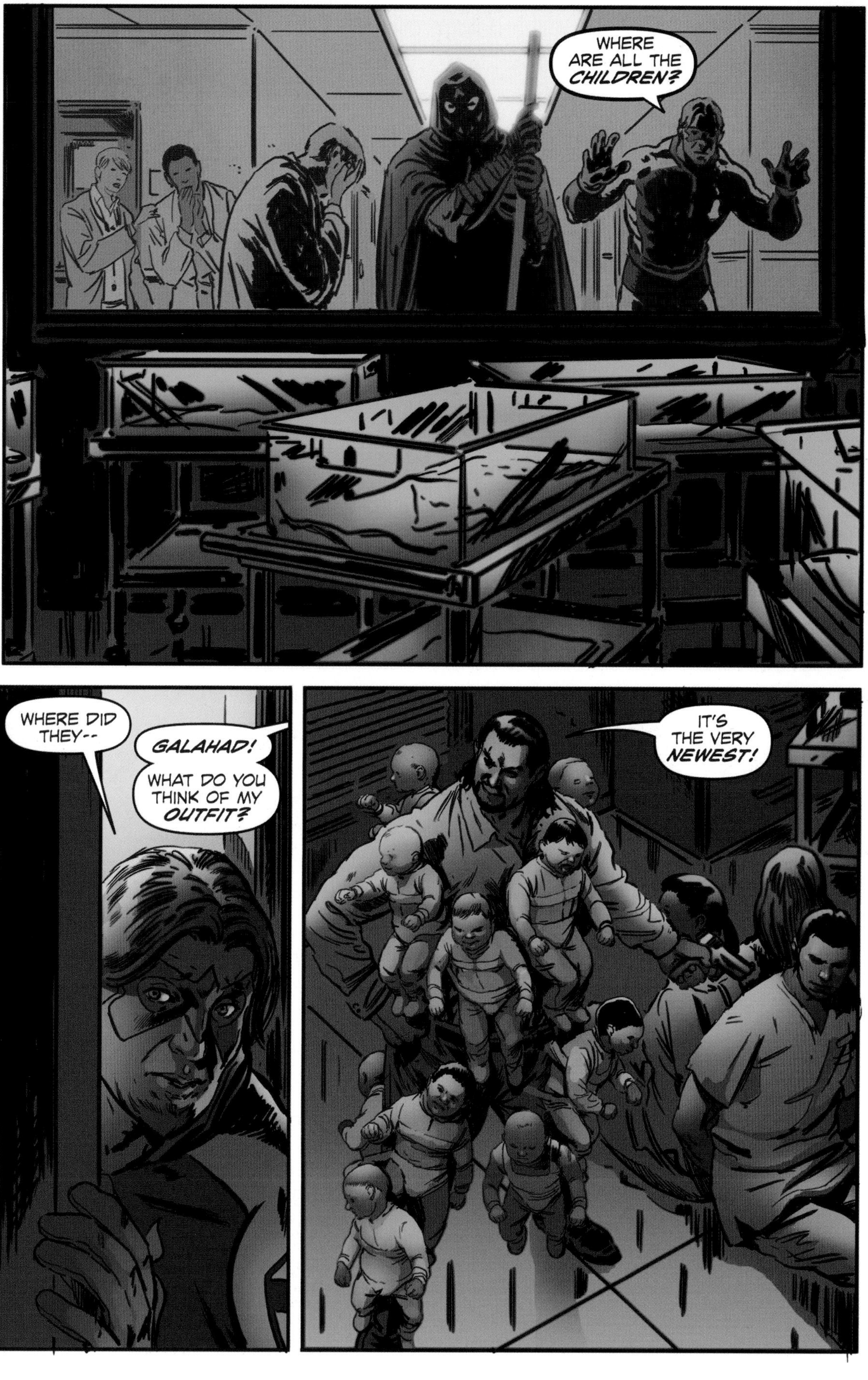
WHERE ARE ALL THE CHILDREN?
WHERE DID THEY--
GALAHAD!
WHAT DO YOU THINK OF MY OUTFIT?
IT'S THE VERY NEWEST!

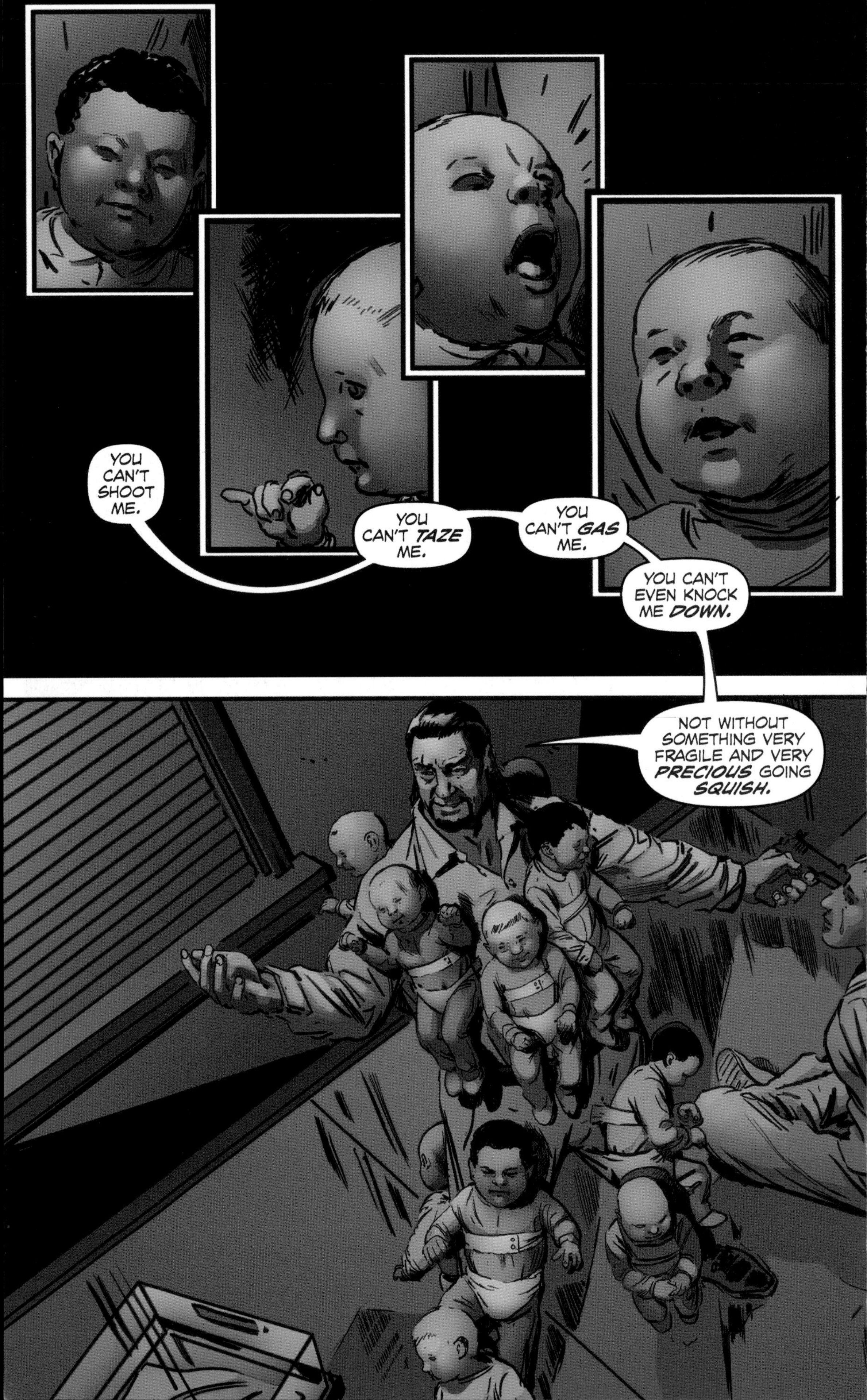

YOU CAN'T SHOOT ME.
YOU CAN'T TAZE ME.
YOU CAN'T GAS ME.
YOU CAN'T EVEN KNOCK ME DOWN.
NOT WITHOUT SOMETHING VERY FRAGILE AND VERY PRECIOUS GOING SQUISH.

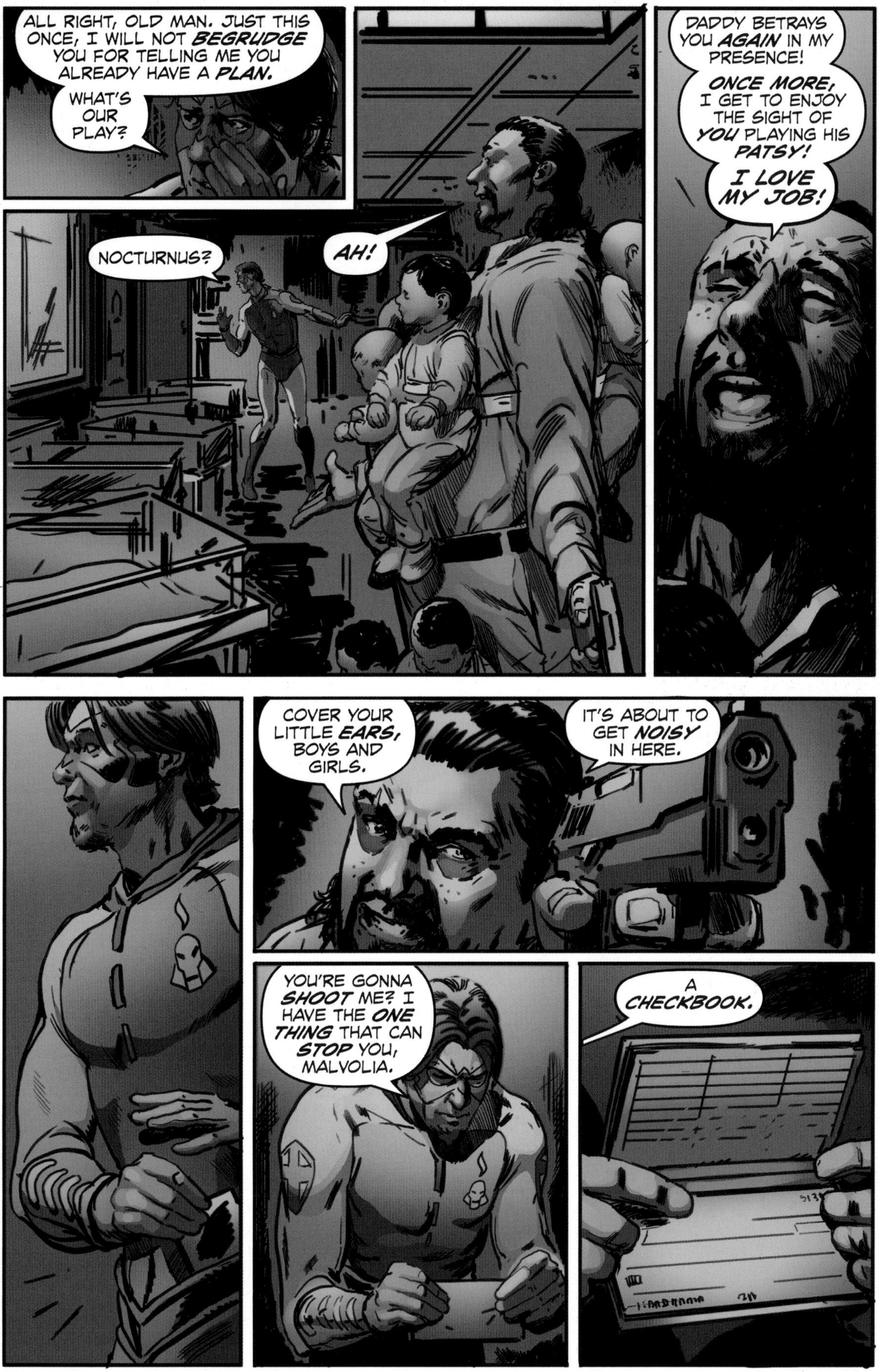
ALL RIGHT, OLD MAN. JUST THIS ONCE, I WILL NOT BEGRUDGE YOU FOR TELLING ME YOU ALREADY HAVE A PLAN.
WHAT'S OUR PLAY?
DADDY BETRAYS YOU AGAIN IN MY PRESENCE!
ONCE MORE, I GET TO ENJOY THE SIGHT OF YOU PLAYING HIS PATSY!
I LOVE MY JOB!
NOCTURNUS?
AH!
COVER YOUR LITTLE EARS, BOYS AND GIRLS.
IT'S ABOUT TO GET NOISY IN HERE.
YOU'RE GONNA SHOOT ME? I HAVE THE ONE THING THAT CAN STOP YOU, MALVOLIA.
A CHECKBOOK.

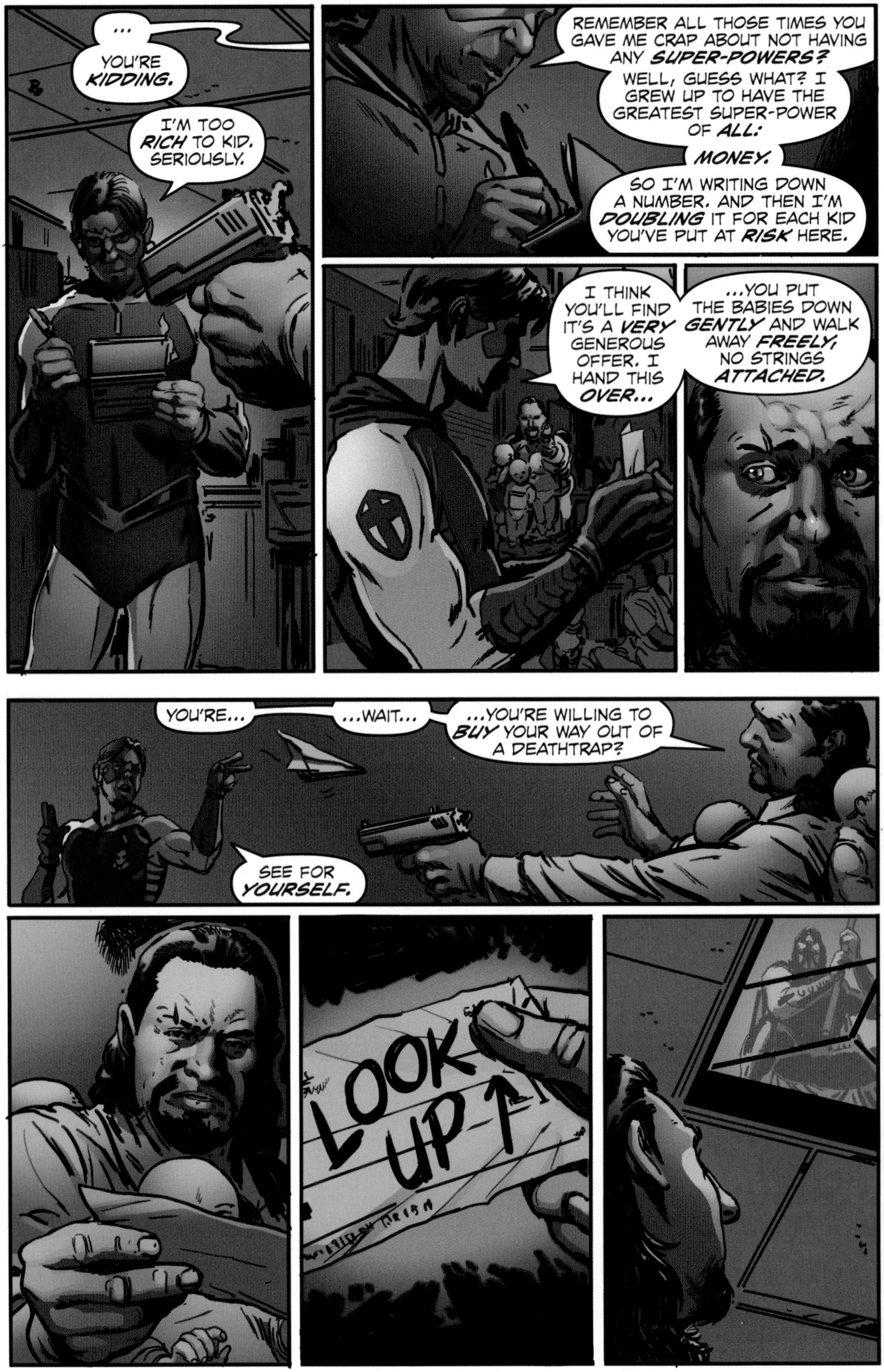
...
YOU'RE KIDDING.
I'M TOO RICH TO KID. SERIOUSLY.
REMEMBER ALL THOSE TIMES YOU GAVE ME CRAP ABOUT NOT HAVING ANY SUPER-POWERS?
WELL, GUESS WHAT? I GREW UP TO HAVE THE GREATEST SUPER-POWER OF ALL:
MONEY.
SO I'M WRITING DOWN A NUMBER. AND THEN I'M DOUBLING IT FOR EACH KID YOU'VE PUT AT RISK HERE.
I THINK YOU'LL FIND IT'S A VERY GENEROUS OFFER. I HAND THIS OVER...
...YOU PUT THE BABIES DOWN GENTLY AND WALK AWAY FREELY, NO STRINGS ATTACHED.
YOU'RE...
...WAIT...
...YOU'RE WILLING TO BUY YOUR WAY OUT OF A DEATHTRAP?
SEE FOR YOURSELF.
LOOK UP ↑

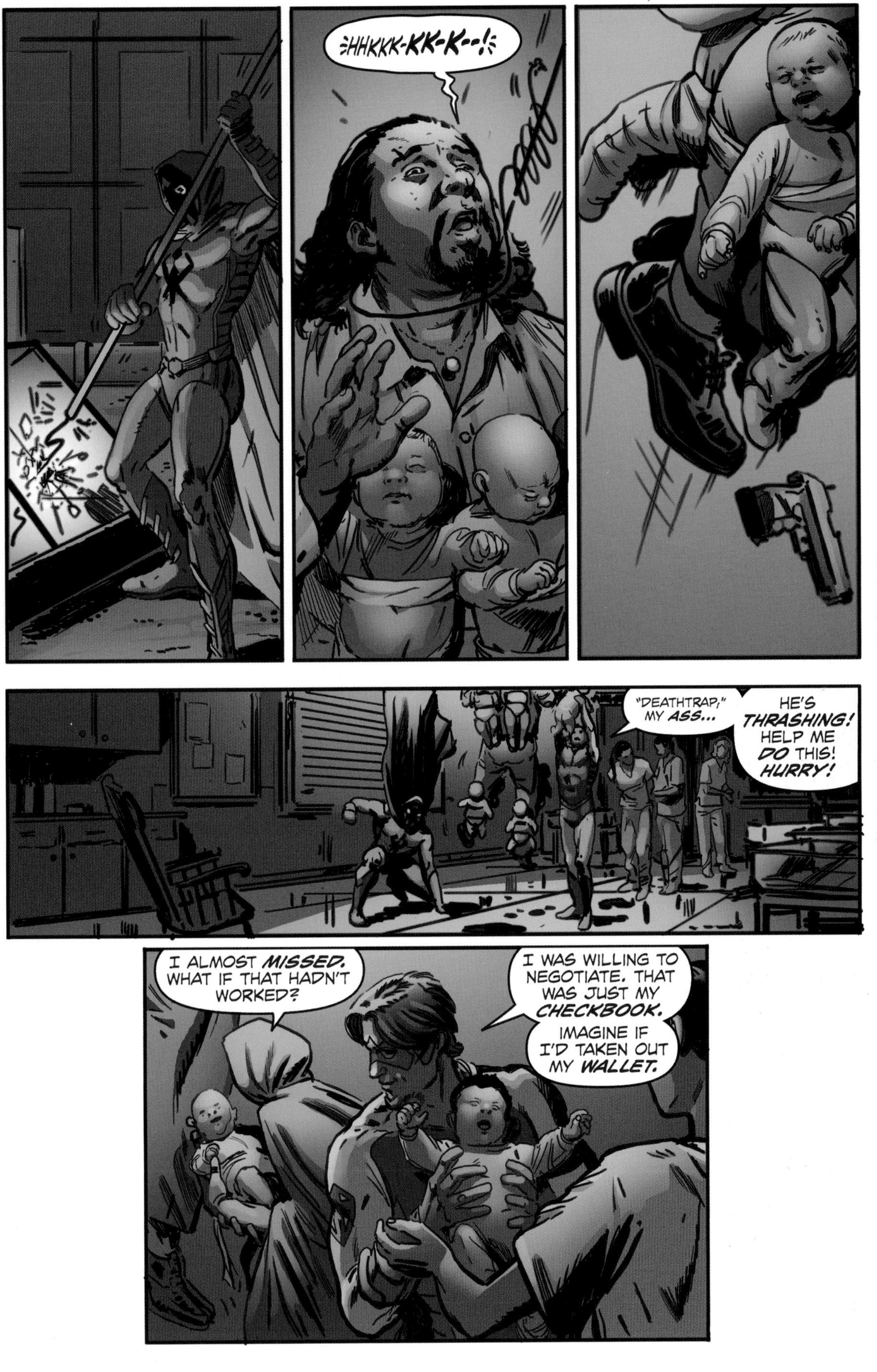

HHKKK-KK-K--!
"DEATHTRAP," MY ASS...
HE'S THRASHING! HELP ME DO THIS! HURRY!
I ALMOST MISSED. WHAT IF THAT HADN'T WORKED?
I WAS WILLING TO NEGOTIATE. THAT WAS JUST MY CHECKBOOK.
IMAGINE IF I'D TAKEN OUT MY WALLET.

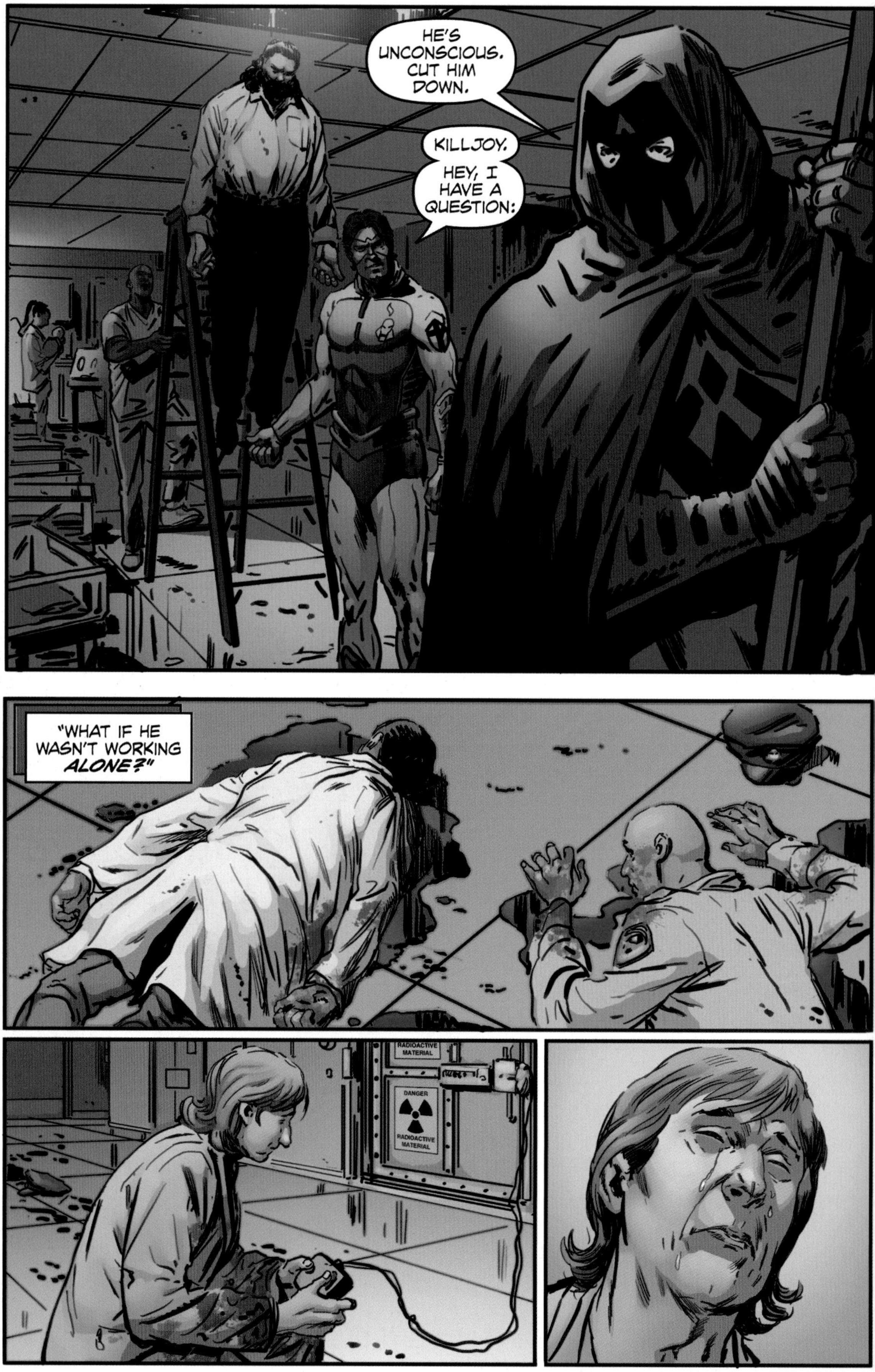
HE'S UNCONSCIOUS. CUT HIM DOWN.
KILLJOY.
HEY, I HAVE A QUESTION:
"WHAT IF HE WASN'T WORKING *ALONE?*"
RADIOACTIVE MATERIAL
DANGER
RADIOACTIVE MATERIAL

CHAPTER SIX

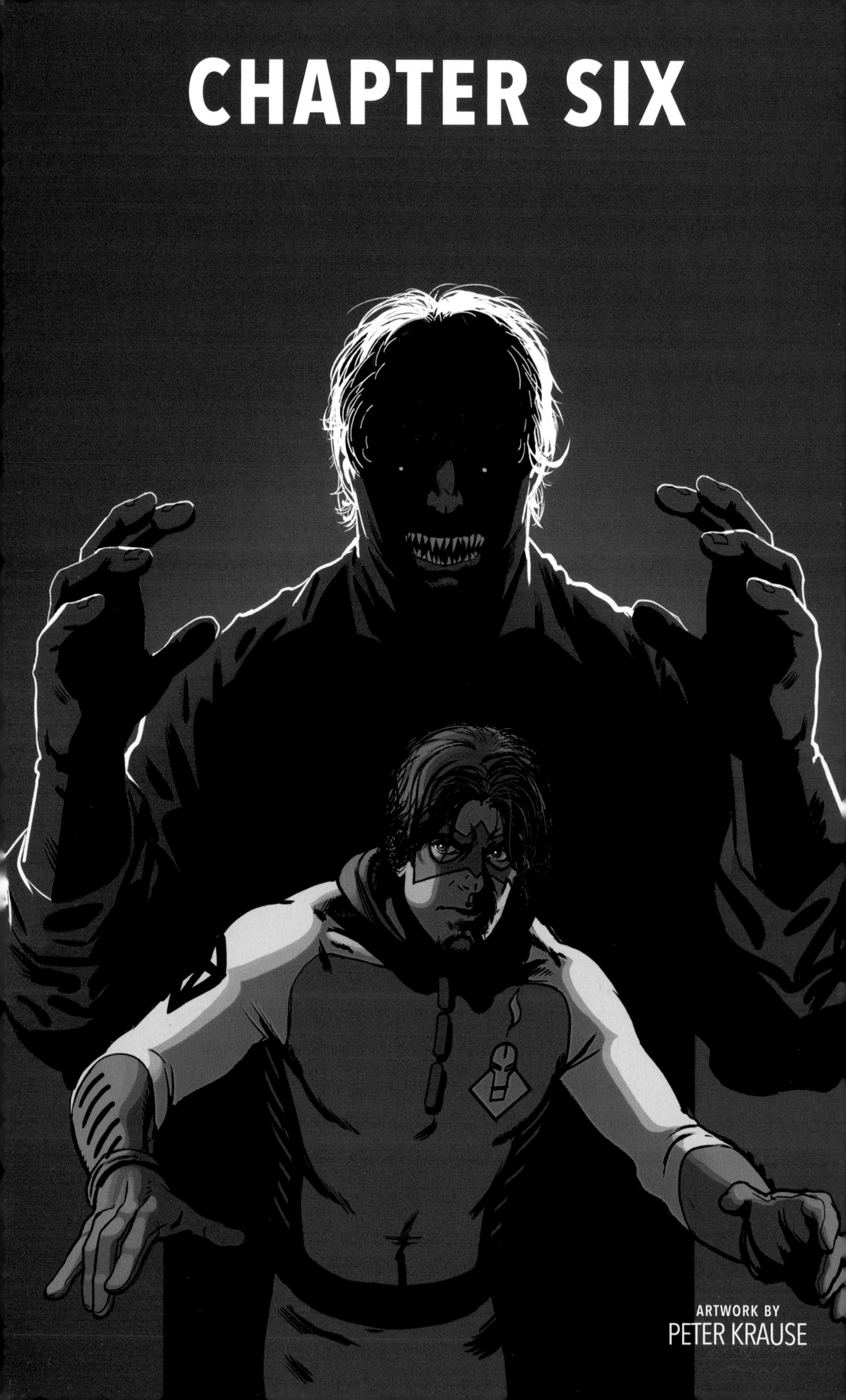

ARTWORK BY
PETER KRAUSE

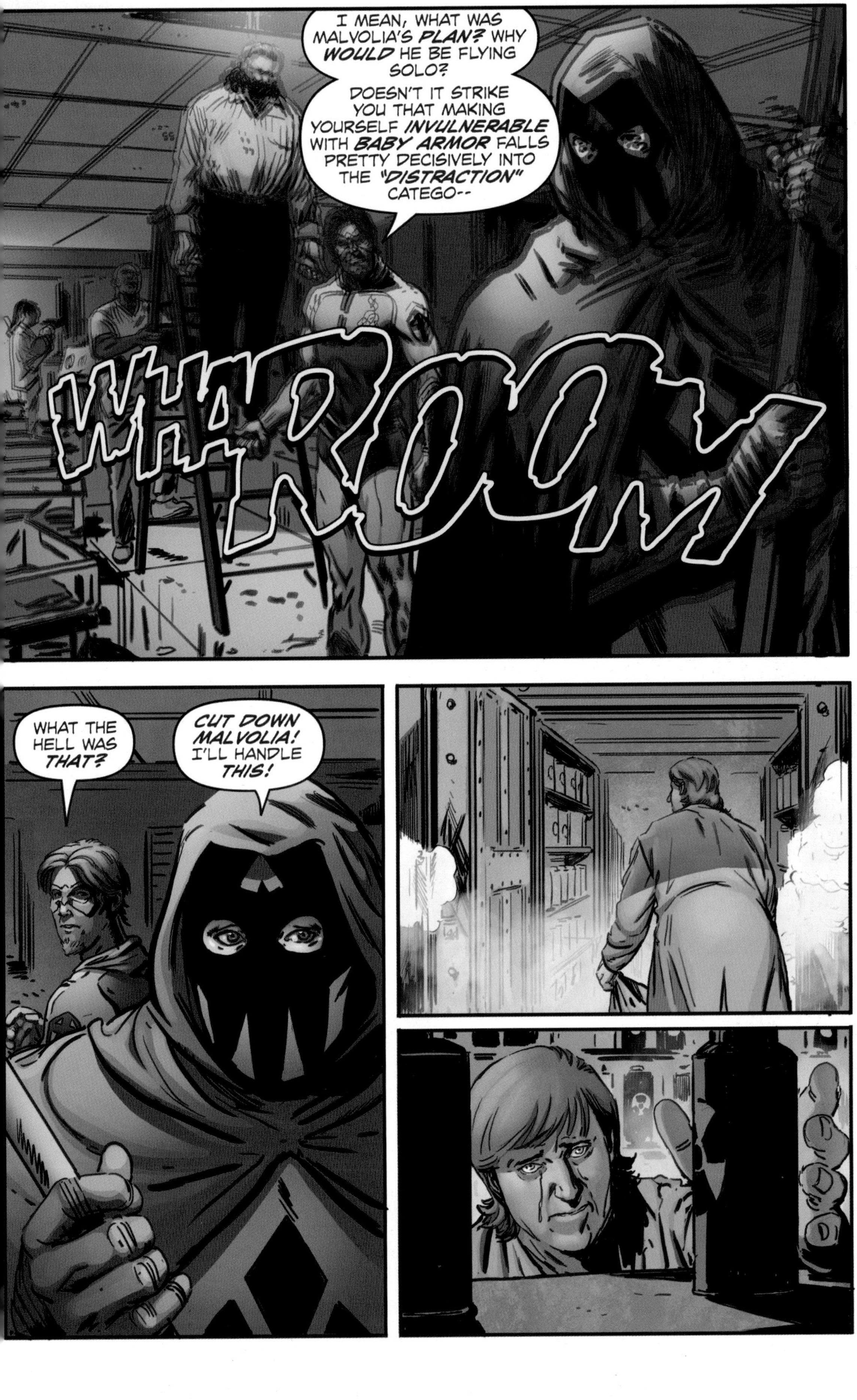
I MEAN, WHAT WAS MALVOLIA'S PLAN? WHY WOULD HE BE FLYING SOLO?
DOESN'T IT STRIKE YOU THAT MAKING YOURSELF INVULNERABLE WITH BABY ARMOR FALLS PRETTY DECISIVELY INTO THE "DISTRACTION" CATEGO--
WHAROOM
WHAT THE HELL WAS THAT?
CUT DOWN MALVOLIA! I'LL HANDLE THIS!

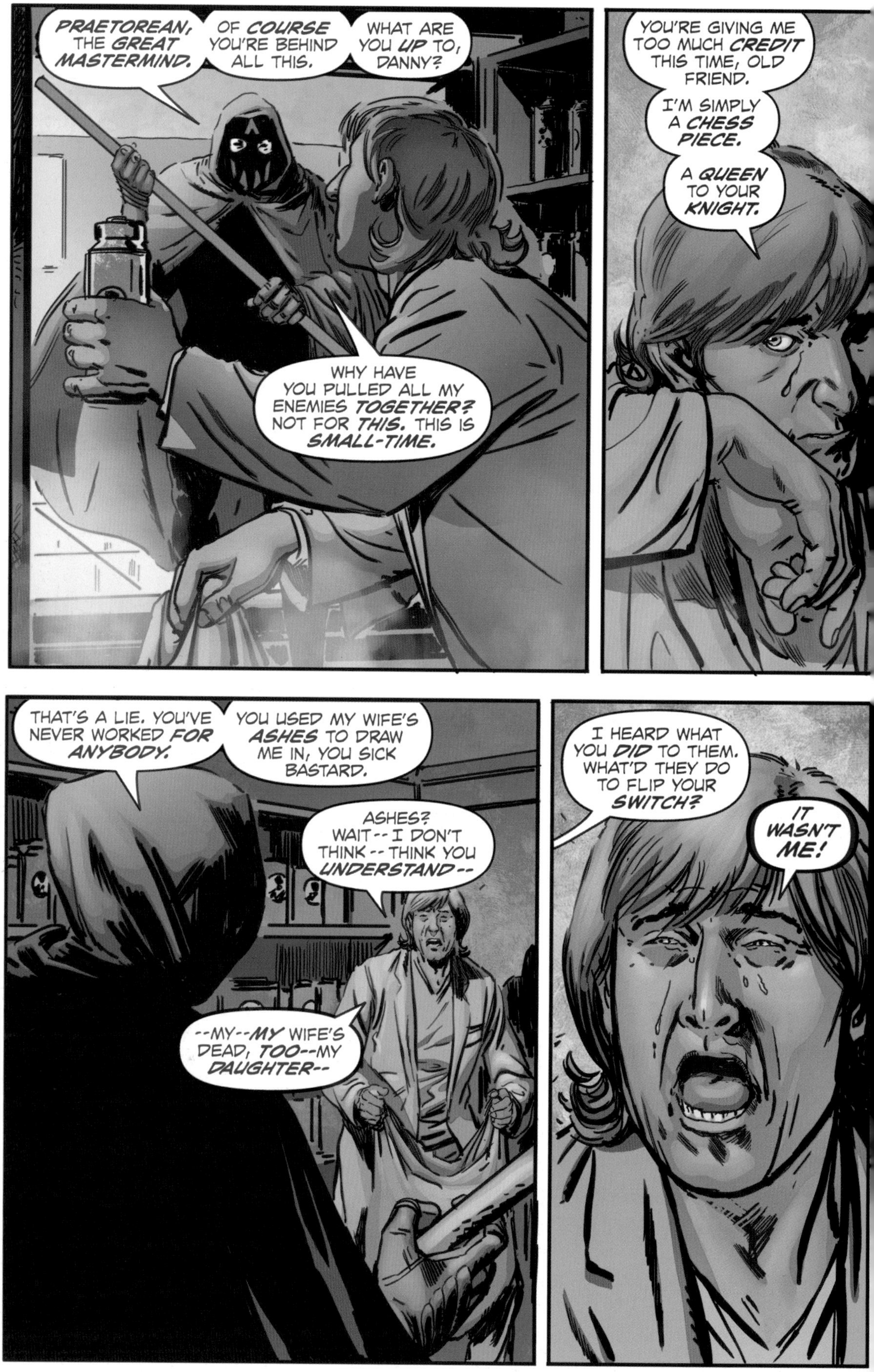
PRAETOREAN, THE GREAT MASTERMIND.
OF COURSE YOU'RE BEHIND ALL THIS.
WHAT ARE YOU UP TO, DANNY?
WHY HAVE YOU PULLED ALL MY ENEMIES TOGETHER? NOT FOR THIS. THIS IS SMALL-TIME.
YOU'RE GIVING ME TOO MUCH CREDIT THIS TIME, OLD FRIEND.
I'M SIMPLY A CHESS PIECE.
A QUEEN TO YOUR KNIGHT.
THAT'S A LIE. YOU'VE NEVER WORKED FOR ANYBODY.
YOU USED MY WIFE'S ASHES TO DRAW ME IN, YOU SICK BASTARD.
ASHES? WAIT--I DON'T THINK--THINK YOU UNDERSTAND--
--MY--MY WIFE'S DEAD, TOO--MY DAUGHTER--
I HEARD WHAT YOU DID TO THEM. WHAT'D THEY DO TO FLIP YOUR SWITCH?
IT WASN'T ME!

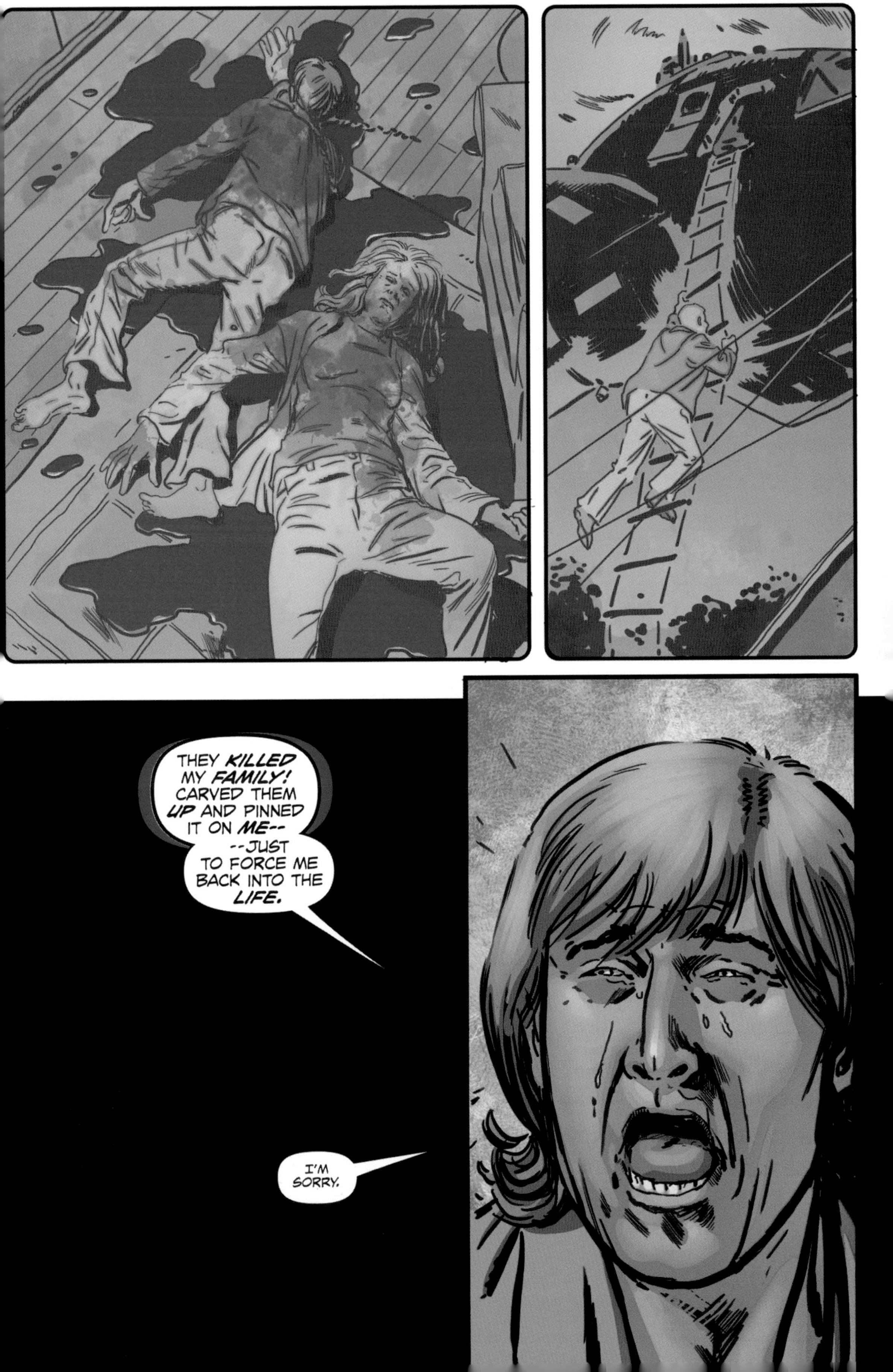
THEY KILLED MY FAMILY! CARVED THEM UP AND PINNED IT ON ME--
--JUST TO FORCE ME BACK INTO THE LIFE.
I'M SORRY.

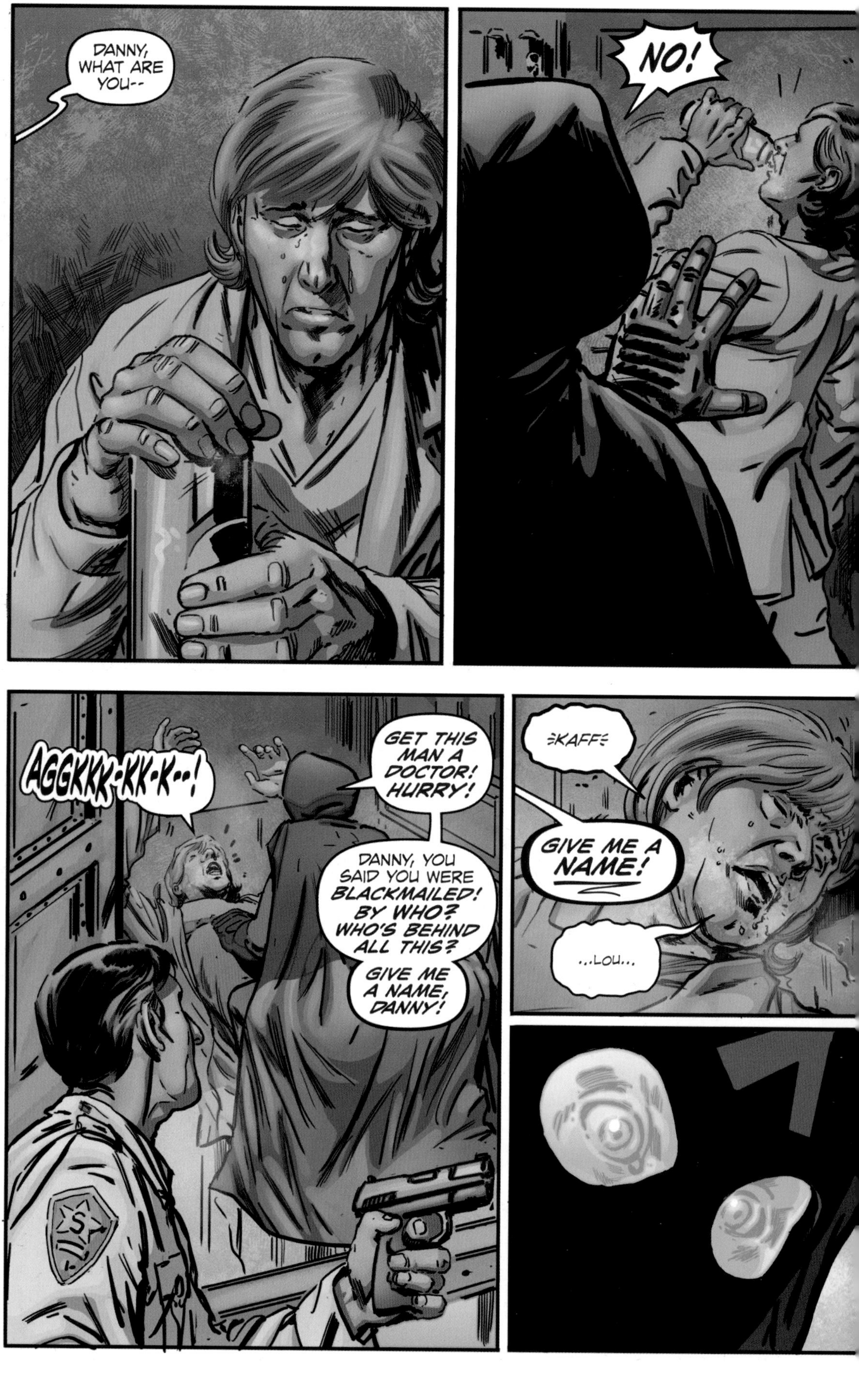
DANNY, WHAT ARE YOU--
NO!
AGGKKK-KK-K--!
GET THIS MAN A DOCTOR! HURRY!
DANNY, YOU SAID YOU WERE BLACKMAILED! BY WHO? WHO'S BEHIND ALL THIS?
GIVE ME A NAME, DANNY!
=KAFF=
GIVE ME A NAME!
...LOU...

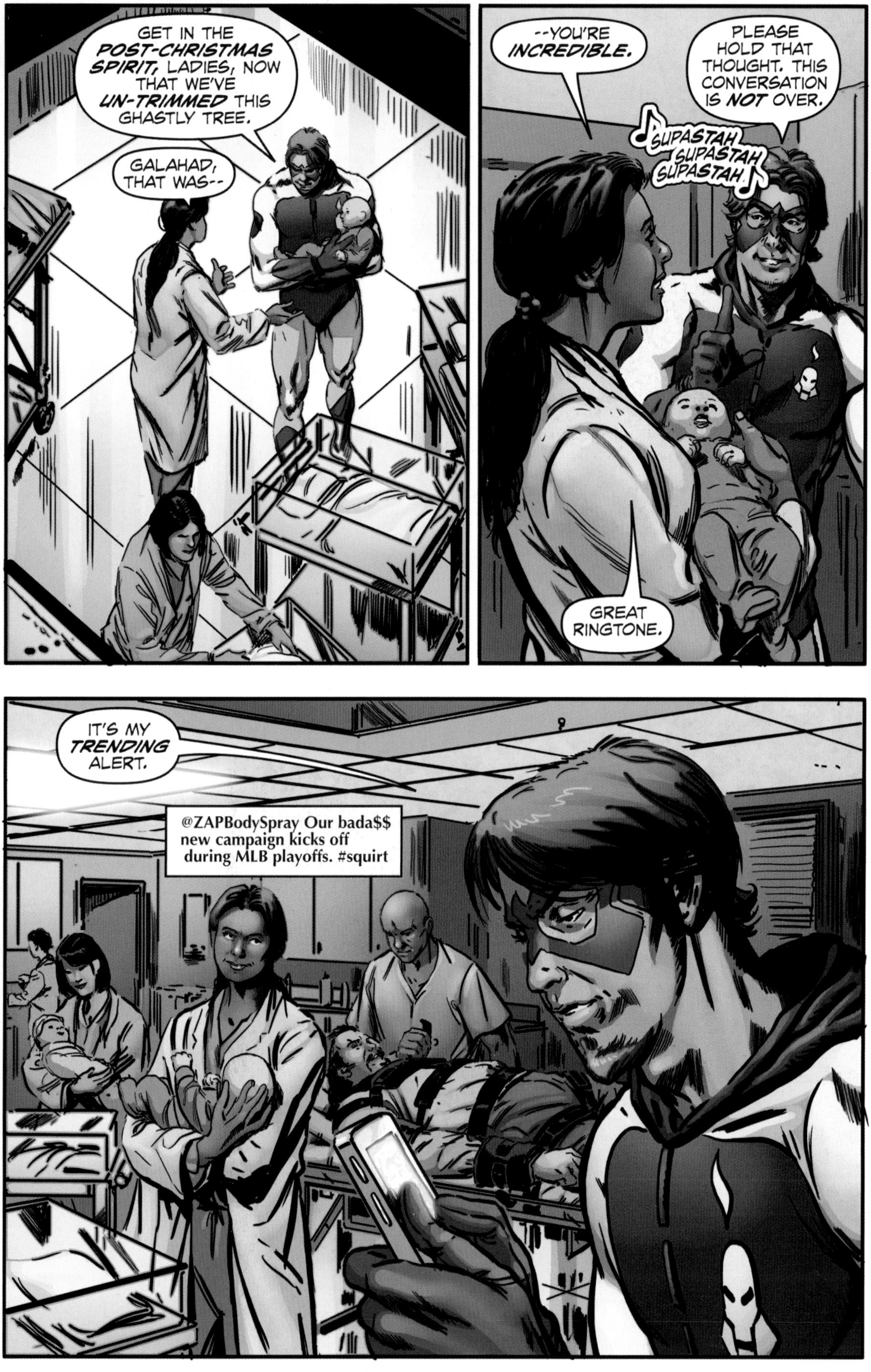
GET IN THE POST-CHRISTMAS SPIRIT, LADIES, NOW THAT WE'VE UN-TRIMMED THIS GHASTLY TREE.
GALAHAD, THAT WAS--
--YOU'RE INCREDIBLE.
PLEASE HOLD THAT THOUGHT. THIS CONVERSATION IS NOT OVER.
SUPASTAH SUPASTAH SUPASTAH
GREAT RINGTONE.
IT'S MY TRENDING ALERT.
@ZAPBodySpray Our bada$$ new campaign kicks off during MLB playoffs. #squirt

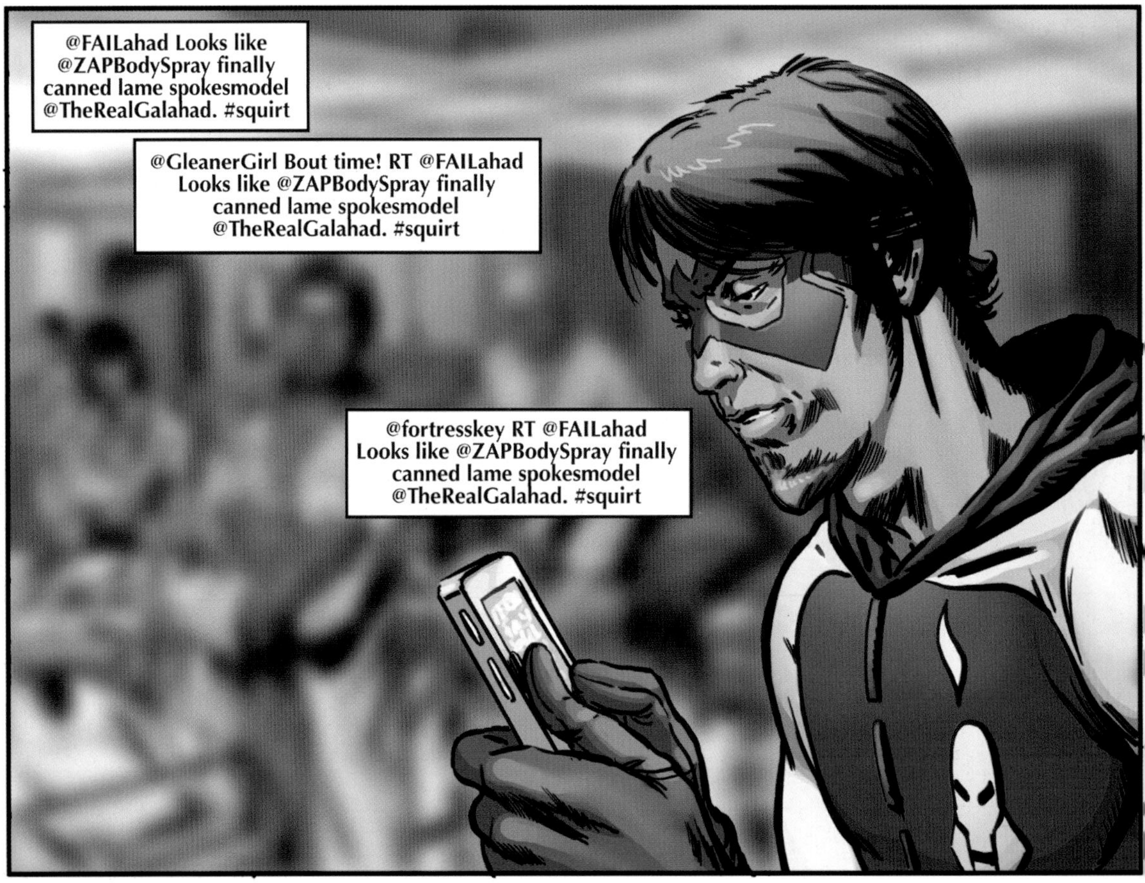
@FAILahad Looks like @ZAPBodySpray finally canned lame spokesmodel @TheRealGalahad. #squirt
@GleanerGirl Bout time! RT @FAILahad Looks like @ZAPBodySpray finally canned lame spokesmodel @TheRealGalahad. #squirt
@fortresskey RT @FAILahad Looks like @ZAPBodySpray finally canned lame spokesmodel @TheRealGalahad. #squirt

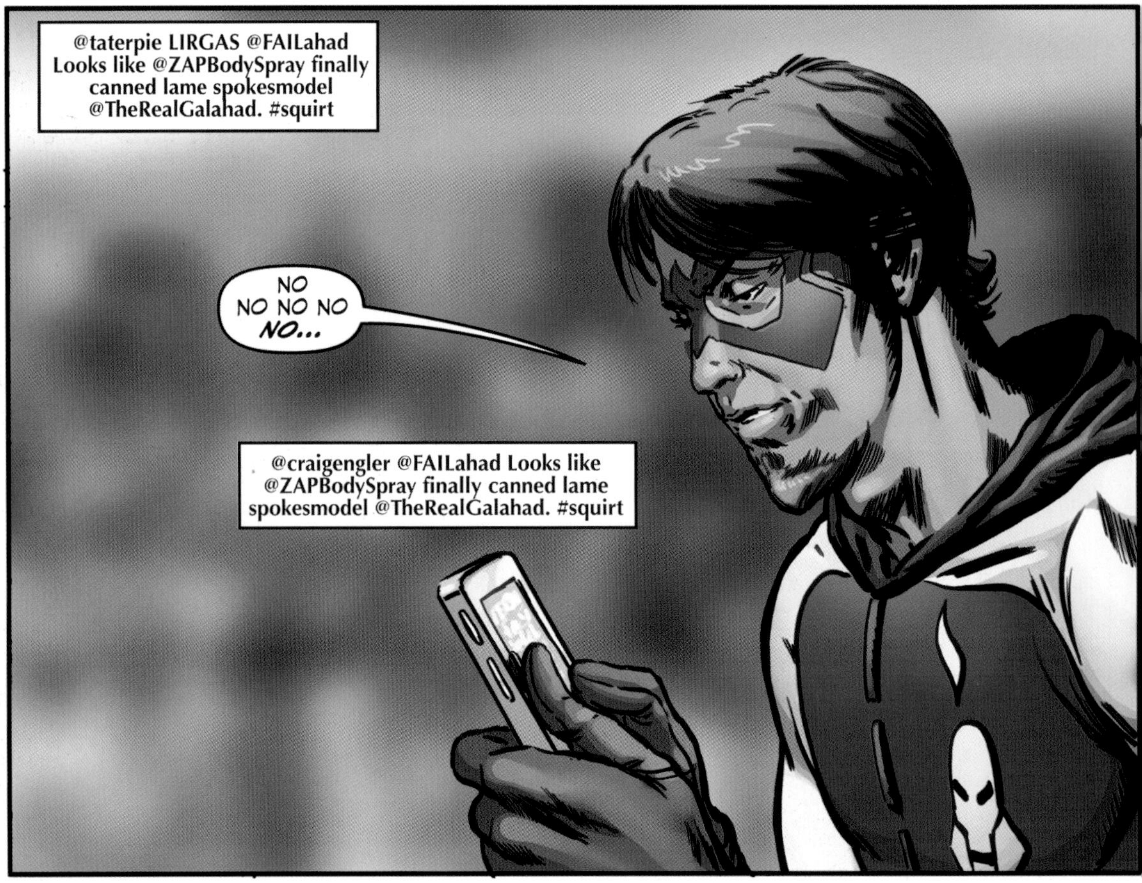
@taterpie LIRGAS @FAILahad Looks like @ZAPBodySpray finally canned lame spokesmodel @TheRealGalahad. #squirt
NO NO NO NO *NO...*
@craigengler @FAILahad Looks like @ZAPBodySpray finally canned lame spokesmodel @TheRealGalahad. #squirt

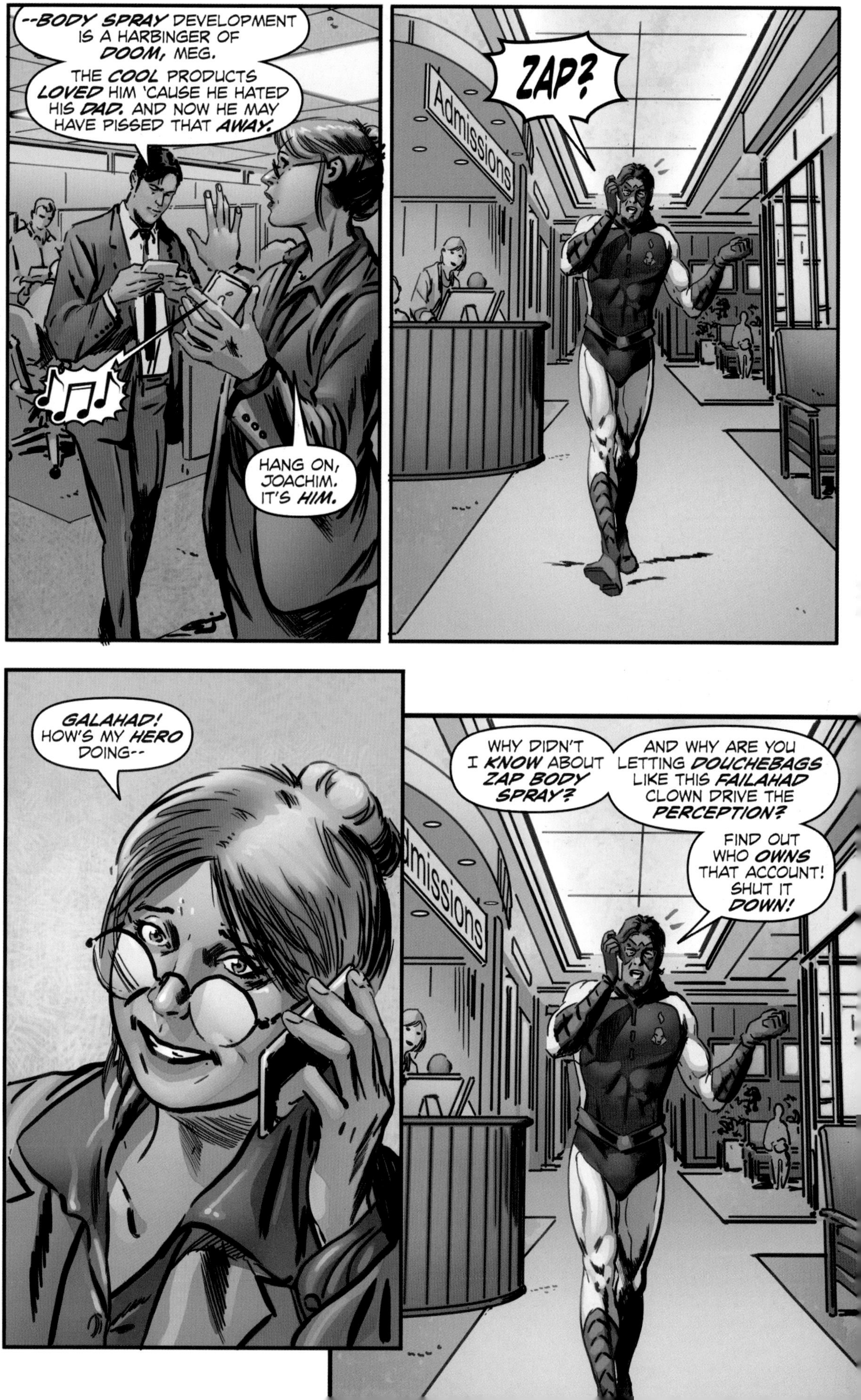
--BODY SPRAY DEVELOPMENT IS A HARBINGER OF DOOM, MEG.
THE COOL PRODUCTS LOVED HIM 'CAUSE HE HATED HIS DAD. AND NOW HE MAY HAVE PISSED THAT AWAY.
HANG ON, JOACHIM. IT'S HIM.
Admissions
ZAP?
GALAHAD! HOW'S MY HERO DOING--
Admissions
WHY DIDN'T I KNOW ABOUT ZAP BODY SPRAY?
AND WHY ARE YOU LETTING DOUCHEBAGS LIKE THIS FAILAHAD CLOWN DRIVE THE PERCEPTION?
FIND OUT WHO OWNS THAT ACCOUNT! SHUT IT DOWN!

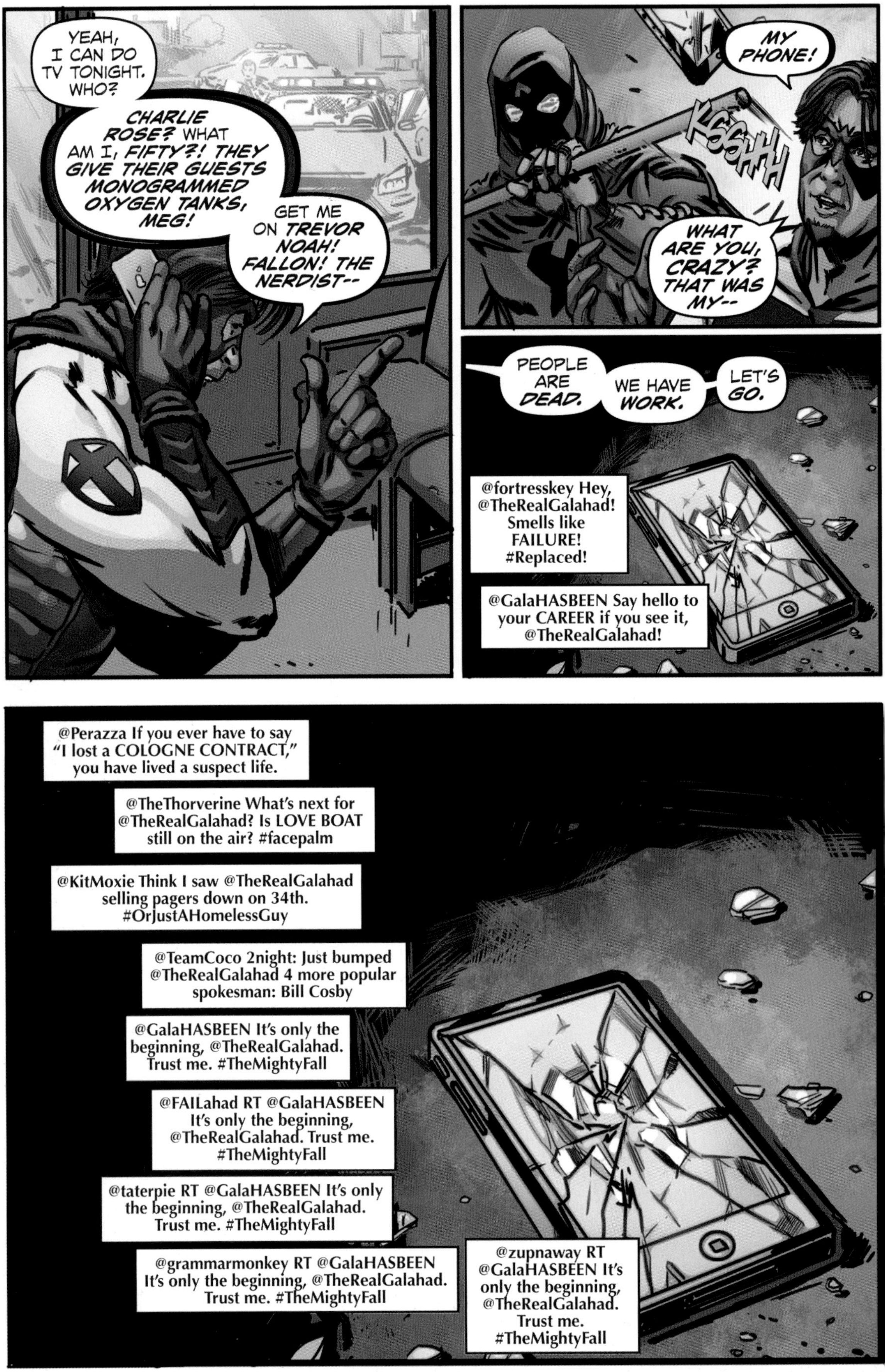
YEAH, I CAN DO TV TONIGHT. WHO?
CHARLIE ROSE? WHAT AM I, FIFTY?! THEY GIVE THEIR GUESTS MONOGRAMMED OXYGEN TANKS, MEG!
GET ME ON TREVOR NOAH! FALLON! THE NERDIST--
MY PHONE!
KSSHHH
WHAT ARE YOU, CRAZY? THAT WAS MY--
PEOPLE ARE DEAD.
WE HAVE WORK.
LET'S GO.
@fortresskey Hey, @TheRealGalahad! Smells like FAILURE! #Replaced!
@GalaHASBEEN Say hello to your CAREER if you see it, @TheRealGalahad!
@Perazza If you ever have to say "I lost a COLOGNE CONTRACT," you have lived a suspect life.
@TheThorverine What's next for @TheRealGalahad? Is LOVE BOAT still on the air? #facepalm
@KitMoxie Think I saw @TheRealGalahad selling pagers down on 34th. #OrJustAHomelessGuy
@TeamCoco 2night: Just bumped @TheRealGalahad 4 more popular spokesman: Bill Cosby
@GalaHASBEEN It's only the beginning, @TheRealGalahad. Trust me. #TheMightyFall
@FAILahad RT @GalaHASBEEN It's only the beginning, @TheRealGalahad. Trust me. #TheMightyFall
@taterpie RT @GalaHASBEEN It's only the beginning, @TheRealGalahad. Trust me. #TheMightyFall
@grammarmonkey RT @GalaHASBEEN It's only the beginning, @TheRealGalahad. Trust me. #TheMightyFall
@zupnaway RT @GalaHASBEEN It's only the beginning, @TheRealGalahad. Trust me. #TheMightyFall

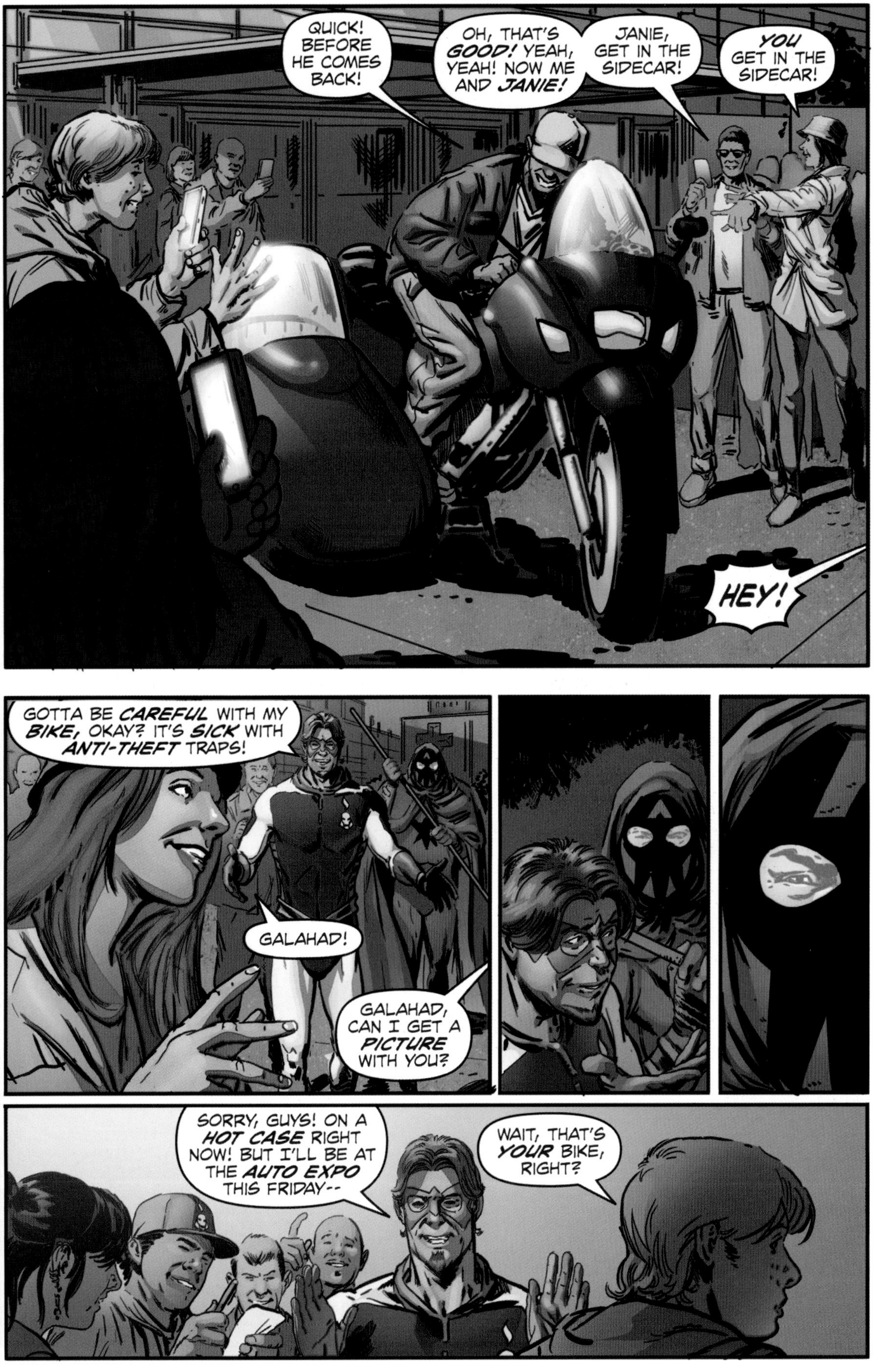
QUICK! BEFORE HE COMES BACK!
OH, THAT'S GOOD! YEAH, YEAH! NOW ME AND JANIE!
JANIE, GET IN THE SIDECAR!
YOU GET IN THE SIDECAR!
HEY!
GOTTA BE CAREFUL WITH MY BIKE, OKAY? IT'S SICK WITH ANTI-THEFT TRAPS!
GALAHAD!
GALAHAD, CAN I GET A PICTURE WITH YOU?
SORRY, GUYS! ON A HOT CASE RIGHT NOW! BUT I'LL BE AT THE AUTO EXPO THIS FRIDAY--
WAIT, THAT'S YOUR BIKE, RIGHT?

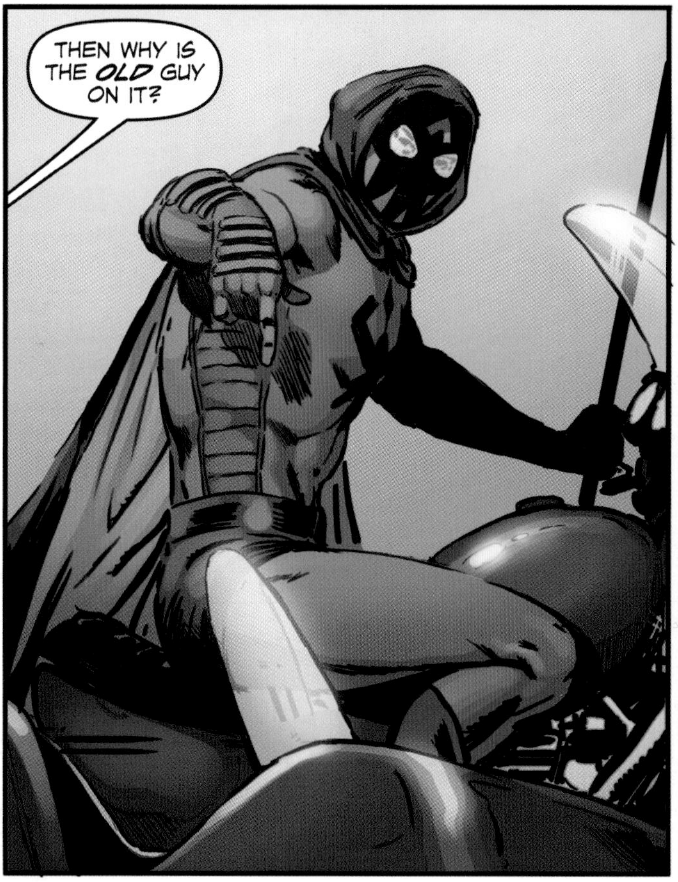
THEN WHY IS THE OLD GUY ON IT?

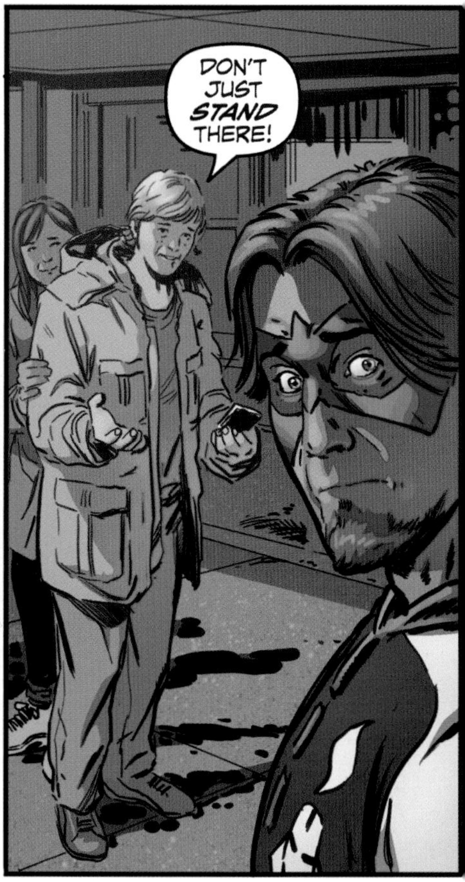
DON'T JUST STAND THERE!

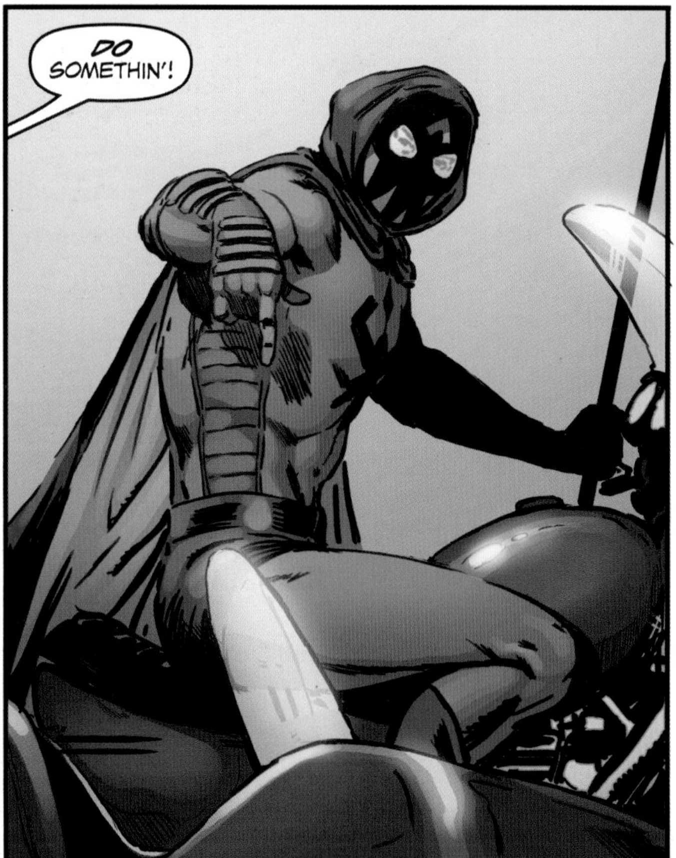
DO SOMETHIN'!

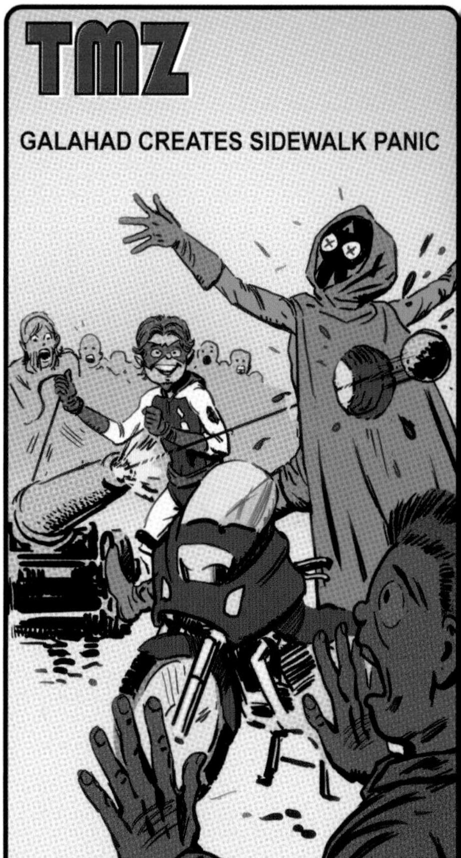
TMZ
GALAHAD CREATES SIDEWALK PANIC

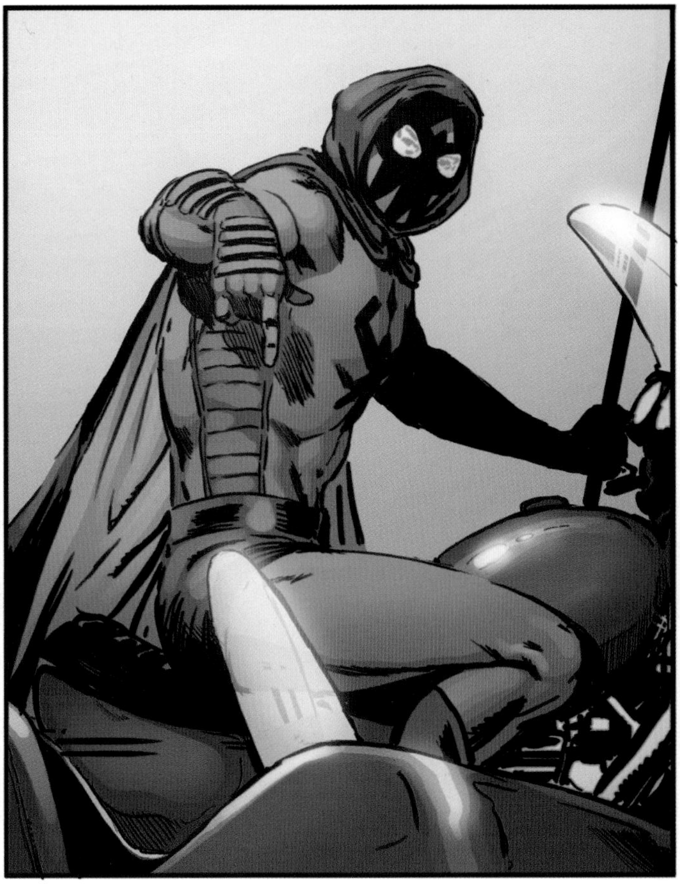

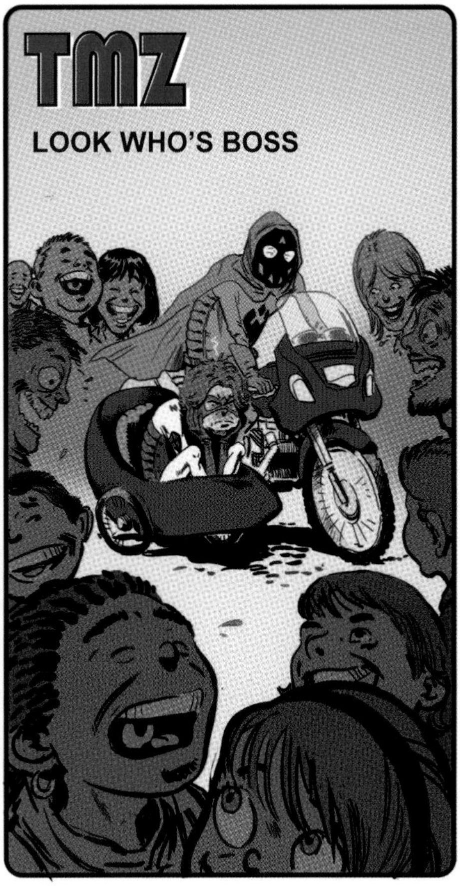
TMZ
LOOK WHO'S BOSS

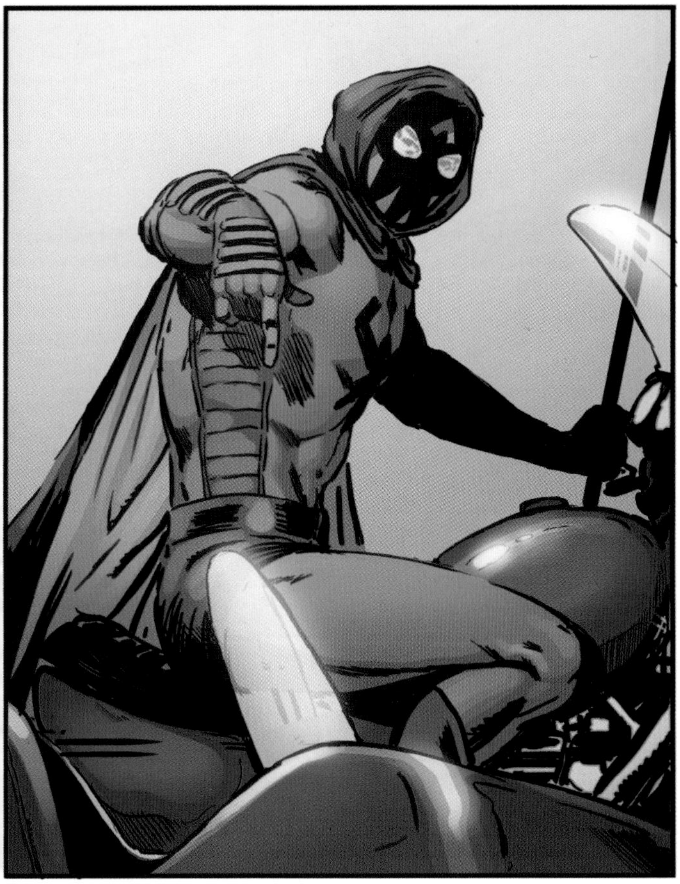

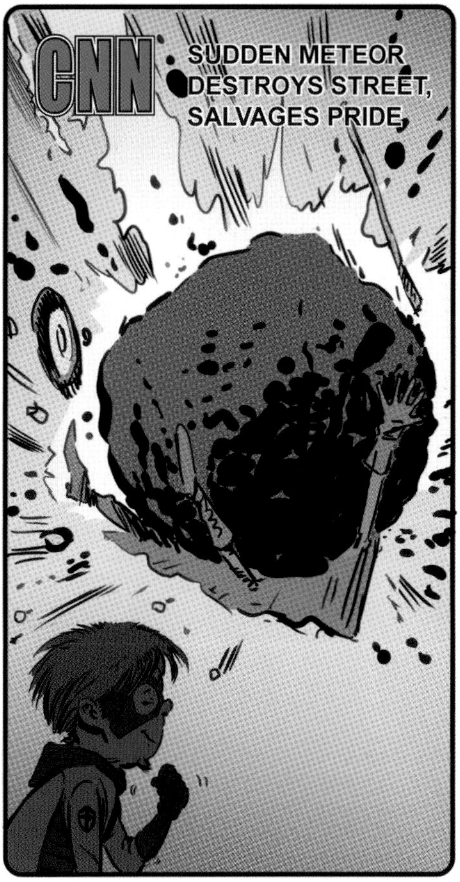
CNN
SUDDEN METEOR DESTROYS STREET, SALVAGES PRIDE

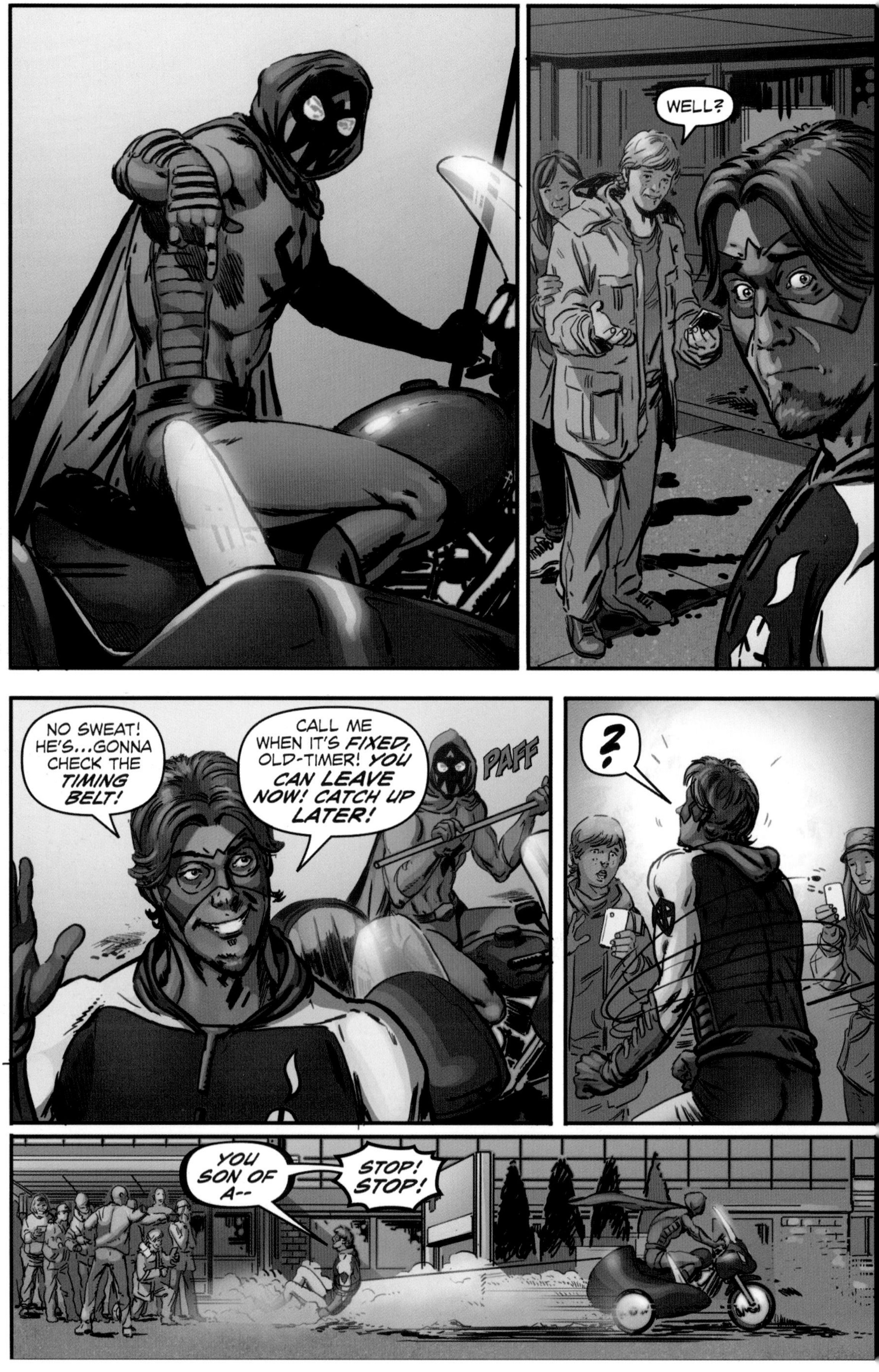
WELL?
NO SWEAT! HE'S...GONNA CHECK THE TIMING BELT!
CALL ME WHEN IT'S FIXED, OLD-TIMER! YOU CAN LEAVE NOW! CATCH UP LATER!
PAFF
?
YOU SON OF A--
STOP! STOP!

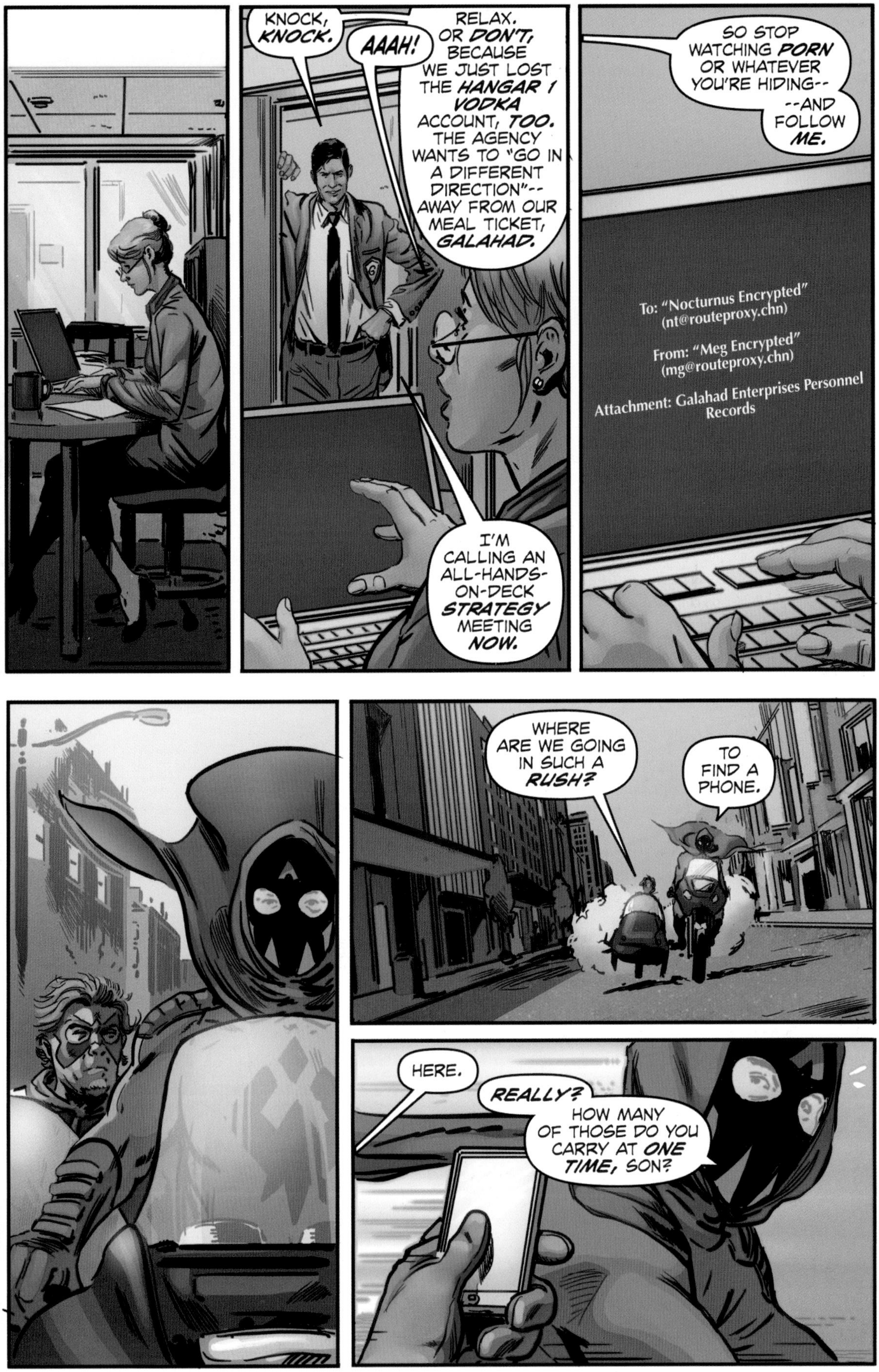
KNOCK, KNOCK.
AAAH!
RELAX. OR DON'T, BECAUSE WE JUST LOST THE HANGAR 1 VODKA ACCOUNT, TOO. THE AGENCY WANTS TO "GO IN A DIFFERENT DIRECTION"-- AWAY FROM OUR MEAL TICKET, GALAHAD.
I'M CALLING AN ALL-HANDS-ON-DECK STRATEGY MEETING NOW.
SO STOP WATCHING PORN OR WHATEVER YOU'RE HIDING--
--AND FOLLOW ME.
To: "Nocturnus Encrypted" (nt@routeproxy.chn)
From: "Meg Encrypted" (mg@routeproxy.chn)
Attachment: Galahad Enterprises Personnel Records
WHERE ARE WE GOING IN SUCH A RUSH?
TO FIND A PHONE.
HERE.
REALLY? HOW MANY OF THOSE DO YOU CARRY AT ONE TIME, SON?

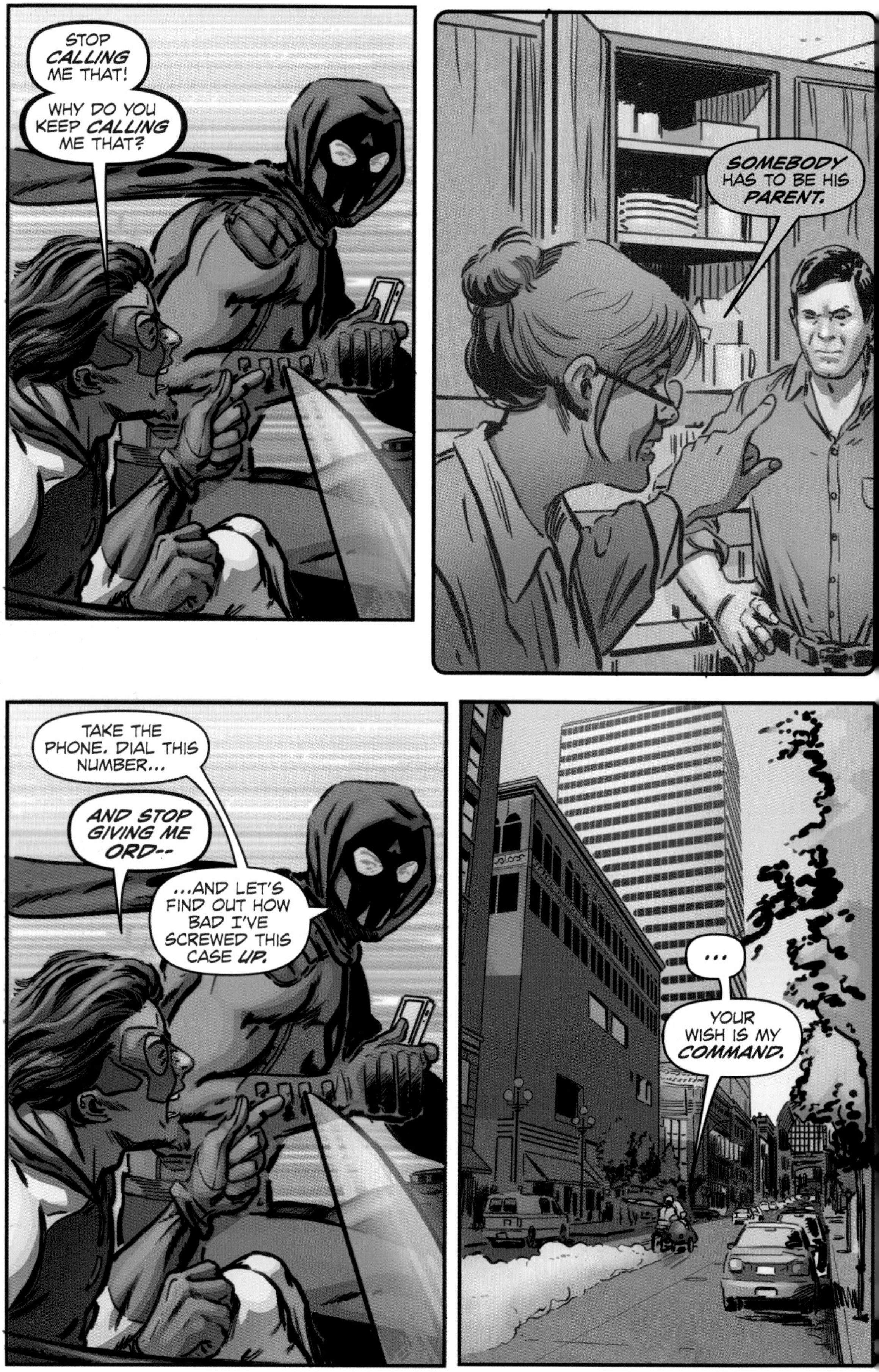

STOP CALLING ME THAT!
WHY DO YOU KEEP CALLING ME THAT?
SOMEBODY HAS TO BE HIS PARENT.
TAKE THE PHONE. DIAL THIS NUMBER...
AND STOP GIVING ME ORD--
...AND LET'S FIND OUT HOW BAD I'VE SCREWED THIS CASE UP.
...
YOUR WISH IS MY COMMAND.

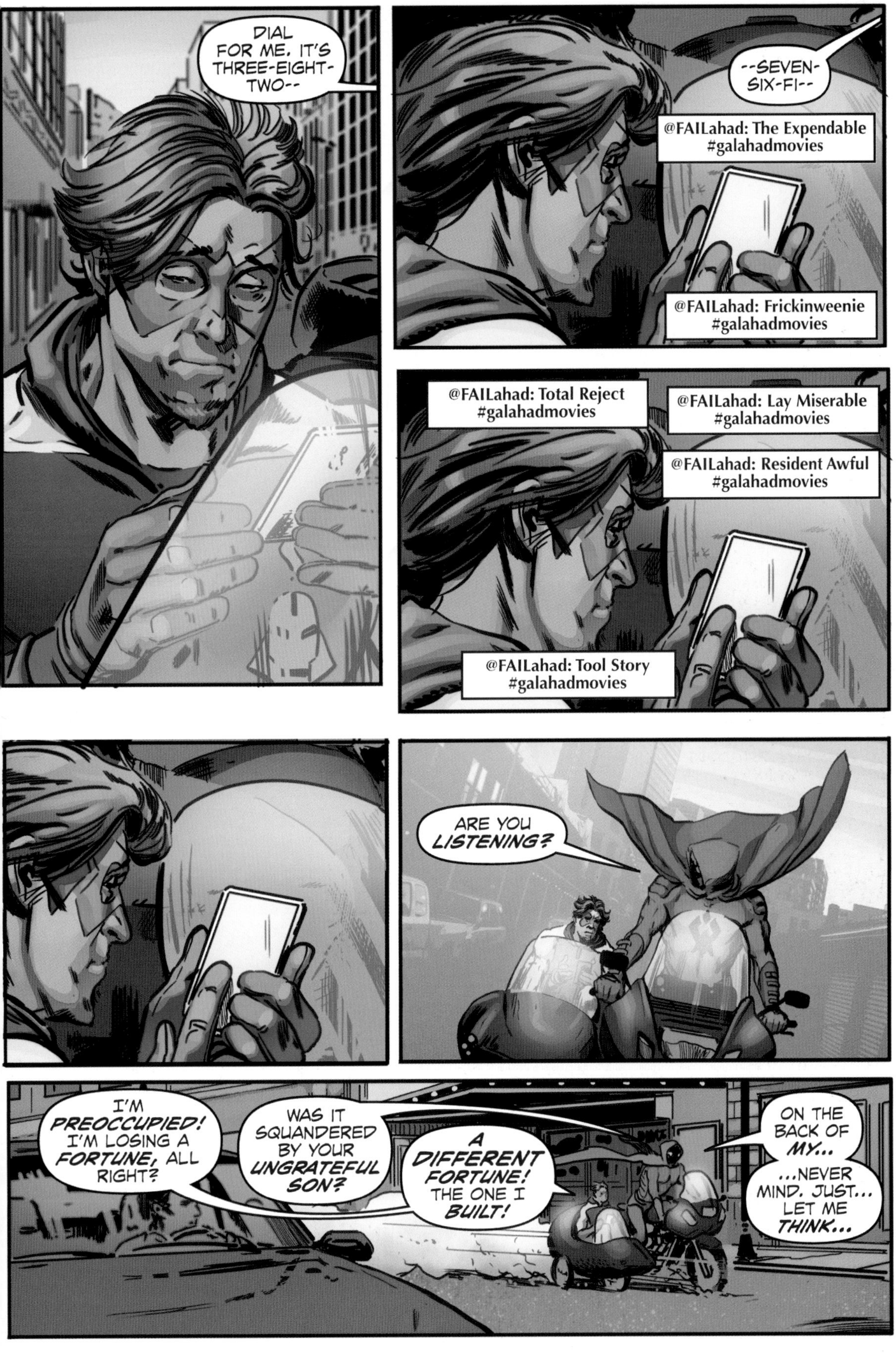

DIAL FOR ME. IT'S THREE-EIGHT-TWO--
--SEVEN-SIX-FI--
@FAILahad: The Expendable #galahadmovies
@FAILahad: Frickinweenie #galahadmovies
@FAILahad: Total Reject #galahadmovies
@FAILahad: Lay Miserable #galahadmovies
@FAILahad: Resident Awful #galahadmovies
@FAILahad: Tool Story #galahadmovies
ARE YOU LISTENING?
I'M PREOCCUPIED! I'M LOSING A FORTUNE, ALL RIGHT?
WAS IT SQUANDERED BY YOUR UNGRATEFUL SON?
A DIFFERENT FORTUNE! THE ONE I BUILT!
ON THE BACK OF MY...
...NEVER MIND. JUST... LET ME THINK...

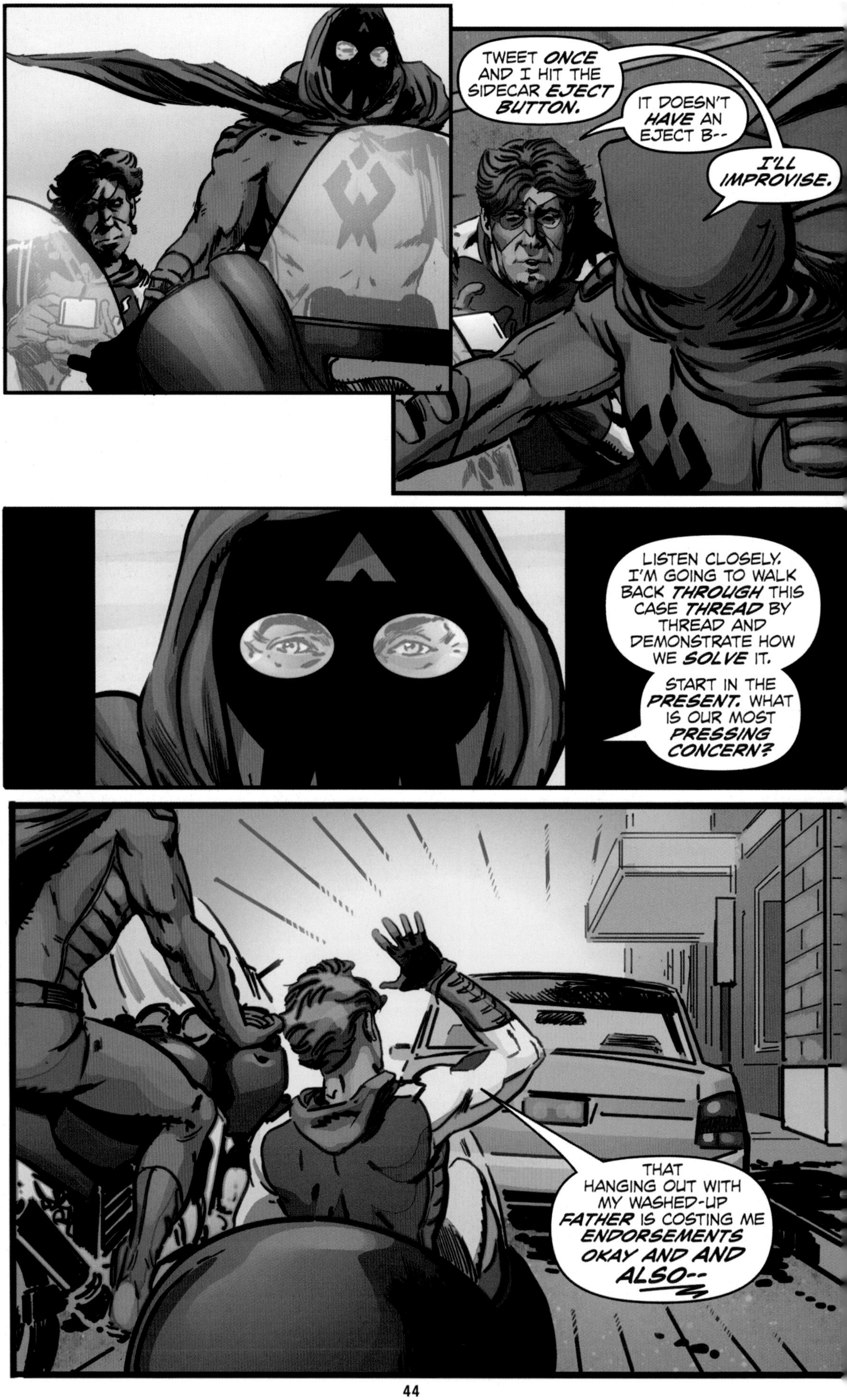
TWEET ONCE AND I HIT THE SIDECAR EJECT BUTTON.
IT DOESN'T HAVE AN EJECT B--
I'LL IMPROVISE.
LISTEN CLOSELY. I'M GOING TO WALK BACK THROUGH THIS CASE THREAD BY THREAD AND DEMONSTRATE HOW WE SOLVE IT.
START IN THE PRESENT. WHAT IS OUR MOST PRESSING CONCERN?
THAT HANGING OUT WITH MY WASHED-UP FATHER IS COSTING ME ENDORSEMENTS OKAY AND AND ALSO--

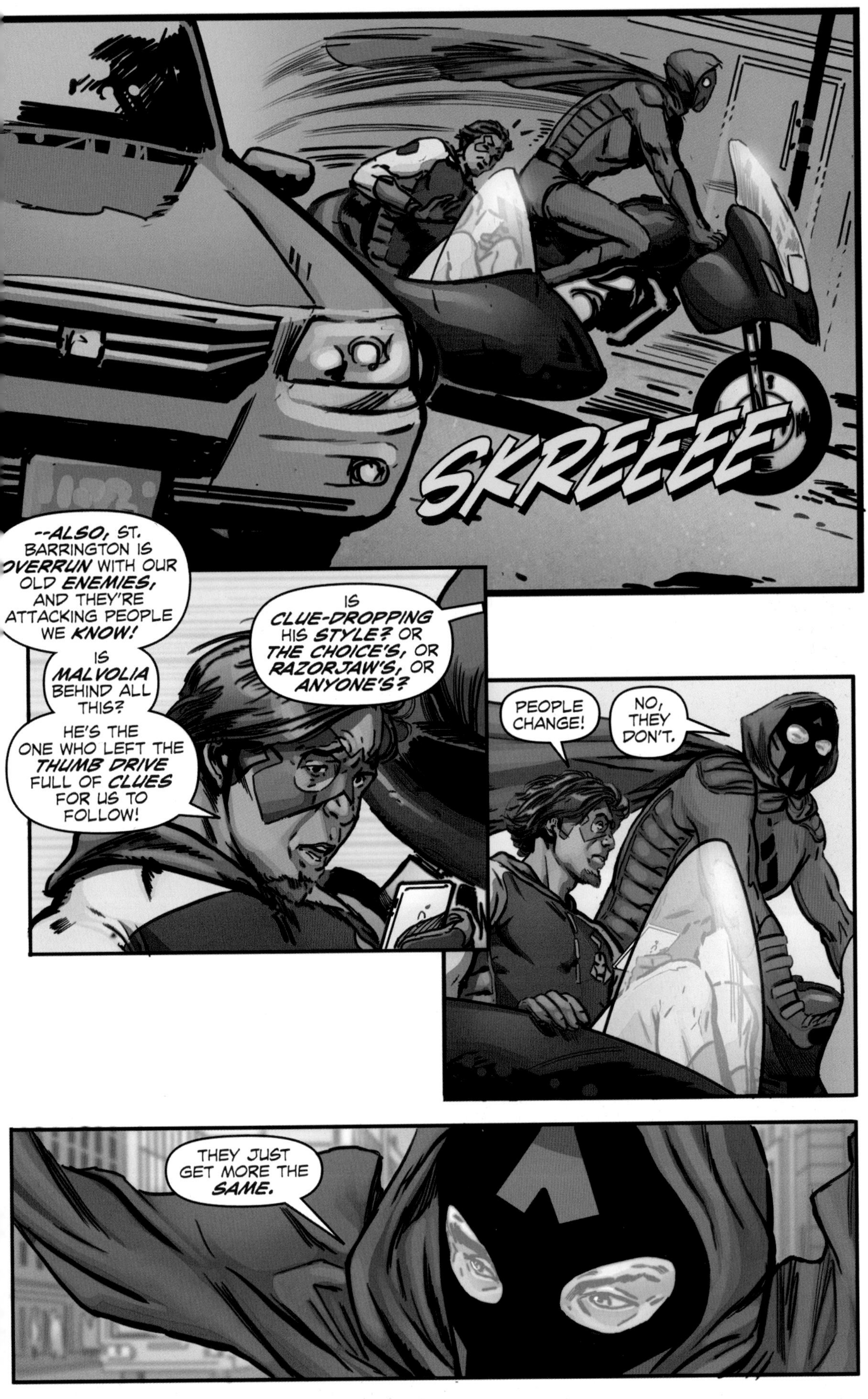
SKREEEEE
--ALSO, ST. BARRINGTON IS OVERRUN WITH OUR OLD ENEMIES, AND THEY'RE ATTACKING PEOPLE WE KNOW!
IS MALVOLIA BEHIND ALL THIS?
HE'S THE ONE WHO LEFT THE THUMB DRIVE FULL OF CLUES FOR US TO FOLLOW!
IS CLUE-DROPPING HIS STYLE? OR THE CHOICE'S, OR RAZORJAW'S, OR ANYONE'S?
PEOPLE CHANGE!
NO, THEY DON'T.
THEY JUST GET MORE THE SAME.

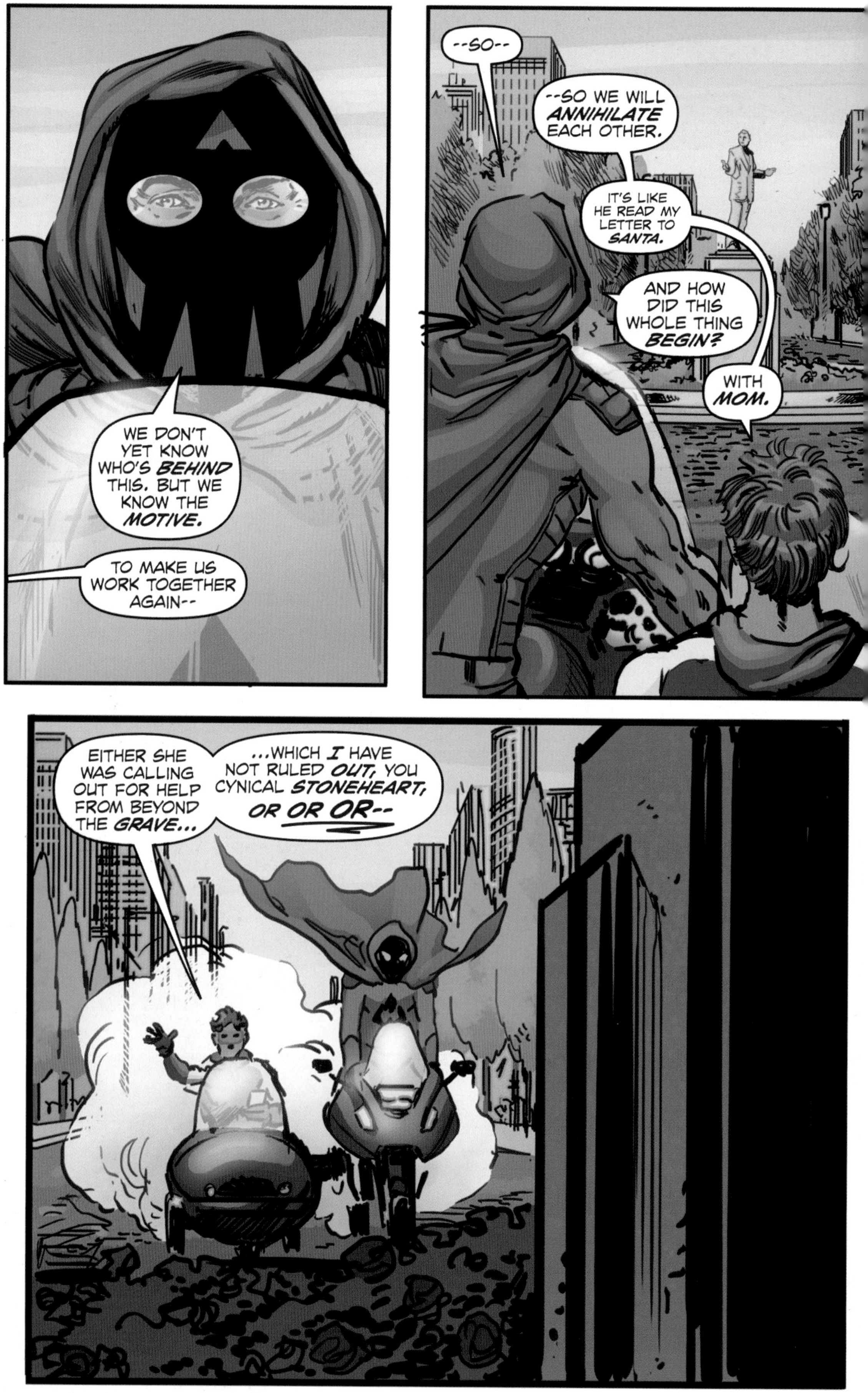
WE DON'T YET KNOW WHO'S *BEHIND* THIS. BUT WE KNOW THE *MOTIVE.*
TO MAKE US WORK TOGETHER AGAIN--
--SO--
--SO WE WILL *ANNIHILATE* EACH OTHER.
IT'S LIKE HE READ MY LETTER TO *SANTA.*
AND HOW DID THIS WHOLE THING *BEGIN?*
WITH *MOM.*
EITHER SHE WAS CALLING OUT FOR HELP FROM BEYOND THE *GRAVE...*
...WHICH *I* HAVE NOT RULED *OUT,* YOU CYNICAL *STONEHEART,* *OR OR OR--*

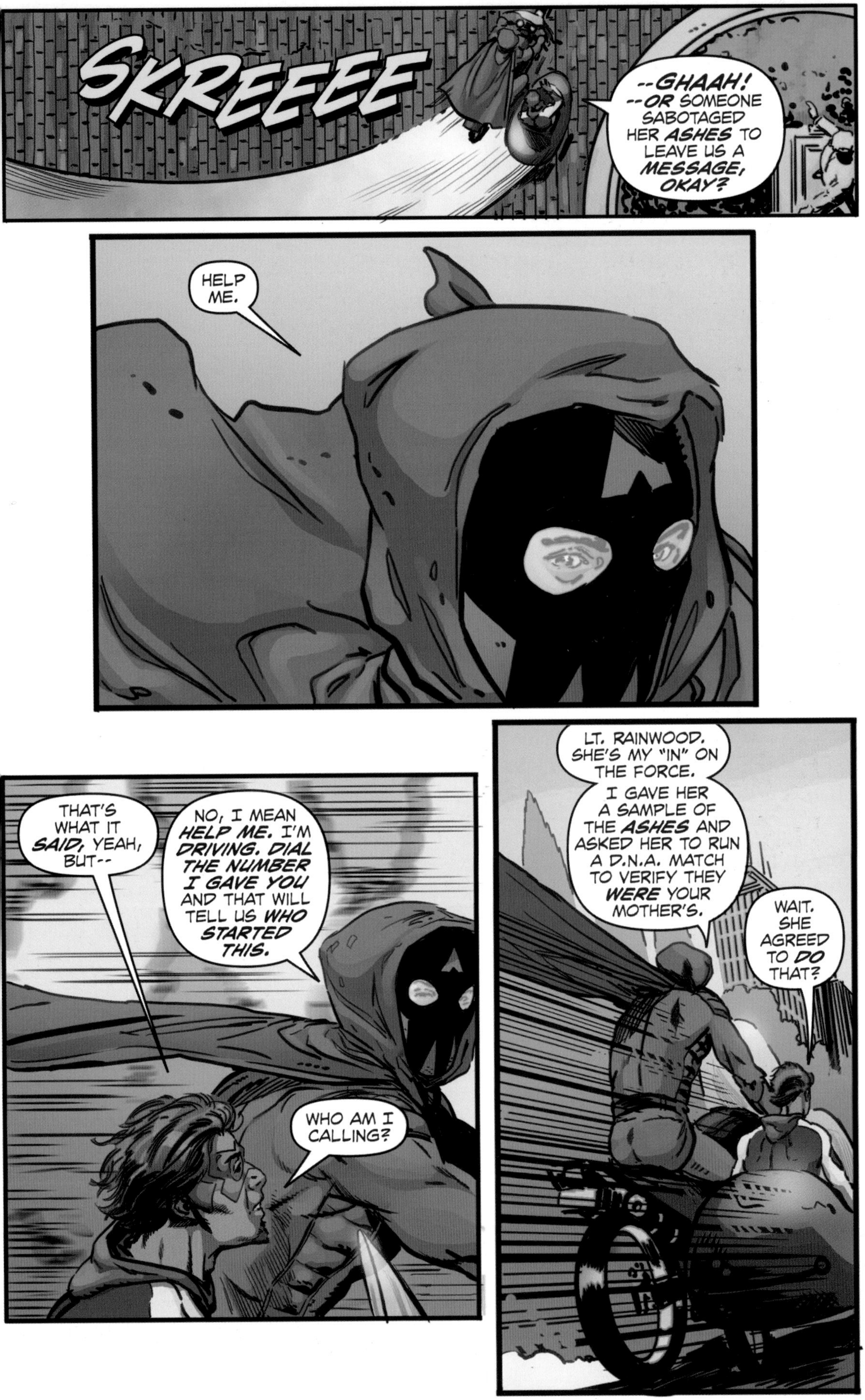
SKREEEE
--GHAAH! --OR SOMEONE SABOTAGED HER ASHES TO LEAVE US A MESSAGE, OKAY?
HELP ME.
THAT'S WHAT IT SAID, YEAH, BUT--
NO, I MEAN HELP ME. I'M DRIVING. DIAL THE NUMBER I GAVE YOU AND THAT WILL TELL US WHO STARTED THIS.
WHO AM I CALLING?
LT. RAINWOOD. SHE'S MY "IN" ON THE FORCE.
I GAVE HER A SAMPLE OF THE ASHES AND ASKED HER TO RUN A D.N.A. MATCH TO VERIFY THEY WERE YOUR MOTHER'S.
WAIT. SHE AGREED TO DO THAT?

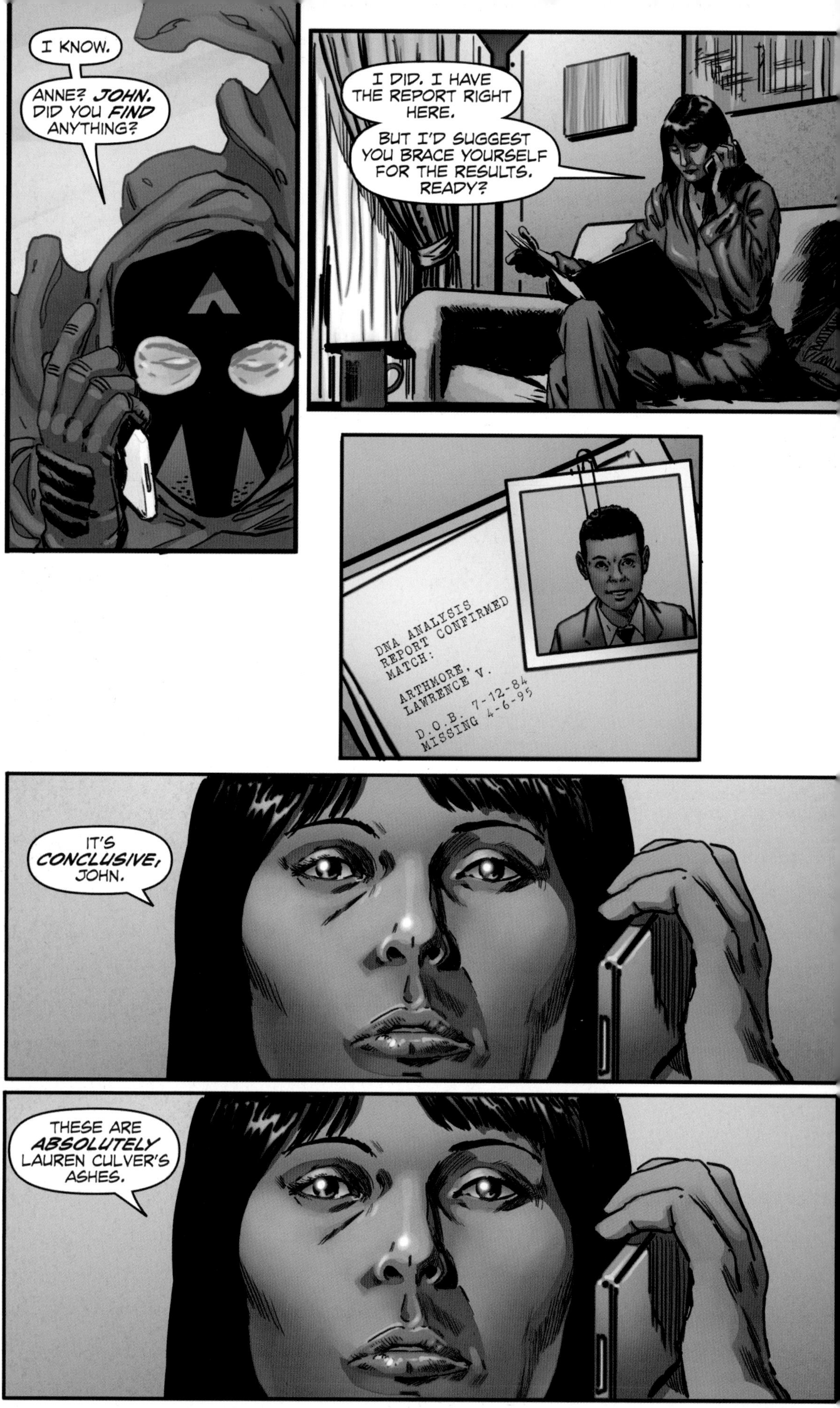
I KNOW.
ANNE? JOHN. DID YOU FIND ANYTHING?
I DID. I HAVE THE REPORT RIGHT HERE.
BUT I'D SUGGEST YOU BRACE YOURSELF FOR THE RESULTS. READY?
DNA ANALYSIS
REPORT CONFIRMED
MATCH:
ARTHMORE,
LAWRENCE V.
D.O.B. 7-12-84
MISSING 4-6-95
IT'S CONCLUSIVE, JOHN.
THESE ARE ABSOLUTELY LAUREN CULVER'S ASHES.

CHAPTER SEVEN

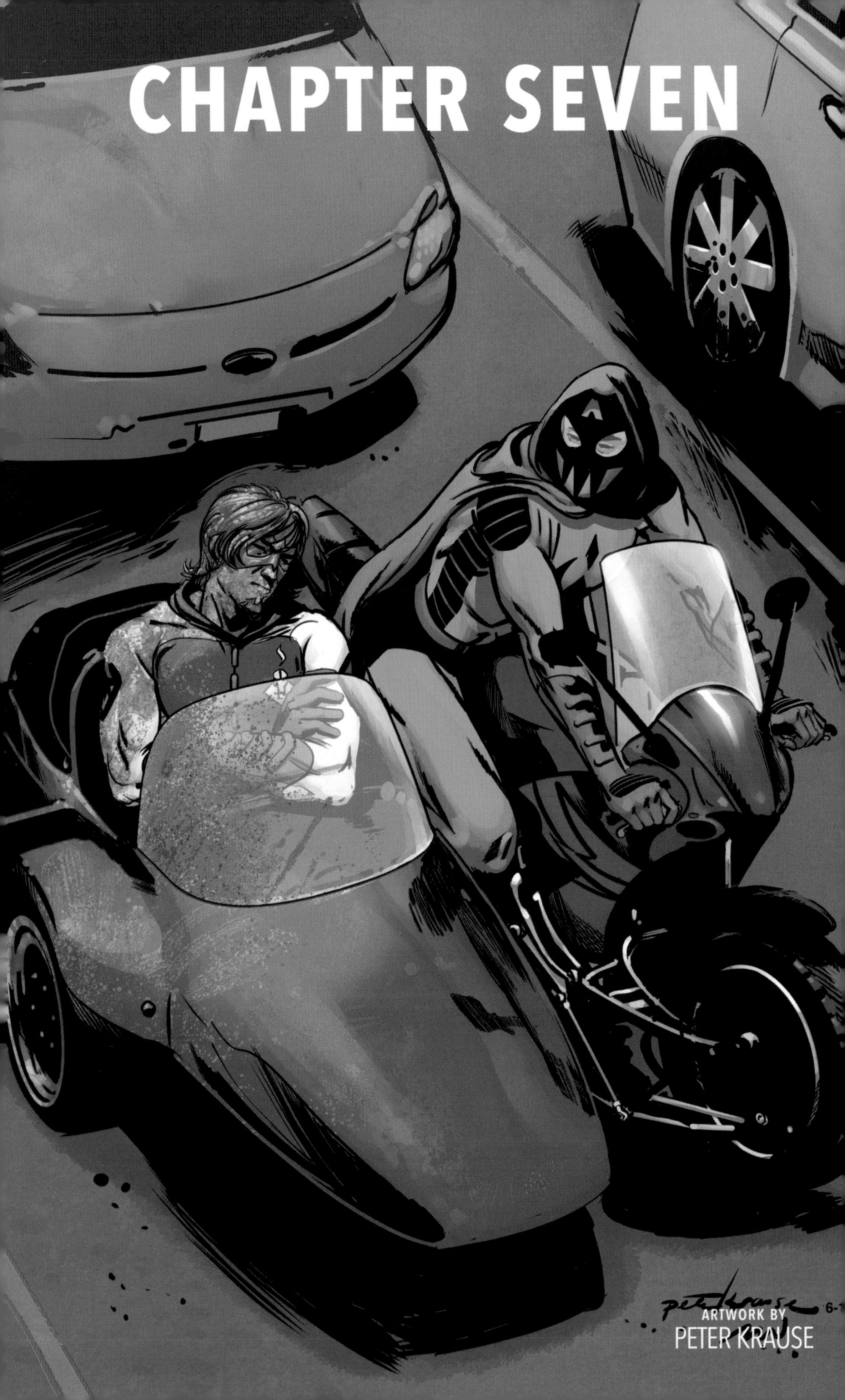

ARTWORK BY
PETER KRAUSE

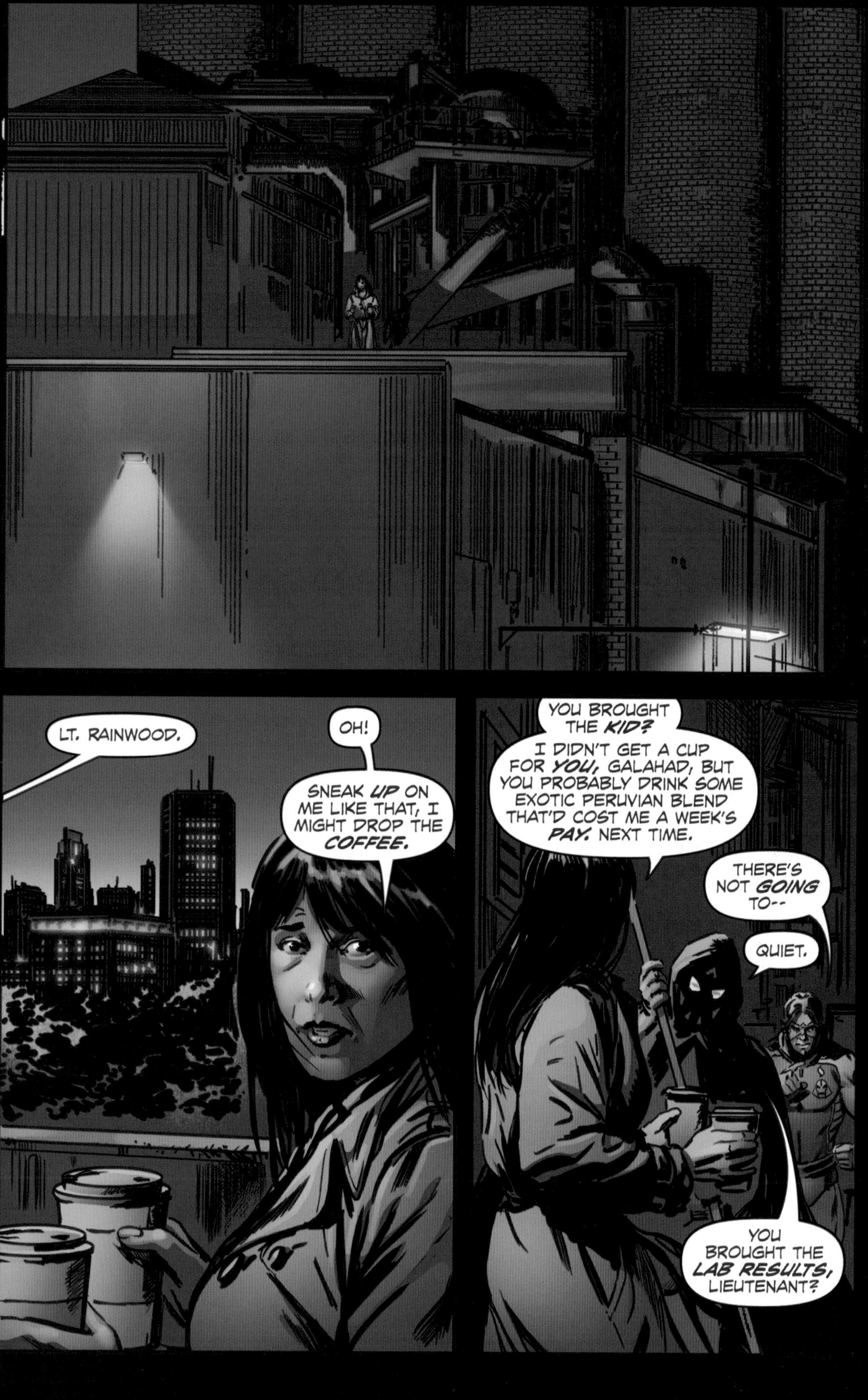
LT. RAINWOOD.
OH!
SNEAK UP ON ME LIKE THAT, I MIGHT DROP THE COFFEE.
YOU BROUGHT THE KID?
I DIDN'T GET A CUP FOR YOU, GALAHAD, BUT YOU PROBABLY DRINK SOME EXOTIC PERUVIAN BLEND THAT'D COST ME A WEEK'S PAY. NEXT TIME.
THERE'S NOT GOING TO--
QUIET.
YOU BROUGHT THE LAB RESULTS, LIEUTENANT?

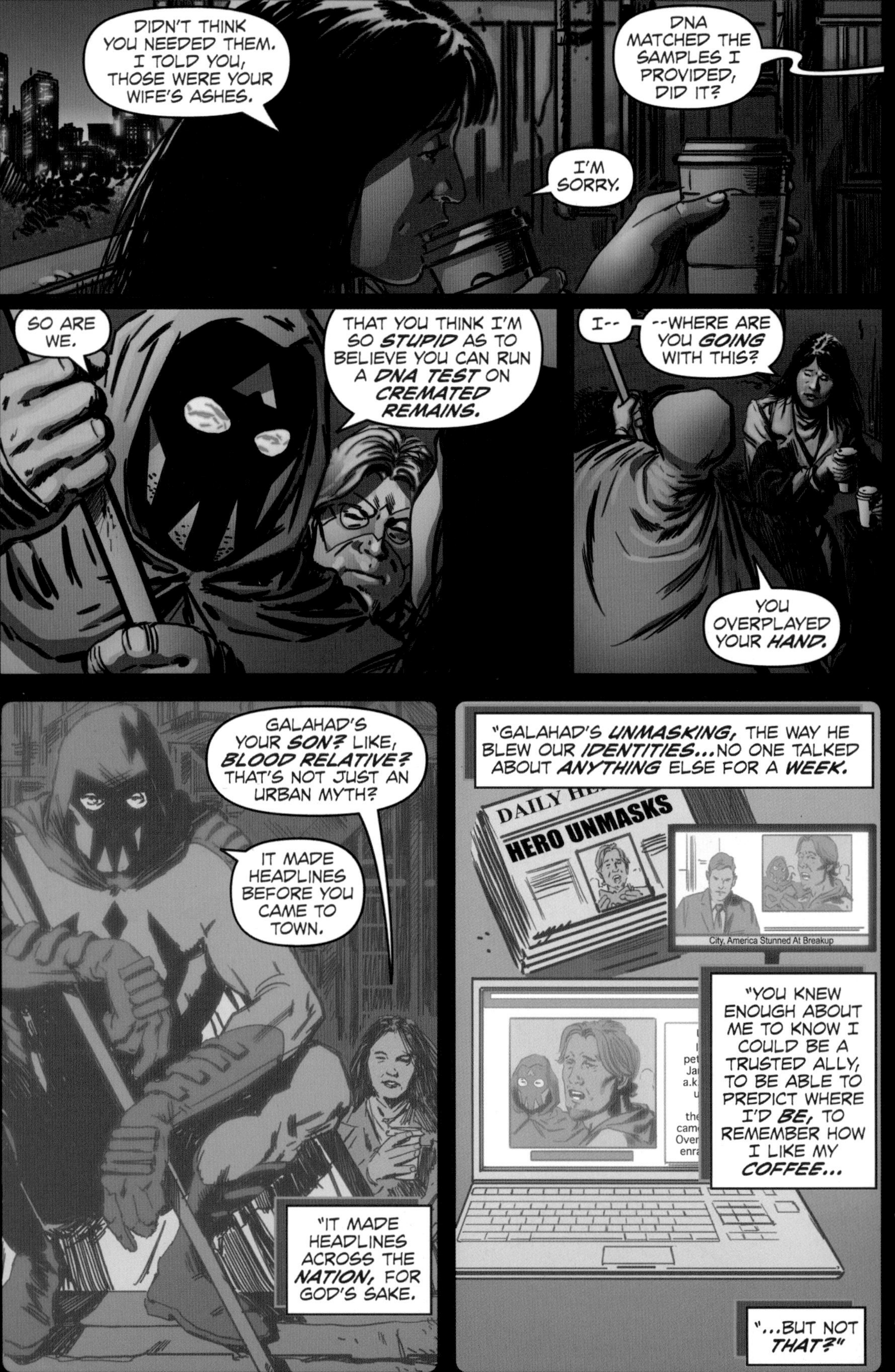
DIDN'T THINK YOU NEEDED THEM. I TOLD YOU, THOSE WERE YOUR WIFE'S ASHES.
DNA MATCHED THE SAMPLES I PROVIDED, DID IT?
I'M SORRY.
SO ARE WE.
THAT YOU THINK I'M SO STUPID AS TO BELIEVE YOU CAN RUN A DNA TEST ON CREMATED REMAINS.
I--
--WHERE ARE YOU GOING WITH THIS?
YOU OVERPLAYED YOUR HAND.
GALAHAD'S YOUR SON? LIKE, BLOOD RELATIVE? THAT'S NOT JUST AN URBAN MYTH?
IT MADE HEADLINES BEFORE YOU CAME TO TOWN.
"IT MADE HEADLINES ACROSS THE NATION, FOR GOD'S SAKE.
"GALAHAD'S UNMASKING, THE WAY HE BLEW OUR IDENTITIES...NO ONE TALKED ABOUT ANYTHING ELSE FOR A WEEK.
DAILY HE
HERO UNMASKS
City, America Stunned At Breakup
"YOU KNEW ENOUGH ABOUT ME TO KNOW I COULD BE A TRUSTED ALLY, TO BE ABLE TO PREDICT WHERE I'D BE, TO REMEMBER HOW I LIKE MY COFFEE...
"...BUT NOT THAT?"

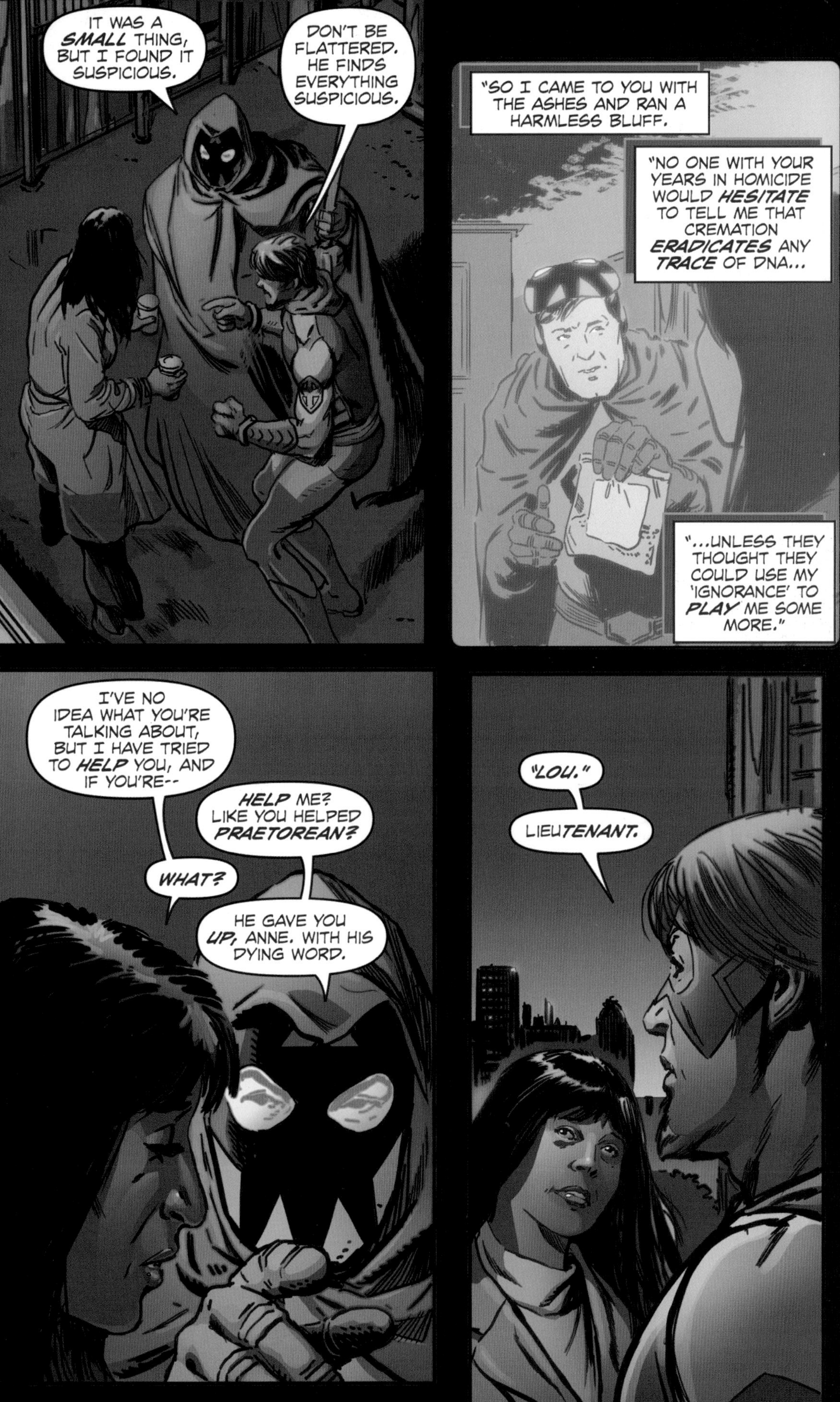
IT WAS A SMALL THING, BUT I FOUND IT SUSPICIOUS.
DON'T BE FLATTERED. HE FINDS EVERYTHING SUSPICIOUS.
"SO I CAME TO YOU WITH THE ASHES AND RAN A HARMLESS BLUFF.
"NO ONE WITH YOUR YEARS IN HOMICIDE WOULD HESITATE TO TELL ME THAT CREMATION ERADICATES ANY TRACE OF DNA...
"...UNLESS THEY THOUGHT THEY COULD USE MY 'IGNORANCE' TO PLAY ME SOME MORE."
I'VE NO IDEA WHAT YOU'RE TALKING ABOUT, BUT I HAVE TRIED TO HELP YOU, AND IF YOU'RE--
HELP ME? LIKE YOU HELPED PRAETOREAN?
WHAT?
HE GAVE YOU UP, ANNE. WITH HIS DYING WORD.
"LOU."
LIEUTENANT.

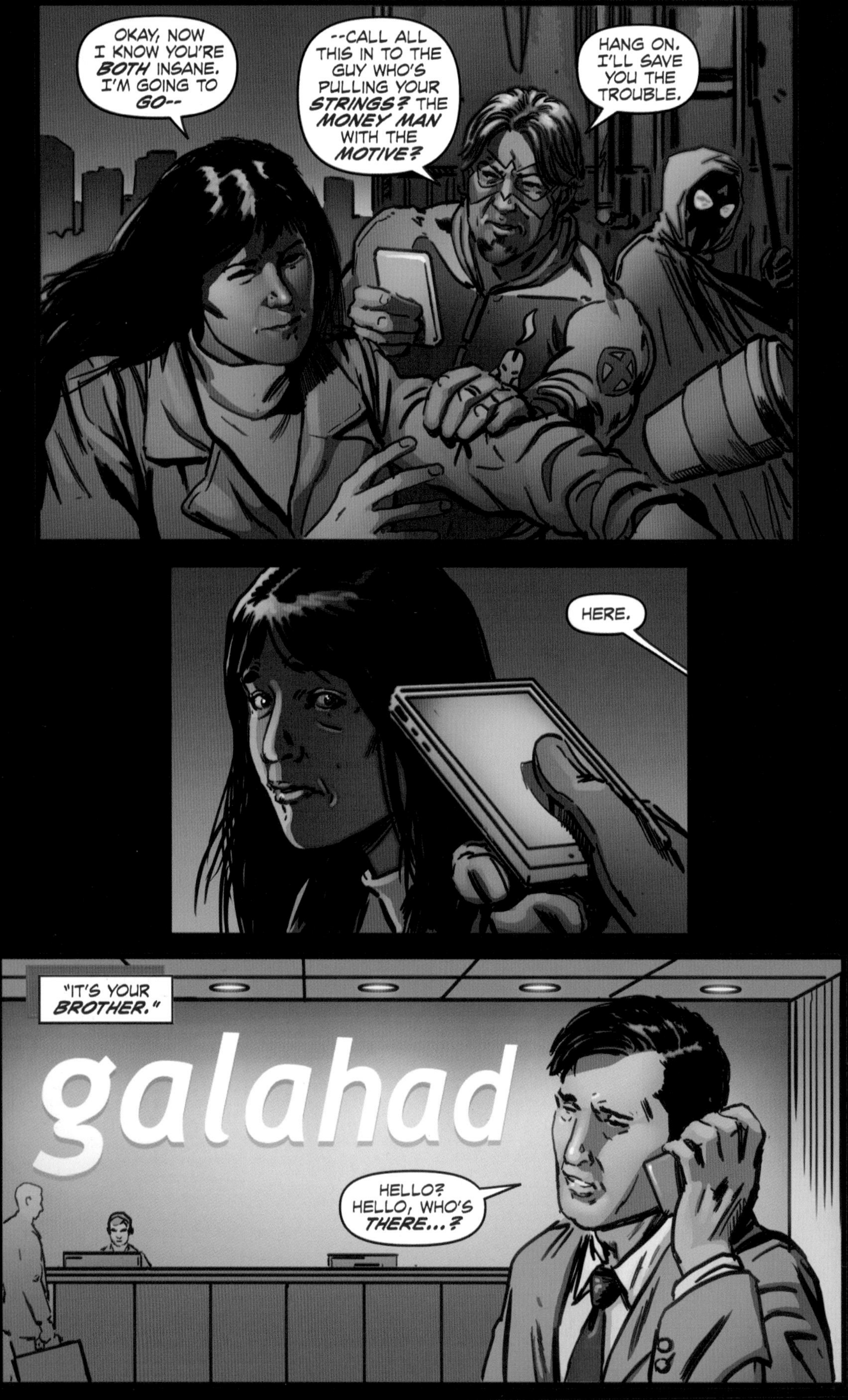
OKAY, NOW I KNOW YOU'RE *BOTH* INSANE. I'M GOING TO *GO--*
--CALL ALL THIS IN TO THE GUY WHO'S PULLING YOUR *STRINGS?* THE *MONEY MAN* WITH THE *MOTIVE?*
HANG ON. I'LL SAVE YOU THE TROUBLE.
HERE.
"IT'S YOUR *BROTHER.*"
galahad
HELLO? HELLO, WHO'S *THERE...?*

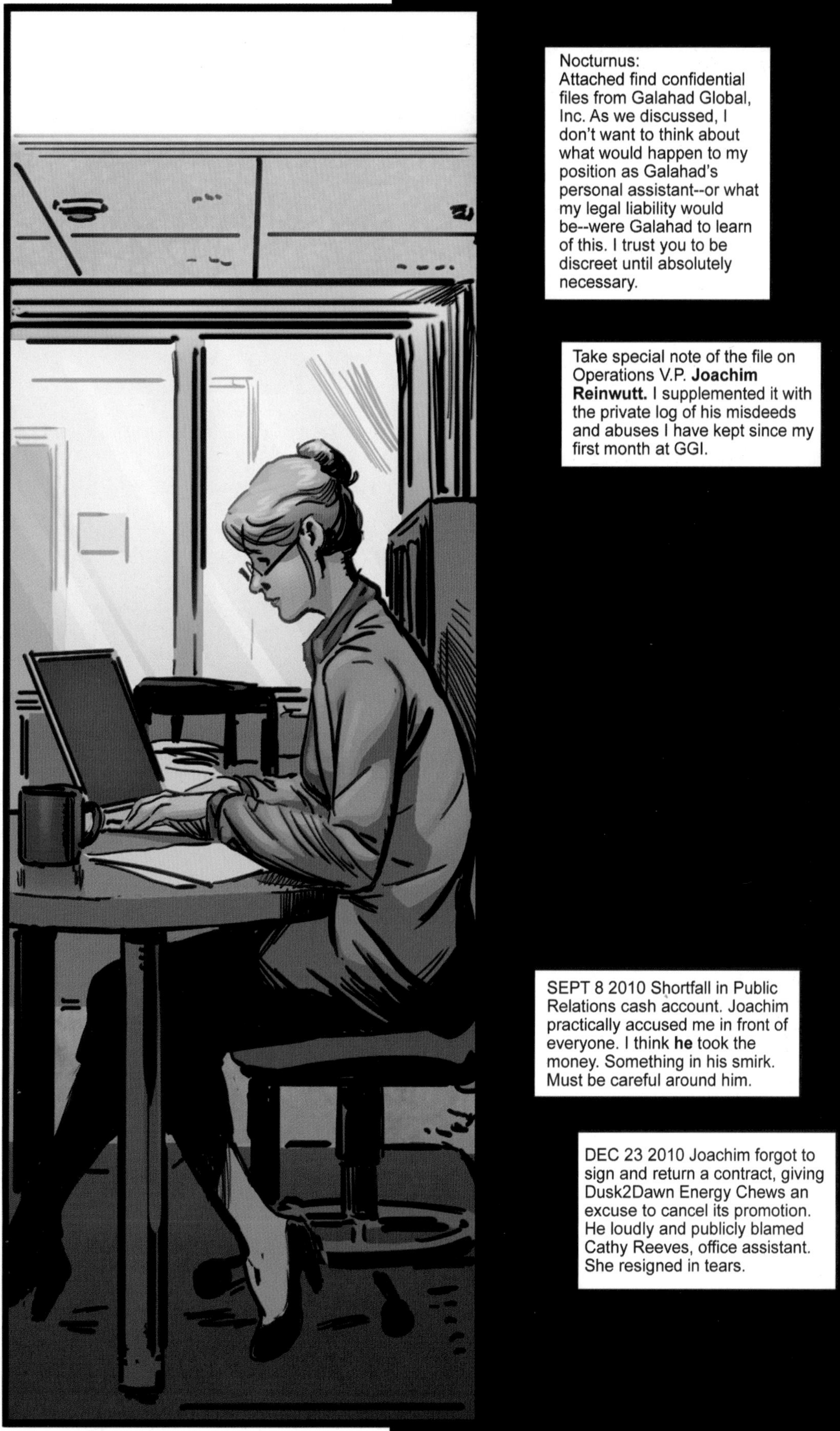
Nocturnus:
Attached find confidential files from Galahad Global, Inc. As we discussed, I don't want to think about what would happen to my position as Galahad's personal assistant--or what my legal liability would be--were Galahad to learn of this. I trust you to be discreet until absolutely necessary.
Take special note of the file on Operations V.P. **Joachim Reinwutt.** I supplemented it with the private log of his misdeeds and abuses I have kept since my first month at GGI.
SEPT 8 2010 Shortfall in Public Relations cash account. Joachim practically accused me in front of everyone. I think **he** took the money. Something in his smirk. Must be careful around him.
DEC 23 2010 Joachim forgot to sign and return a contract, giving Dusk2Dawn Energy Chews an excuse to cancel its promotion. He loudly and publicly blamed Cathy Reeves, office assistant. She resigned in tears.

JAN 3 2011 Joachim hired a new assistant, James. Early 20s, maybe 400 lbs. His size is a constant source of delight to Joachim. After the office closed on Friday, I spied James in the break room, crying.

FEB 11 2011 Joachim spent two afternoons arranging a free ski weekend in Aspen, promising "a 90% chance" Galahad would join him there. Somehow failed to mention it to Galahad.

FEB 15 2011 Liquor on his breath, Joachim spent the marketing meeting crowing about bad references he's been giving to prospective employers of Cathy's. No one else laughed.

WORKING HARD OR HARDLY WORKING?

!

JUST... CATCHING UP ON E-MAIL.

FEB 24 2011 Deanna from Children's Licensing went on the ski trip with Joachim. Am I reading into it, or did she seem coerced?

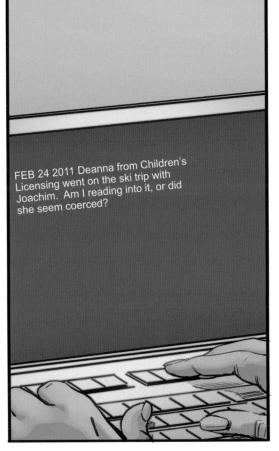

FEB 24 2011 Deanna from Children's Licensing went on the ski trip with Joachim. Am I reading into it, or did she seem coerced?

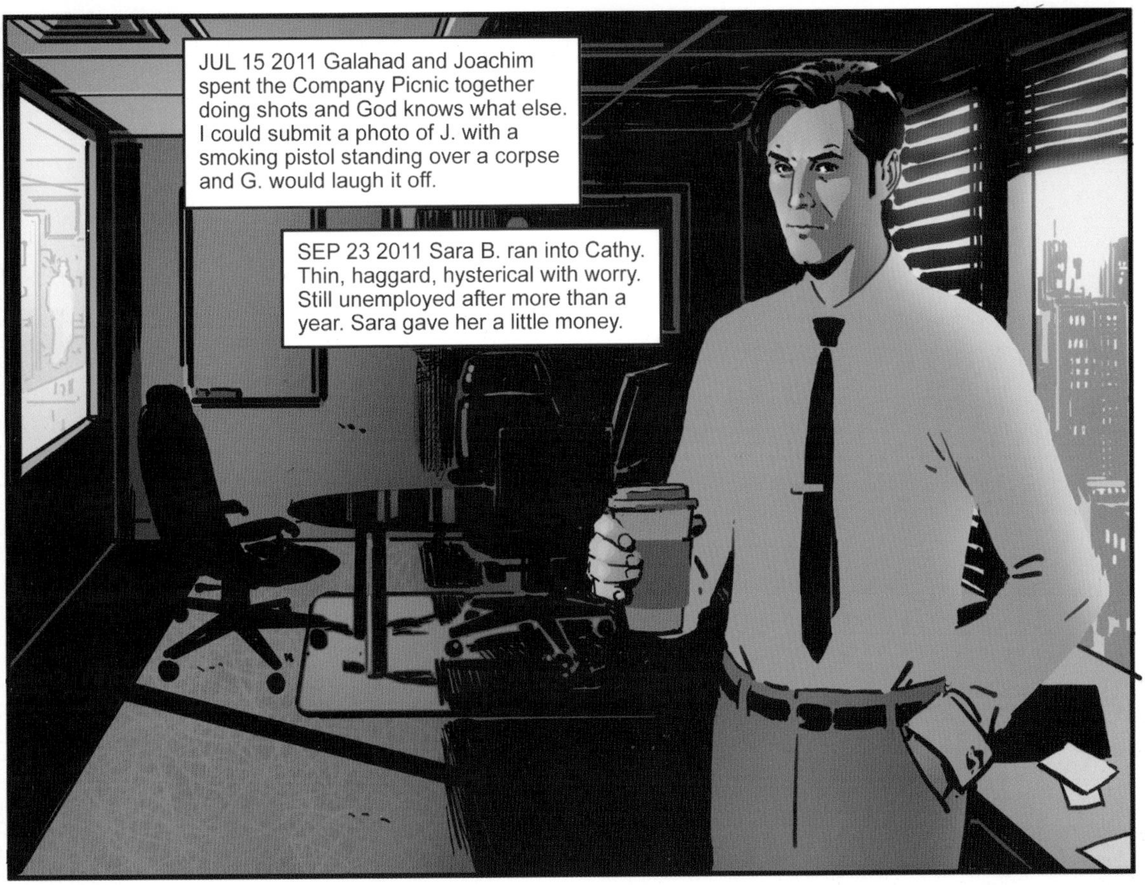
JUL 15 2011 Galahad and Joachim spent the Company Picnic together doing shots and God knows what else. I could submit a photo of J. with a smoking pistol standing over a corpse and G. would laugh it off.
SEP 23 2011 Sara B. ran into Cathy. Thin, haggard, hysterical with worry. Still unemployed after more than a year. Sara gave her a little money.

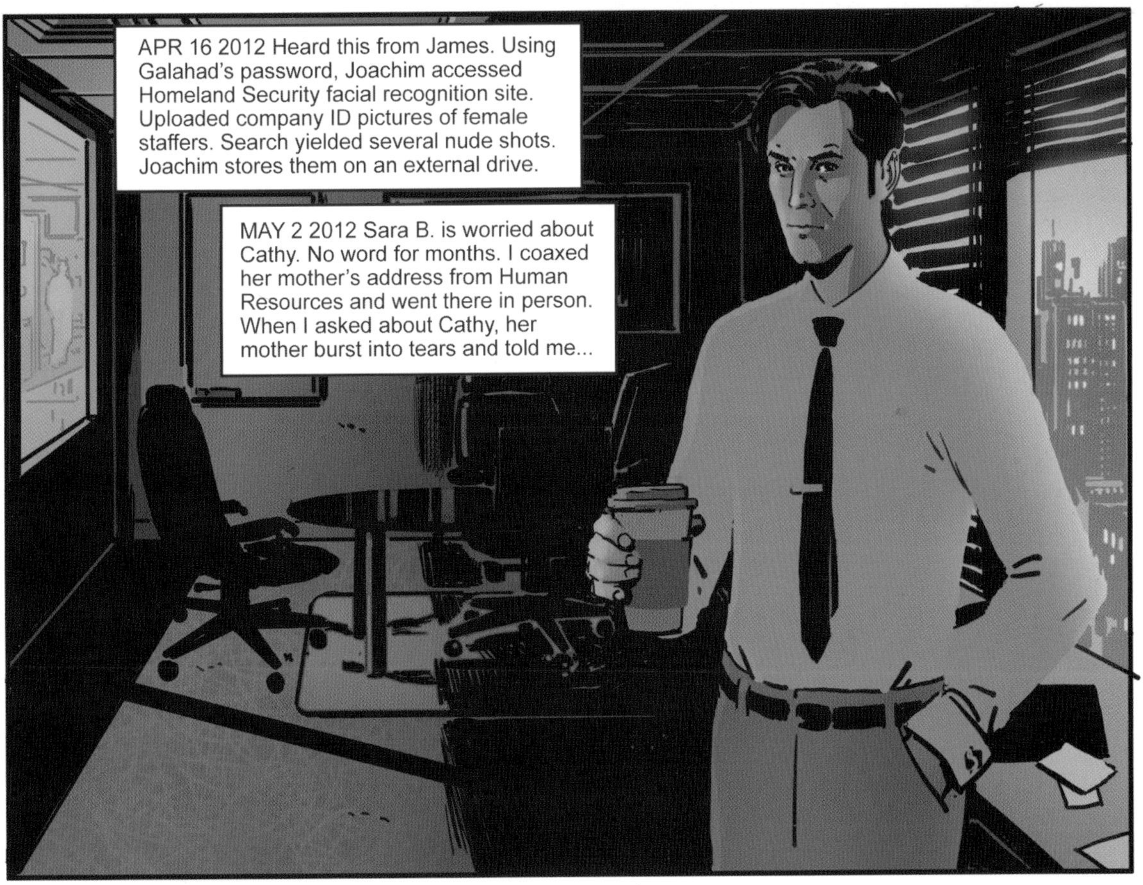
APR 16 2012 Heard this from James. Using Galahad's password, Joachim accessed Homeland Security facial recognition site. Uploaded company ID pictures of female staffers. Search yielded several nude shots. Joachim stores them on an external drive.
MAY 2 2012 Sara B. is worried about Cathy. No word for months. I coaxed her mother's address from Human Resources and went there in person. When I asked about Cathy, her mother burst into tears and told me...

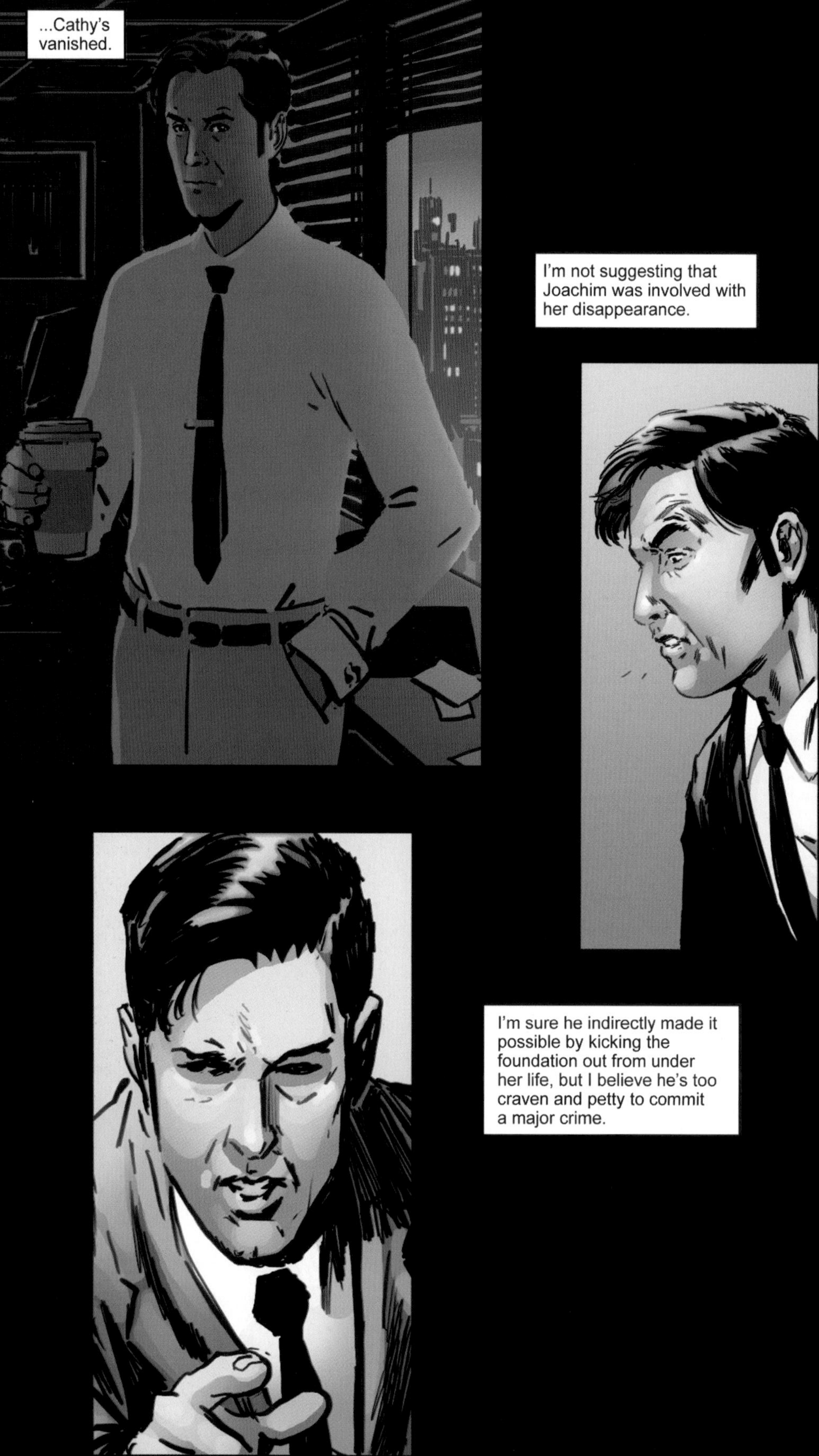
...Cathy's vanished.
I'm not suggesting that Joachim was involved with her disappearance.
I'm sure he indirectly made it possible by kicking the foundation out from under her life, but I believe he's too craven and petty to commit a major crime.

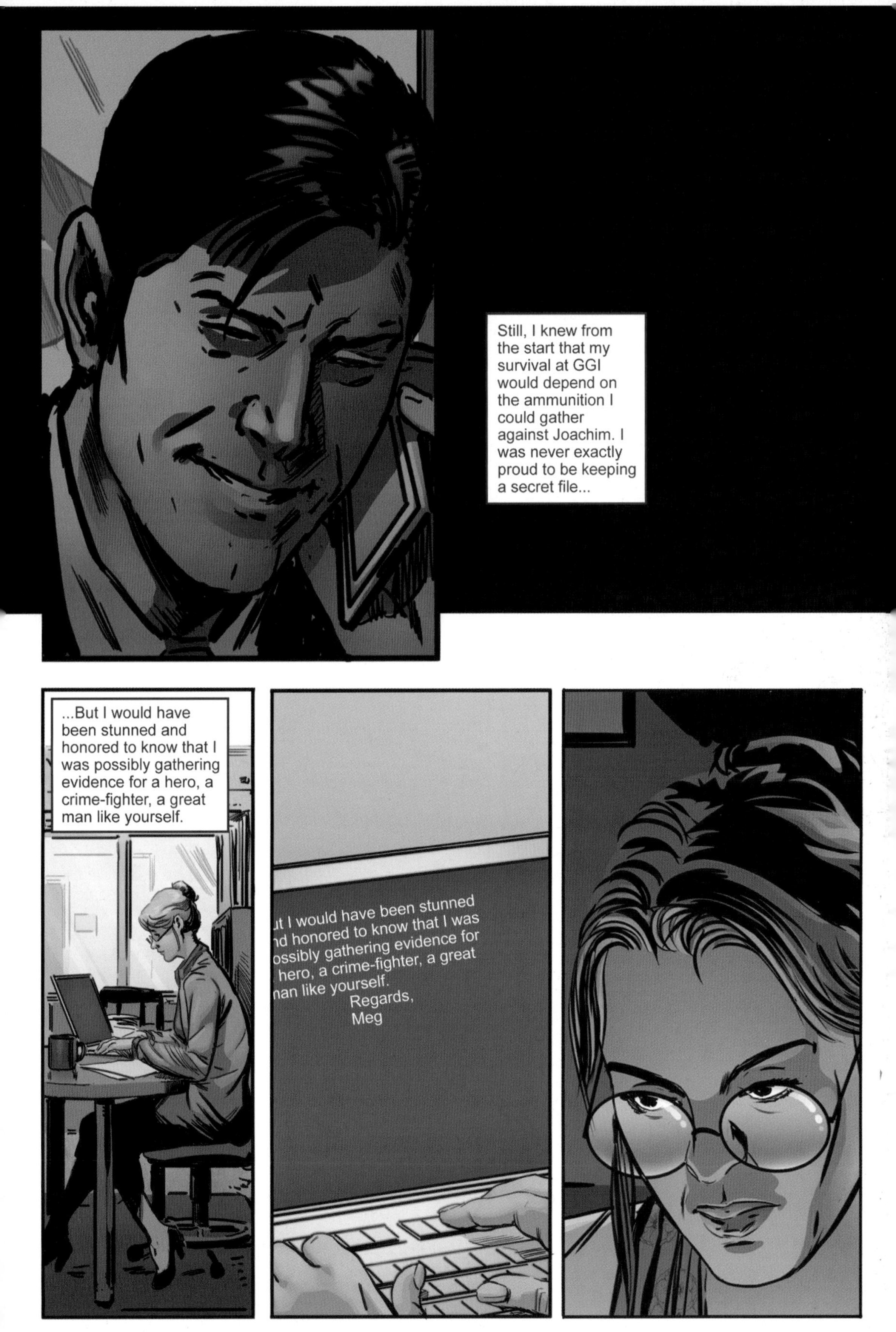
Still, I knew from the start that my survival at GGI would depend on the ammunition I could gather against Joachim. I was never exactly proud to be keeping a secret file...
...But I would have been stunned and honored to know that I was possibly gathering evidence for a hero, a crime-fighter, a great man like yourself.
ut I would have been stunned
nd honored to know that I was
ossibly gathering evidence for
hero, a crime-fighter, a great
nan like yourself.
Regards,
Meg

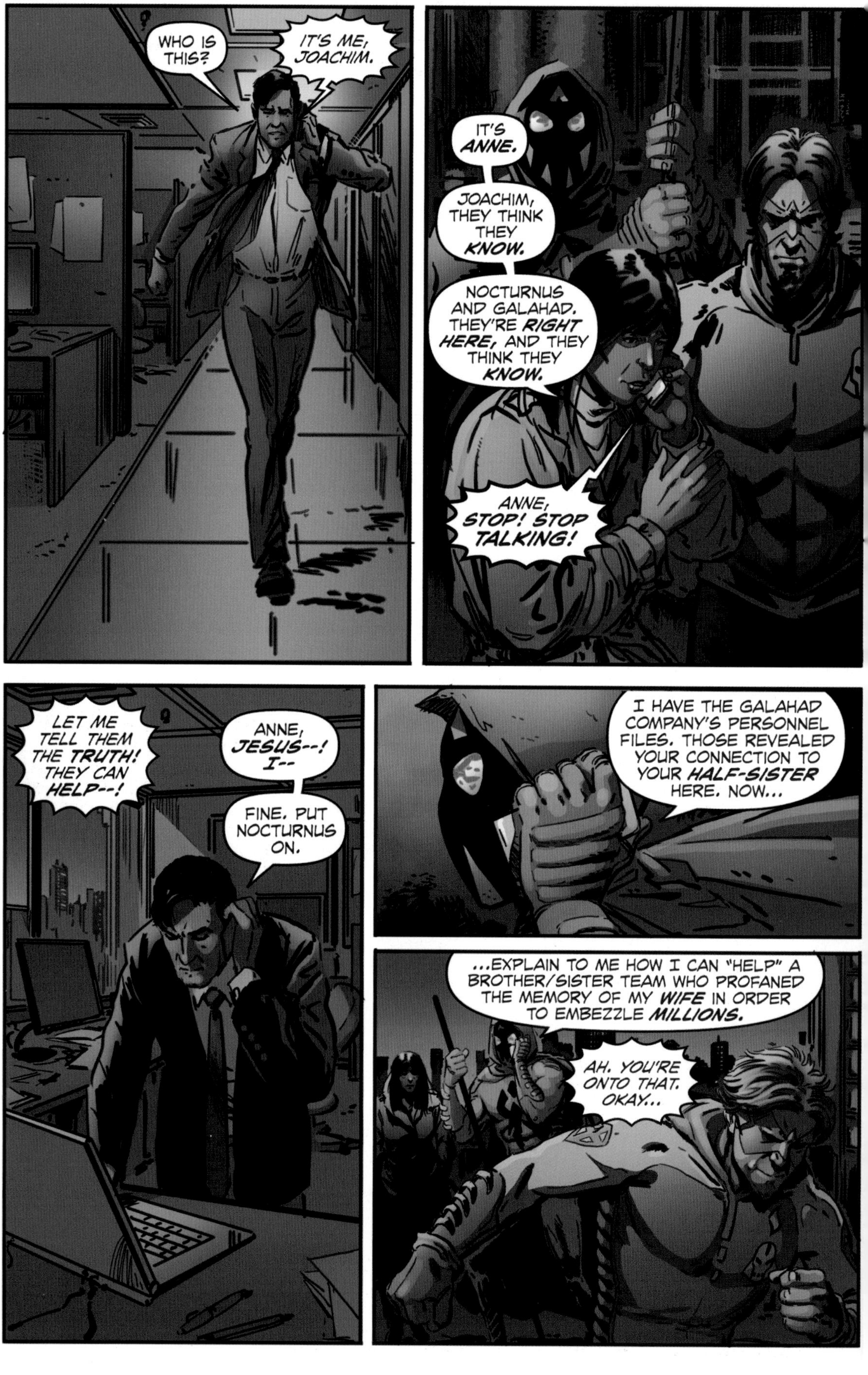
WHO IS THIS?
IT'S ME, JOACHIM.
IT'S ANNE.
JOACHIM, THEY THINK THEY KNOW.
NOCTURNUS AND GALAHAD. THEY'RE RIGHT HERE, AND THEY THINK THEY KNOW.
ANNE, STOP! STOP TALKING!
LET ME TELL THEM THE TRUTH! THEY CAN HELP--!
ANNE, JESUS--! I--
FINE. PUT NOCTURNUS ON.
I HAVE THE GALAHAD COMPANY'S PERSONNEL FILES. THOSE REVEALED YOUR CONNECTION TO YOUR HALF-SISTER HERE. NOW...
...EXPLAIN TO ME HOW I CAN "HELP" A BROTHER/SISTER TEAM WHO PROFANED THE MEMORY OF MY WIFE IN ORDER TO EMBEZZLE MILLIONS.
AH. YOU'RE ONTO THAT. OKAY...

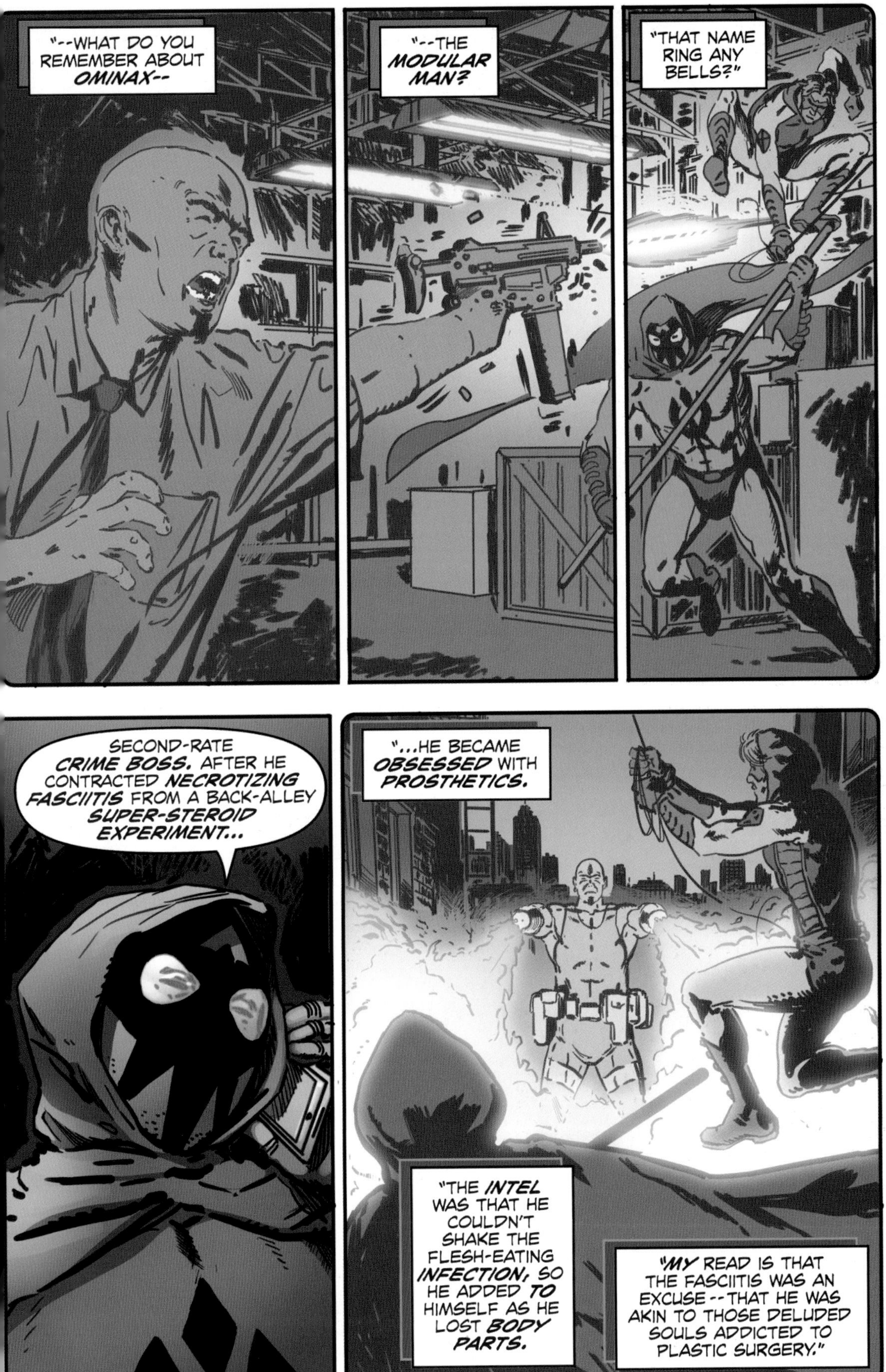
"--WHAT DO YOU REMEMBER ABOUT OMINAX--
"--THE MODULAR MAN?
"THAT NAME RING ANY BELLS?"
SECOND-RATE CRIME BOSS. AFTER HE CONTRACTED NECROTIZING FASCIITIS FROM A BACK-ALLEY SUPER-STEROID EXPERIMENT...
"...HE BECAME OBSESSED WITH PROSTHETICS.
"THE INTEL WAS THAT HE COULDN'T SHAKE THE FLESH-EATING INFECTION, SO HE ADDED TO HIMSELF AS HE LOST BODY PARTS.
"MY READ IS THAT THE FASCIITIS WAS AN EXCUSE--THAT HE WAS AKIN TO THOSE DELUDED SOULS ADDICTED TO PLASTIC SURGERY."

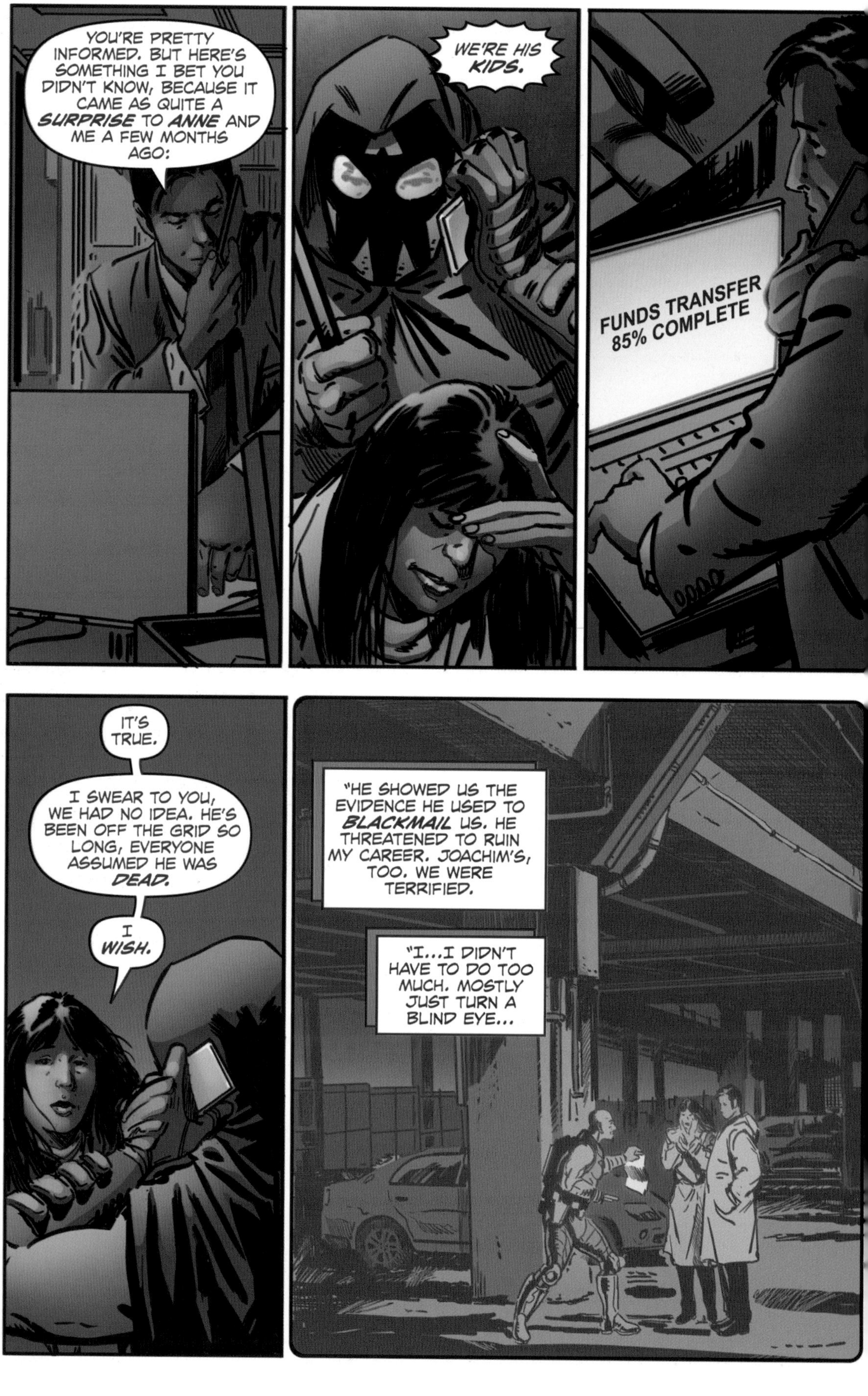
YOU'RE PRETTY INFORMED. BUT HERE'S SOMETHING I BET YOU DIDN'T KNOW, BECAUSE IT CAME AS QUITE A SURPRISE TO ANNE AND ME A FEW MONTHS AGO:
WE'RE HIS KIDS.
FUNDS TRANSFER 85% COMPLETE
IT'S TRUE.
I SWEAR TO YOU, WE HAD NO IDEA. HE'S BEEN OFF THE GRID SO LONG, EVERYONE ASSUMED HE WAS DEAD.
I WISH.
"HE SHOWED US THE EVIDENCE HE USED TO BLACKMAIL US. HE THREATENED TO RUIN MY CAREER. JOACHIM'S, TOO. WE WERE TERRIFIED.
"I...I DIDN'T HAVE TO DO TOO MUCH. MOSTLY JUST TURN A BLIND EYE...

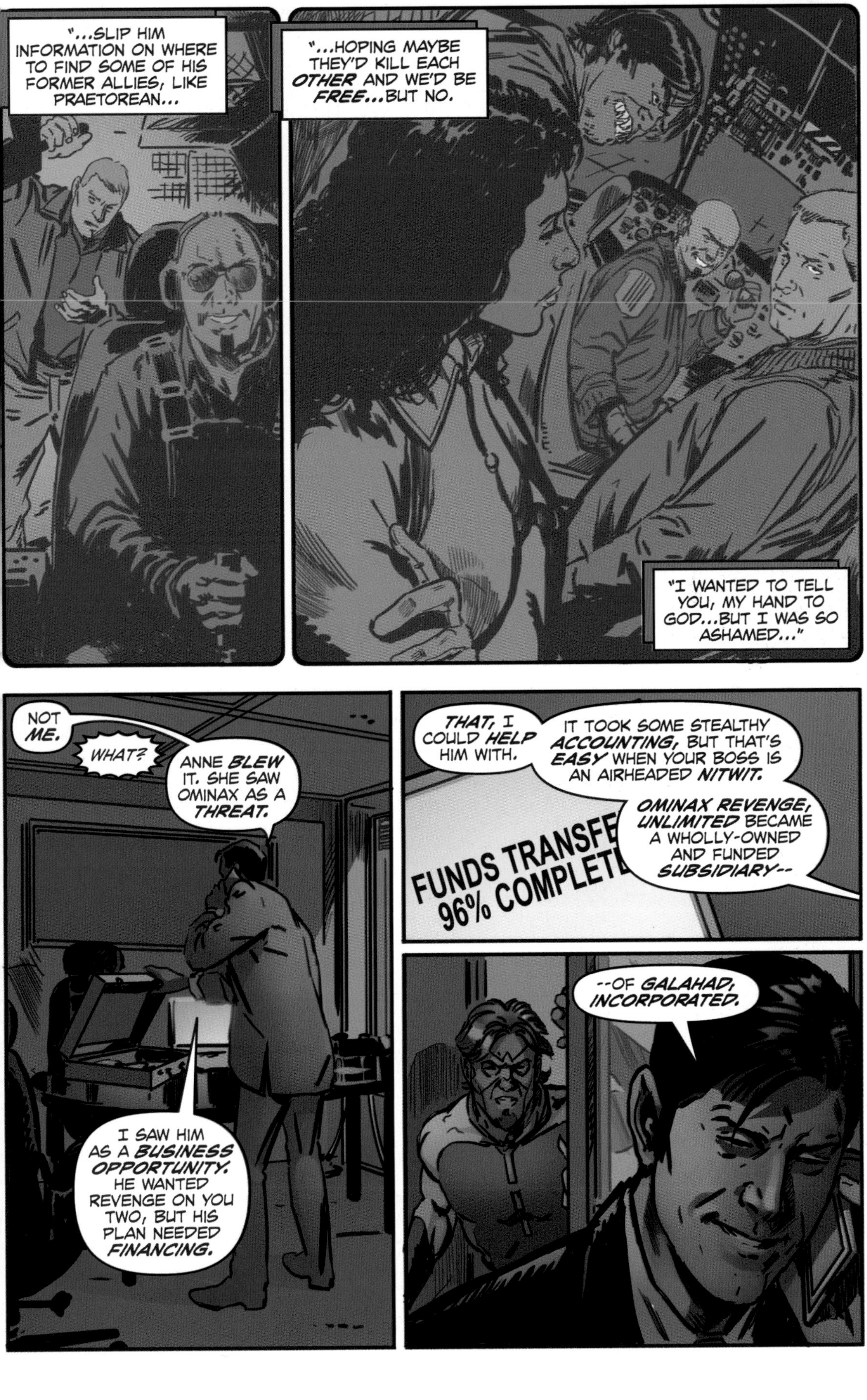
"...SLIP HIM INFORMATION ON WHERE TO FIND SOME OF HIS FORMER ALLIES, LIKE PRAETOREAN...
"...HOPING MAYBE THEY'D KILL EACH OTHER AND WE'D BE FREE...BUT NO.
"I WANTED TO TELL YOU, MY HAND TO GOD...BUT I WAS SO ASHAMED..."
NOT ME.
WHAT?
ANNE BLEW IT. SHE SAW OMINAX AS A THREAT.
I SAW HIM AS A BUSINESS OPPORTUNITY. HE WANTED REVENGE ON YOU TWO, BUT HIS PLAN NEEDED FINANCING.
THAT, I COULD HELP HIM WITH.
IT TOOK SOME STEALTHY ACCOUNTING, BUT THAT'S EASY WHEN YOUR BOSS IS AN AIRHEADED NITWIT.
FUNDS TRANSFE
96% COMPLETE
OMINAX REVENGE, UNLIMITED BECAME A WHOLLY-OWNED AND FUNDED SUBSIDIARY--
--OF GALAHAD, INCORPORATED.

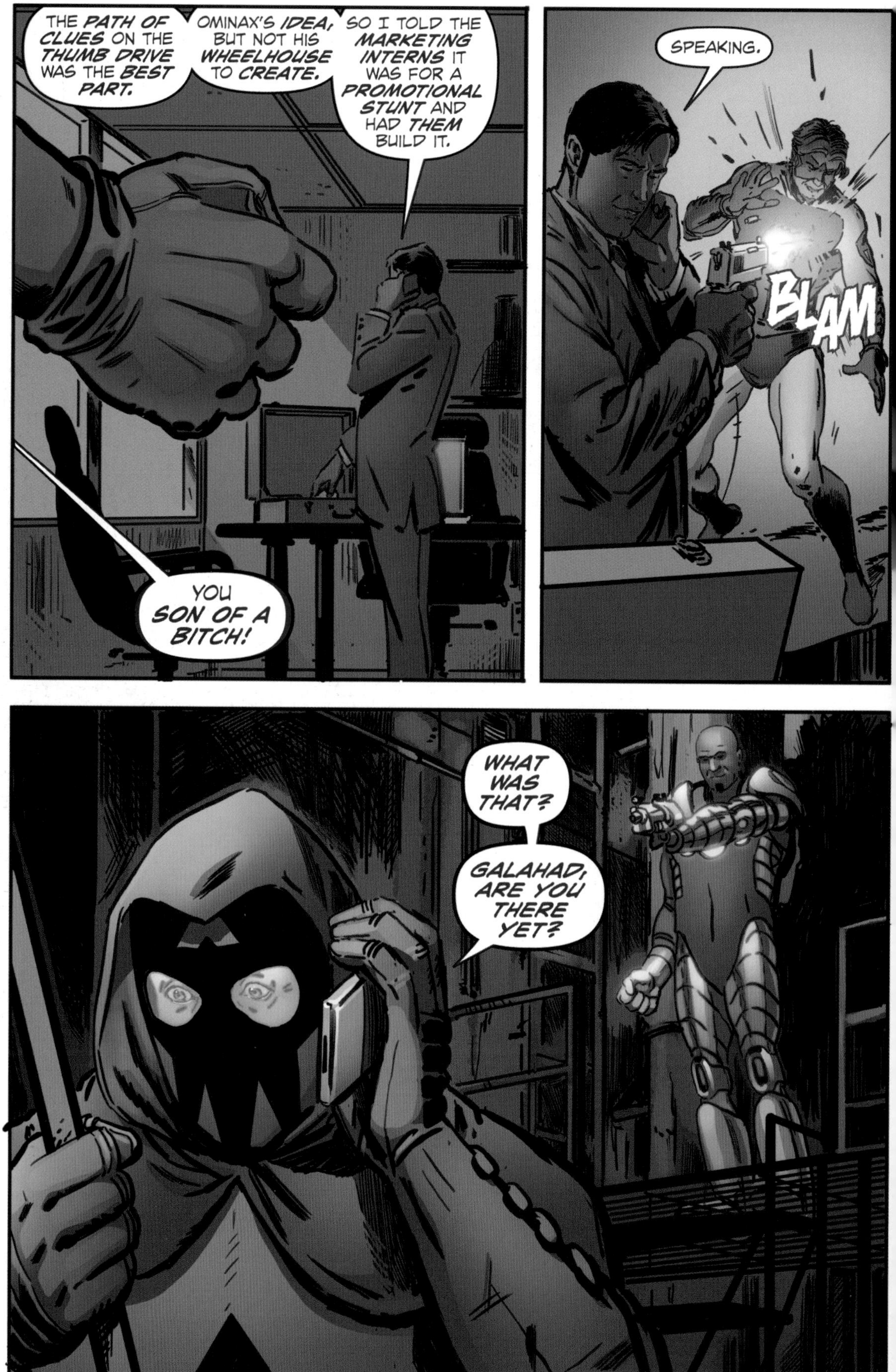
THE PATH OF CLUES ON THE THUMB DRIVE WAS THE BEST PART.
OMINAX'S IDEA, BUT NOT HIS WHEELHOUSE TO CREATE.
SO I TOLD THE MARKETING INTERNS IT WAS FOR A PROMOTIONAL STUNT AND HAD THEM BUILD IT.
YOU SON OF A BITCH!
SPEAKING.
BLAM
WHAT WAS THAT?
GALAHAD, ARE YOU THERE YET?

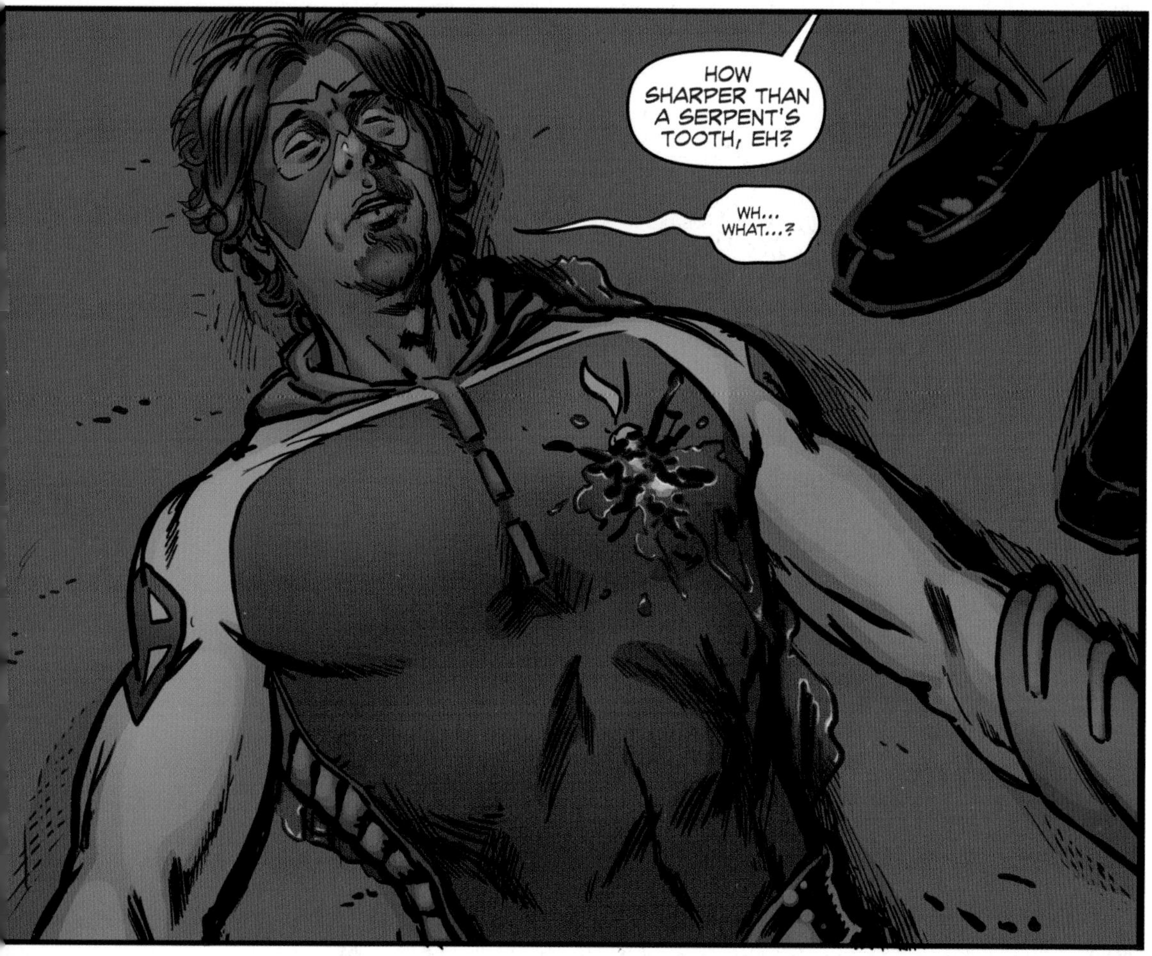
HOW SHARPER THAN A SERPENT'S TOOTH, EH?
WH... WHAT...?

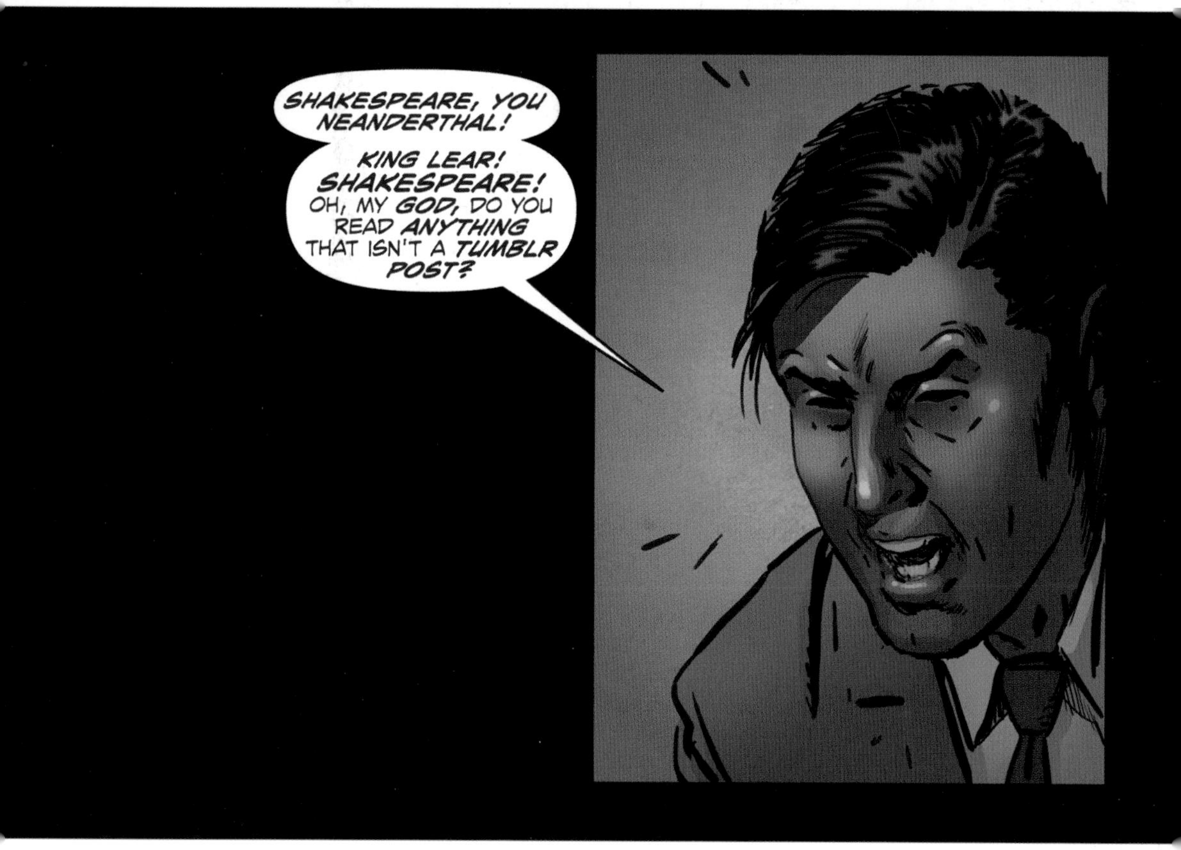
SHAKESPEARE, YOU NEANDERTHAL!
KING LEAR! SHAKESPEARE! OH, MY GOD, DO YOU READ ANYTHING THAT ISN'T A TUMBLR POST?

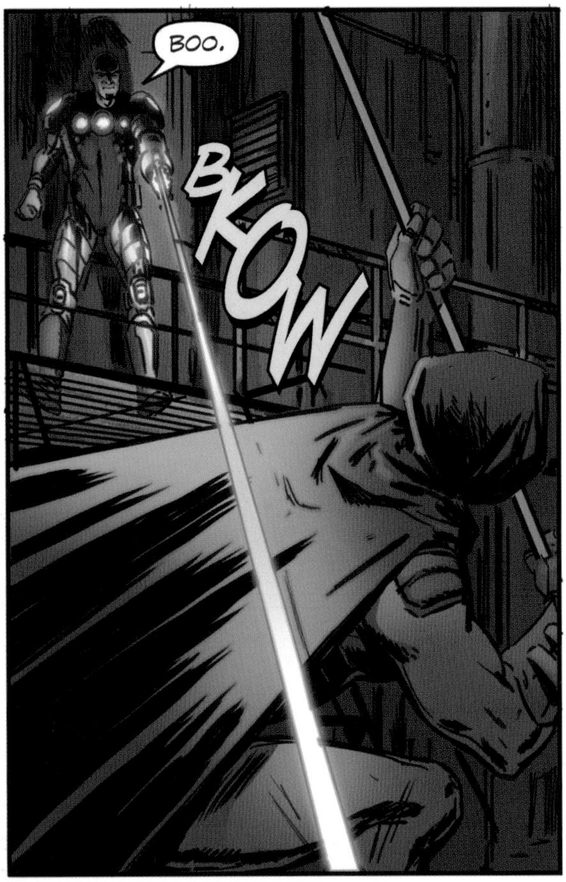
BOO.
BKOW

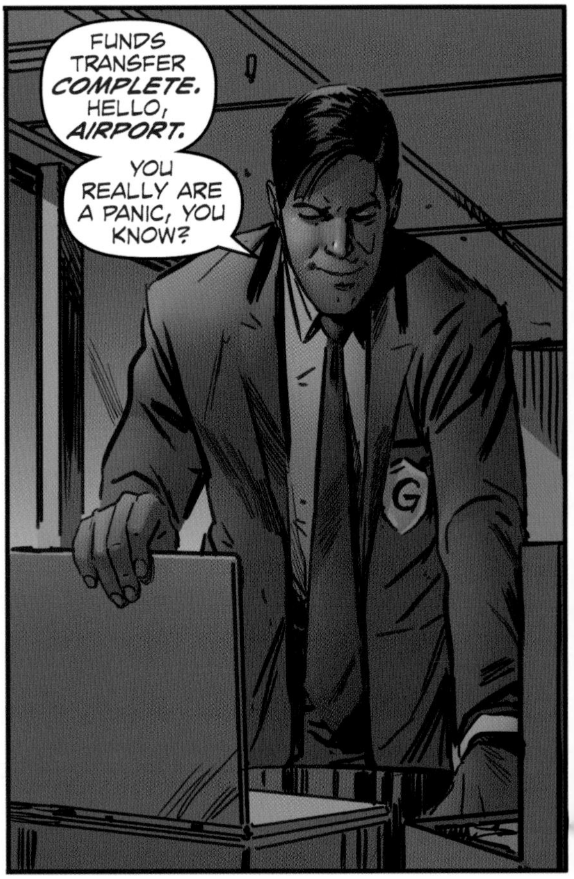
FUNDS TRANSFER COMPLETE. HELLO, AIRPORT.
YOU REALLY ARE A PANIC, YOU KNOW?

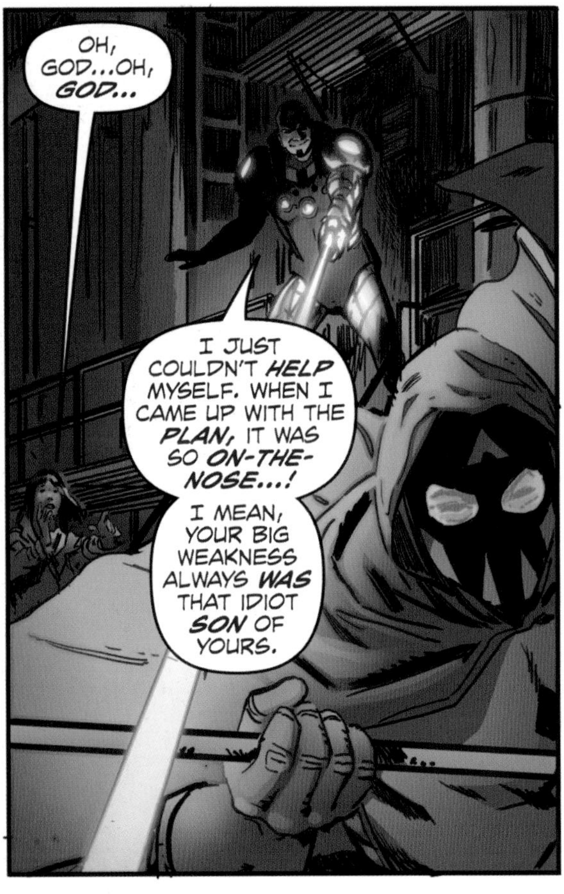
OH, GOD...OH, GOD...
I JUST COULDN'T HELP MYSELF. WHEN I CAME UP WITH THE PLAN, IT WAS SO ON-THE-NOSE...!
I MEAN, YOUR BIG WEAKNESS ALWAYS WAS THAT IDIOT SON OF YOURS.

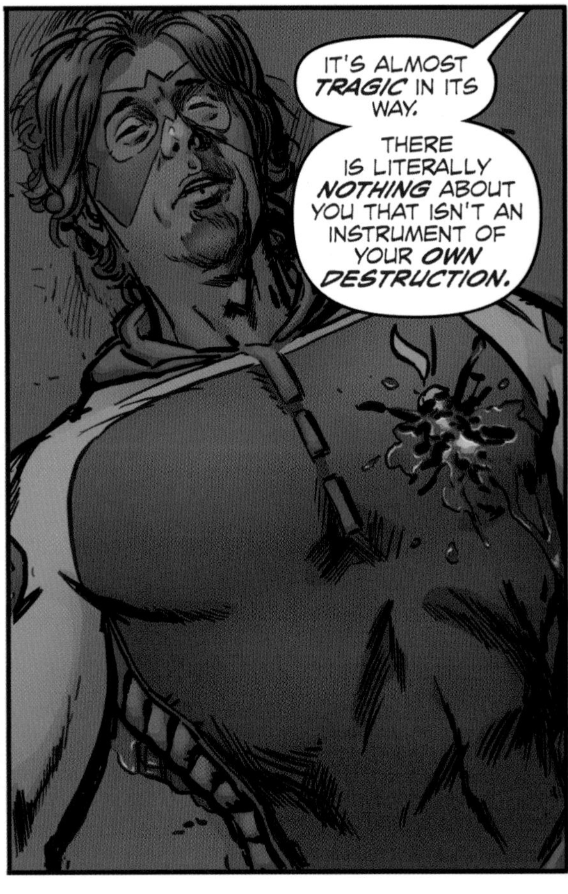
IT'S ALMOST TRAGIC IN ITS WAY.
THERE IS LITERALLY NOTHING ABOUT YOU THAT ISN'T AN INSTRUMENT OF YOUR OWN DESTRUCTION.

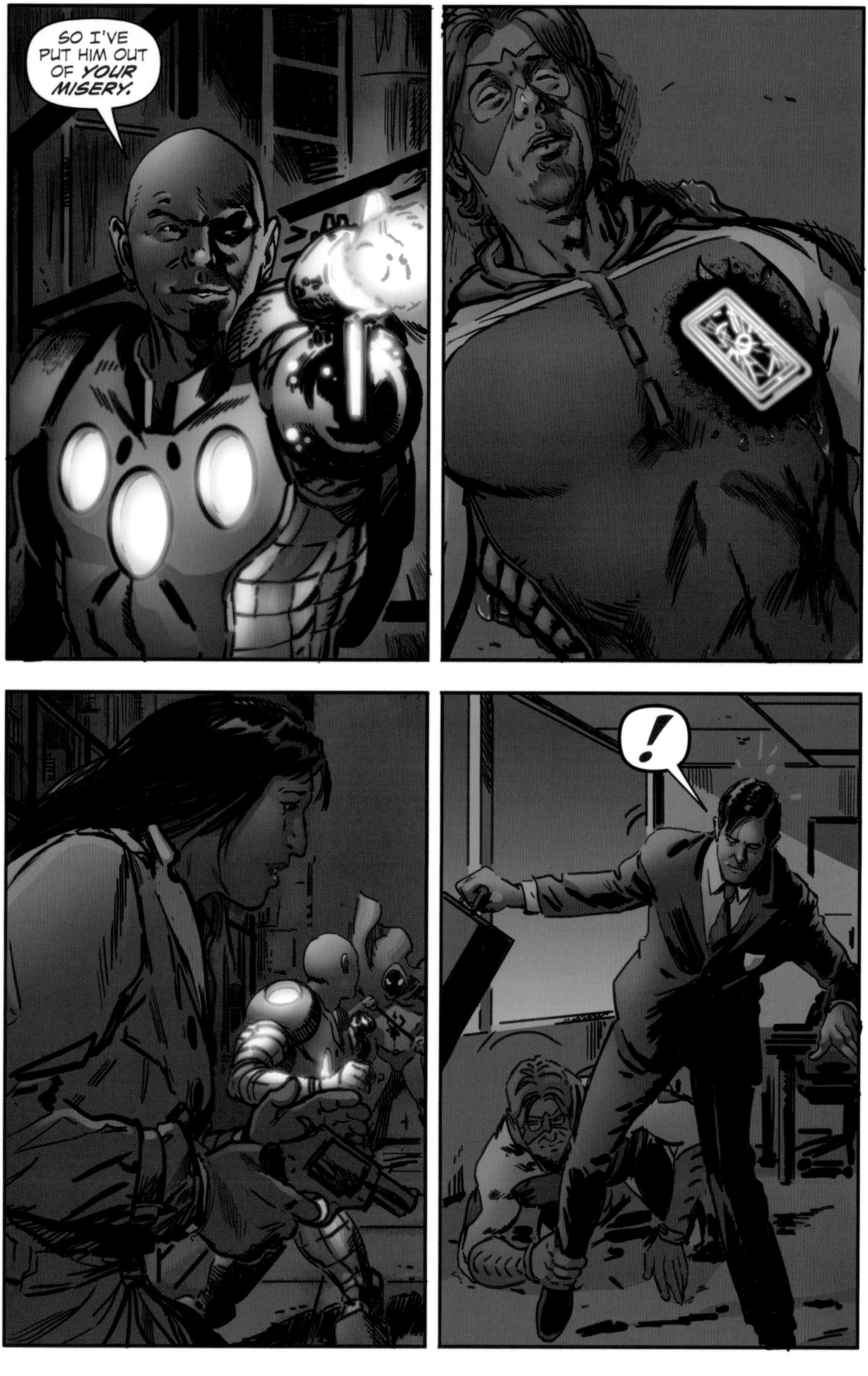
SO I'VE PUT HIM OUT OF *YOUR MISERY.*
!

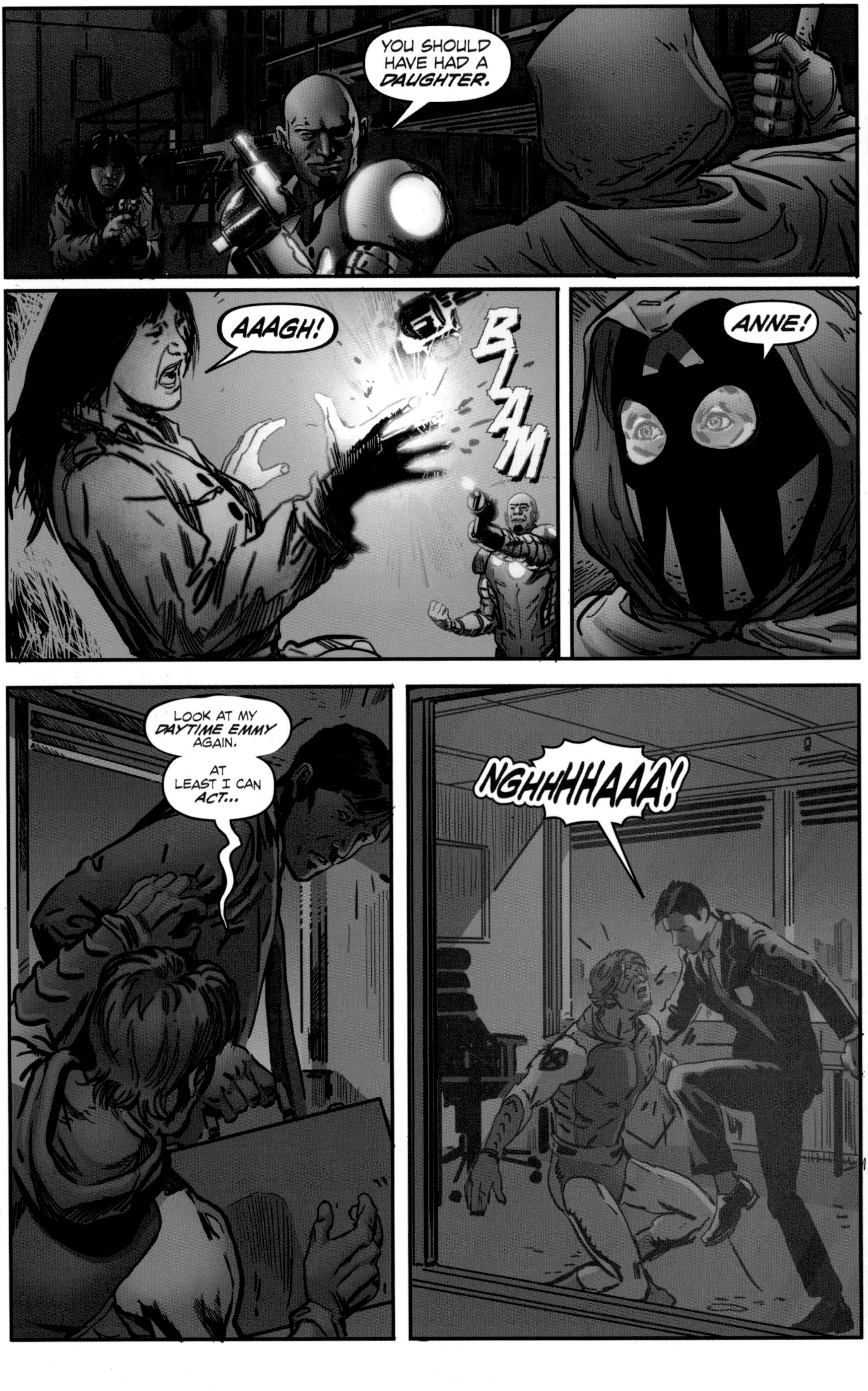

YOU SHOULD HAVE HAD A DAUGHTER.
AAAGH!
BLAM
ANNE!
LOOK AT MY DAYTIME EMMY AGAIN.
AT LEAST I CAN ACT...
NGHHHHAAA!

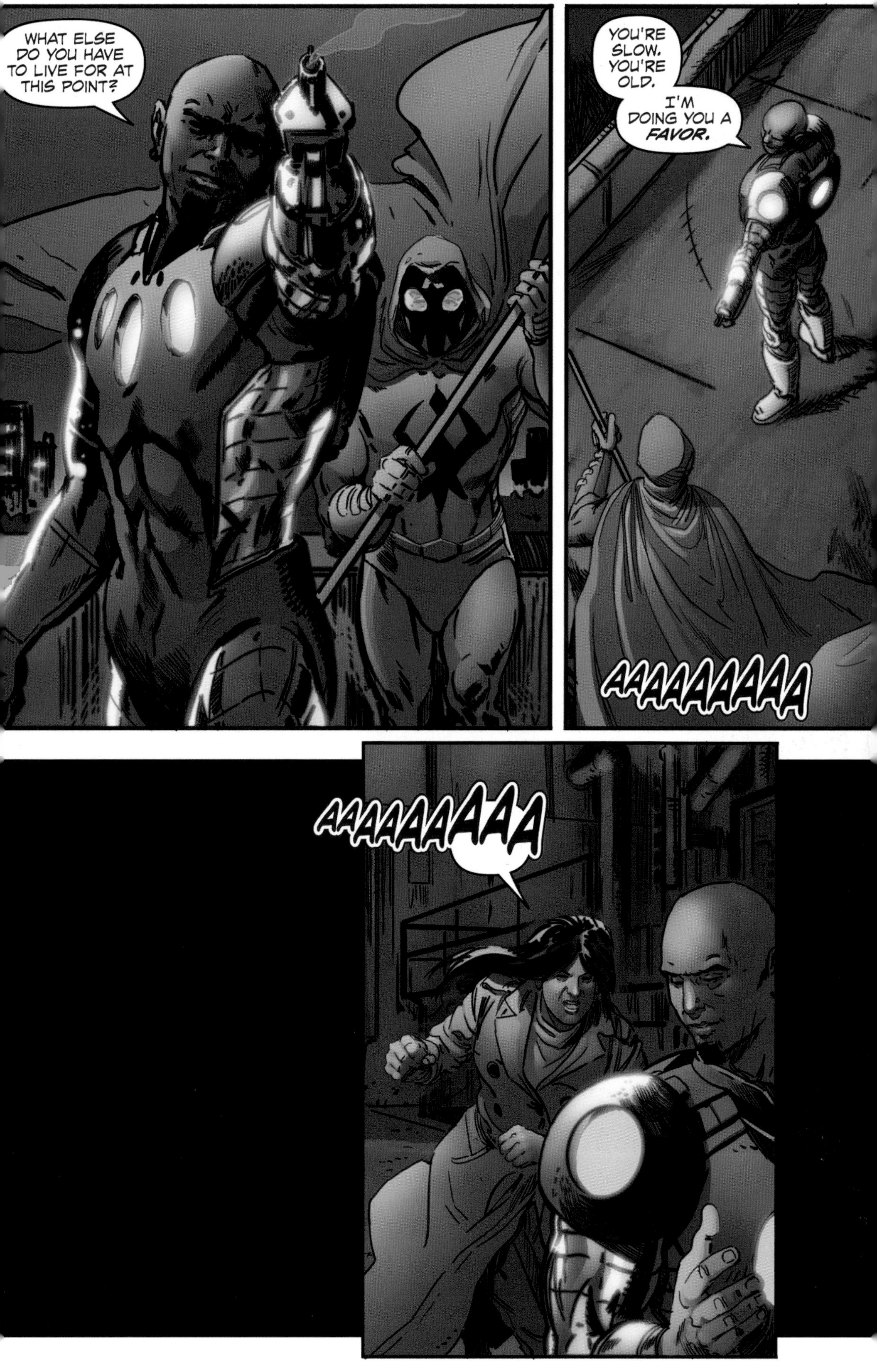
WHAT ELSE DO YOU HAVE TO LIVE FOR AT THIS POINT?
YOU'RE SLOW. YOU'RE OLD.
I'M DOING YOU A *FAVOR.*
AAAAAAAAA
AAAAAAAAA

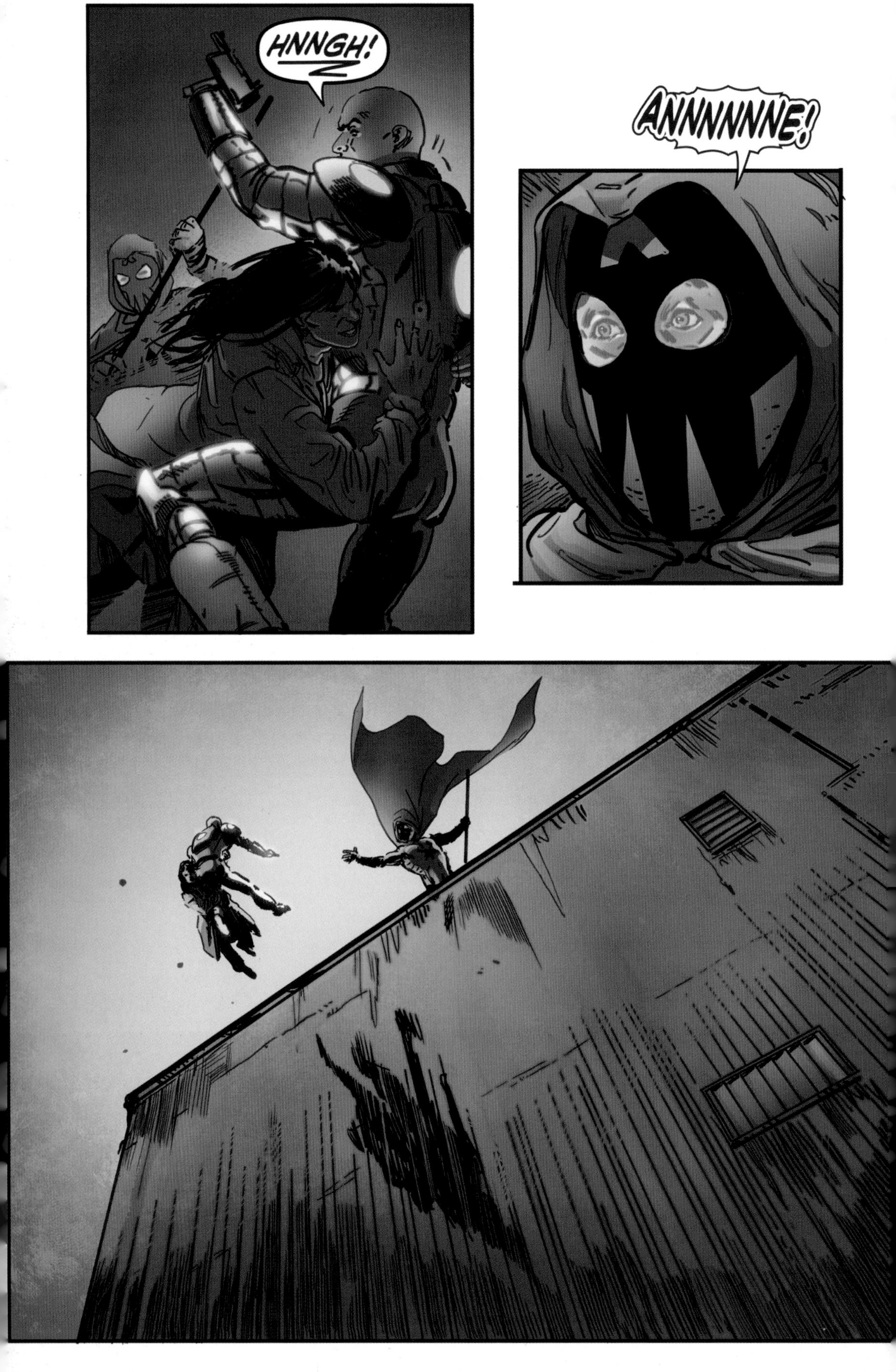
HNNGH!
ANNNNNNE!

CHAPTER EIGHT

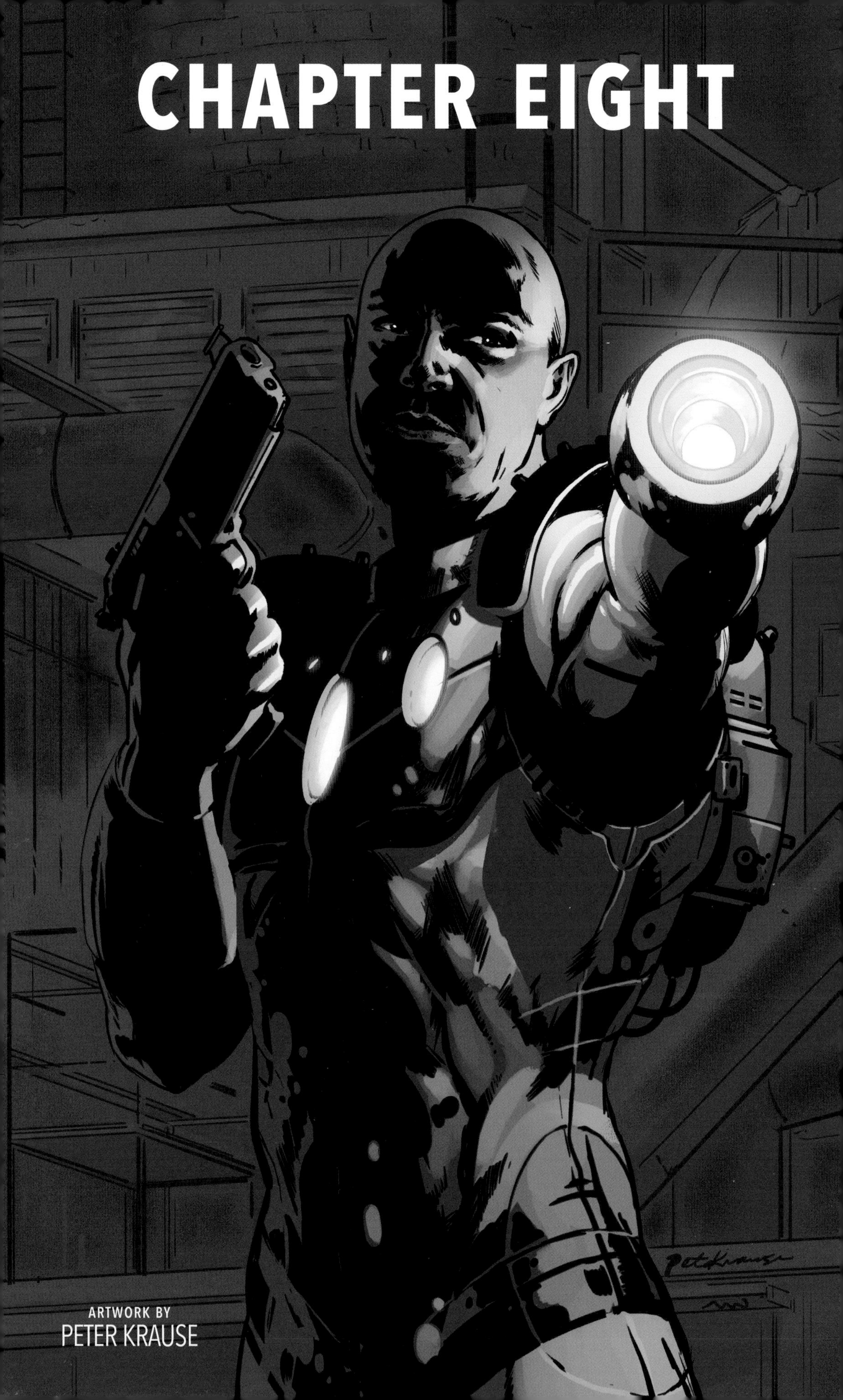

ARTWORK BY
PETER KRAUSE

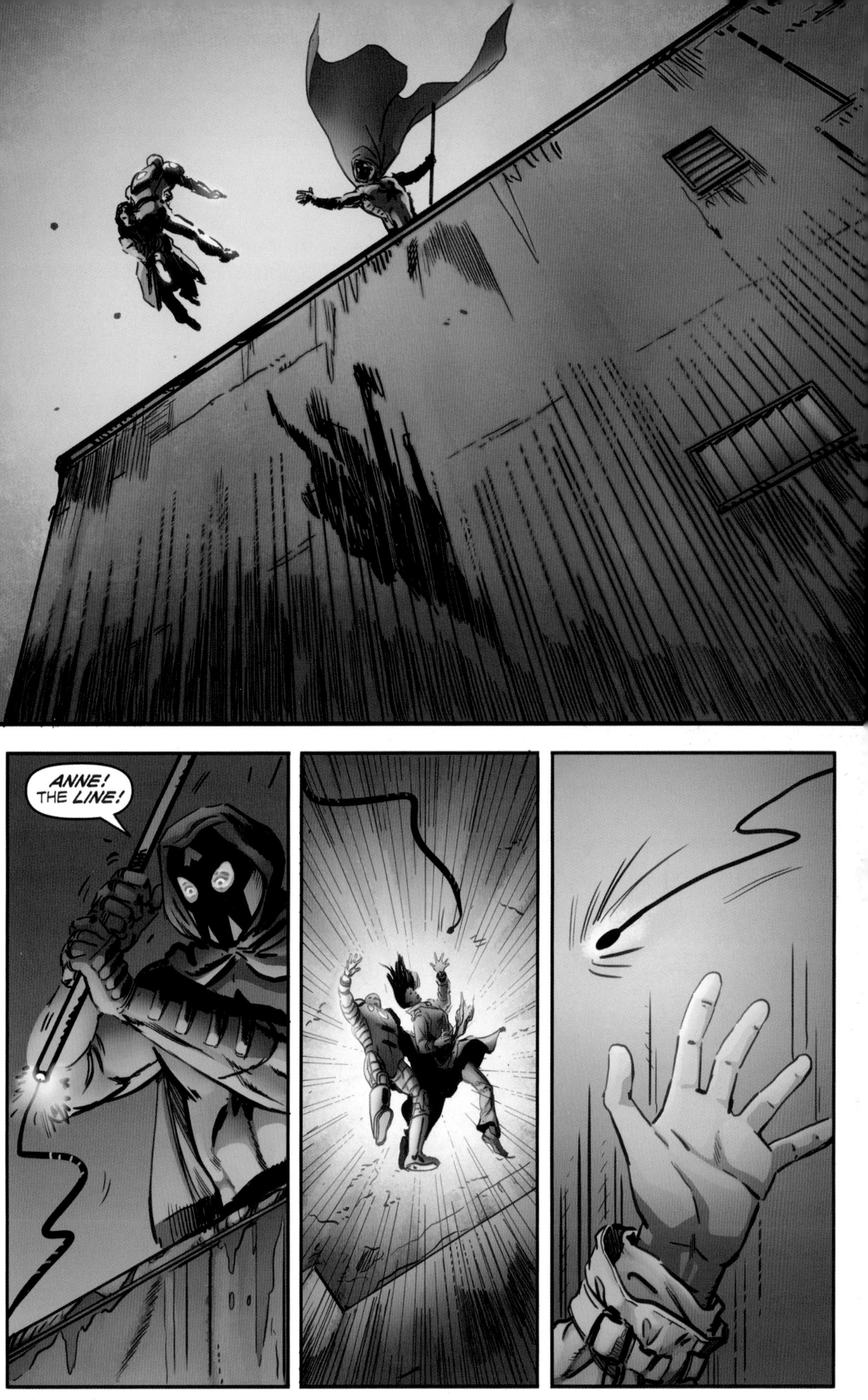
ANNE! THE LINE!

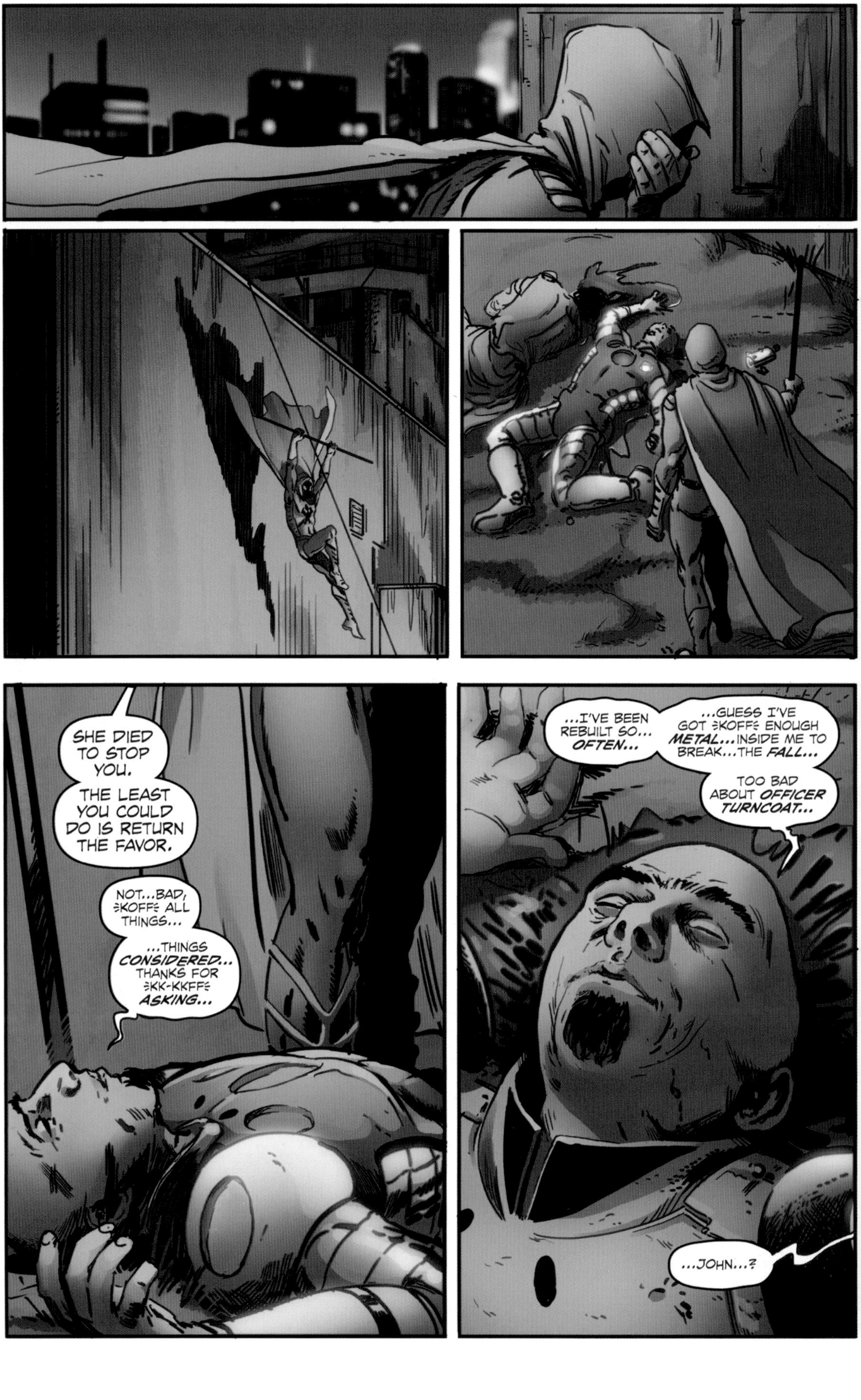
SHE DIED TO STOP YOU.
THE LEAST YOU COULD DO IS RETURN THE FAVOR.
NOT...BAD, ≶KOFF≶ ALL THINGS...
...THINGS CONSIDERED... THANKS FOR ≶KK-KKFF≶ ASKING...
...I'VE BEEN REBUILT SO... OFTEN...
...GUESS I'VE GOT ≶KOFF≶ ENOUGH METAL...INSIDE ME TO BREAK...THE FALL...
TOO BAD ABOUT OFFICER TURNCOAT...
...JOHN...?

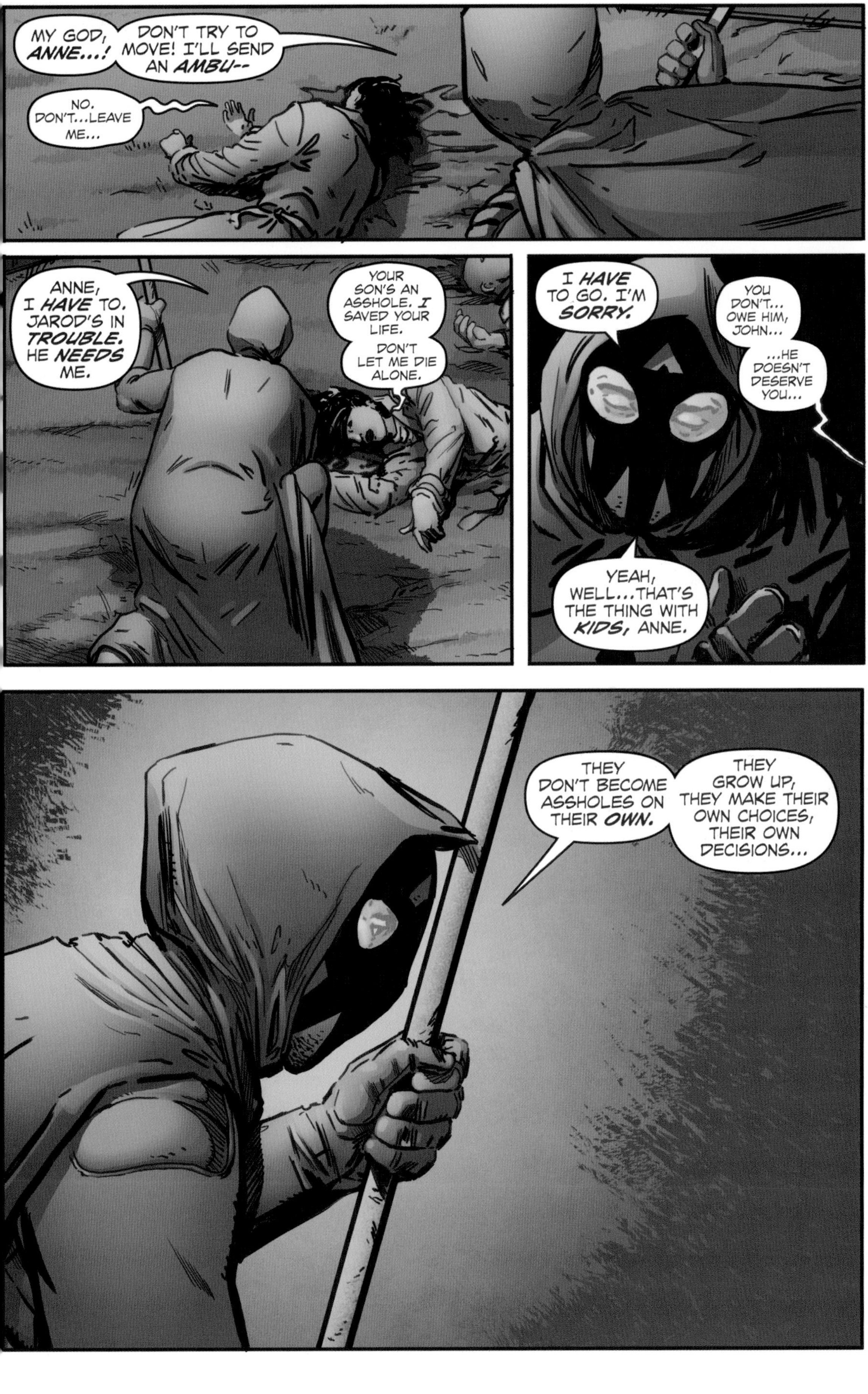
MY GOD, ANNE...!
DON'T TRY TO MOVE! I'LL SEND AN AMBU--
NO. DON'T...LEAVE ME...
ANNE, I HAVE TO. JAROD'S IN TROUBLE. HE NEEDS ME.
YOUR SON'S AN ASSHOLE. I SAVED YOUR LIFE.
DON'T LET ME DIE ALONE.
I HAVE TO GO. I'M SORRY.
YOU DON'T... OWE HIM, JOHN...
...HE DOESN'T DESERVE YOU...
YEAH, WELL...THAT'S THE THING WITH KIDS, ANNE.
THEY GROW UP, THEY MAKE THEIR OWN CHOICES, THEIR OWN DECISIONS...
THEY DON'T BECOME ASSHOLES ON THEIR OWN.

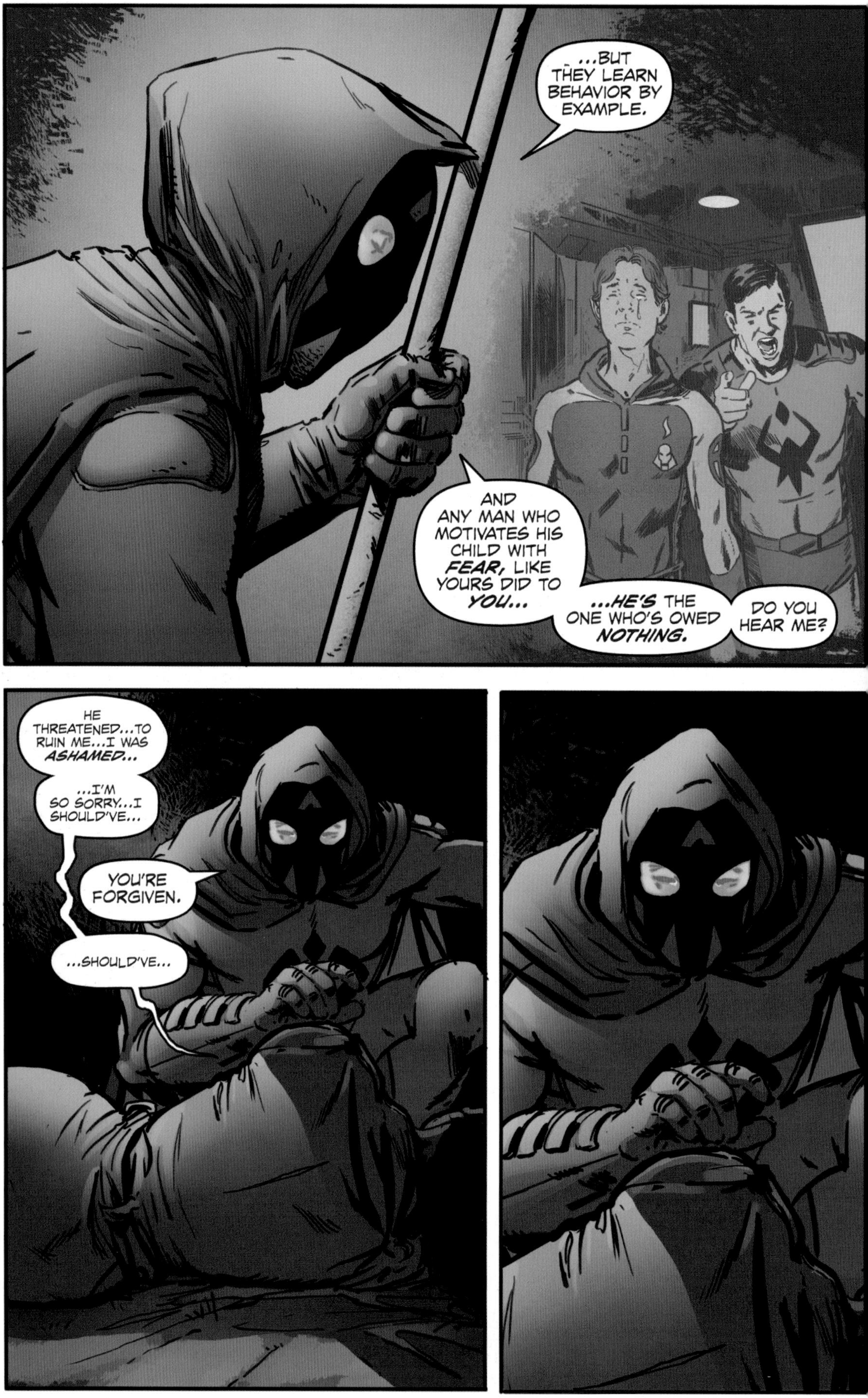
...BUT THEY LEARN BEHAVIOR BY EXAMPLE.
AND ANY MAN WHO MOTIVATES HIS CHILD WITH FEAR, LIKE YOURS DID TO YOU...
...HE'S THE ONE WHO'S OWED NOTHING.
DO YOU HEAR ME?
HE THREATENED...TO RUIN ME...I WAS ASHAMED...
...I'M SO SORRY...I SHOULD'VE...
YOU'RE FORGIVEN.
...SHOULD'VE...

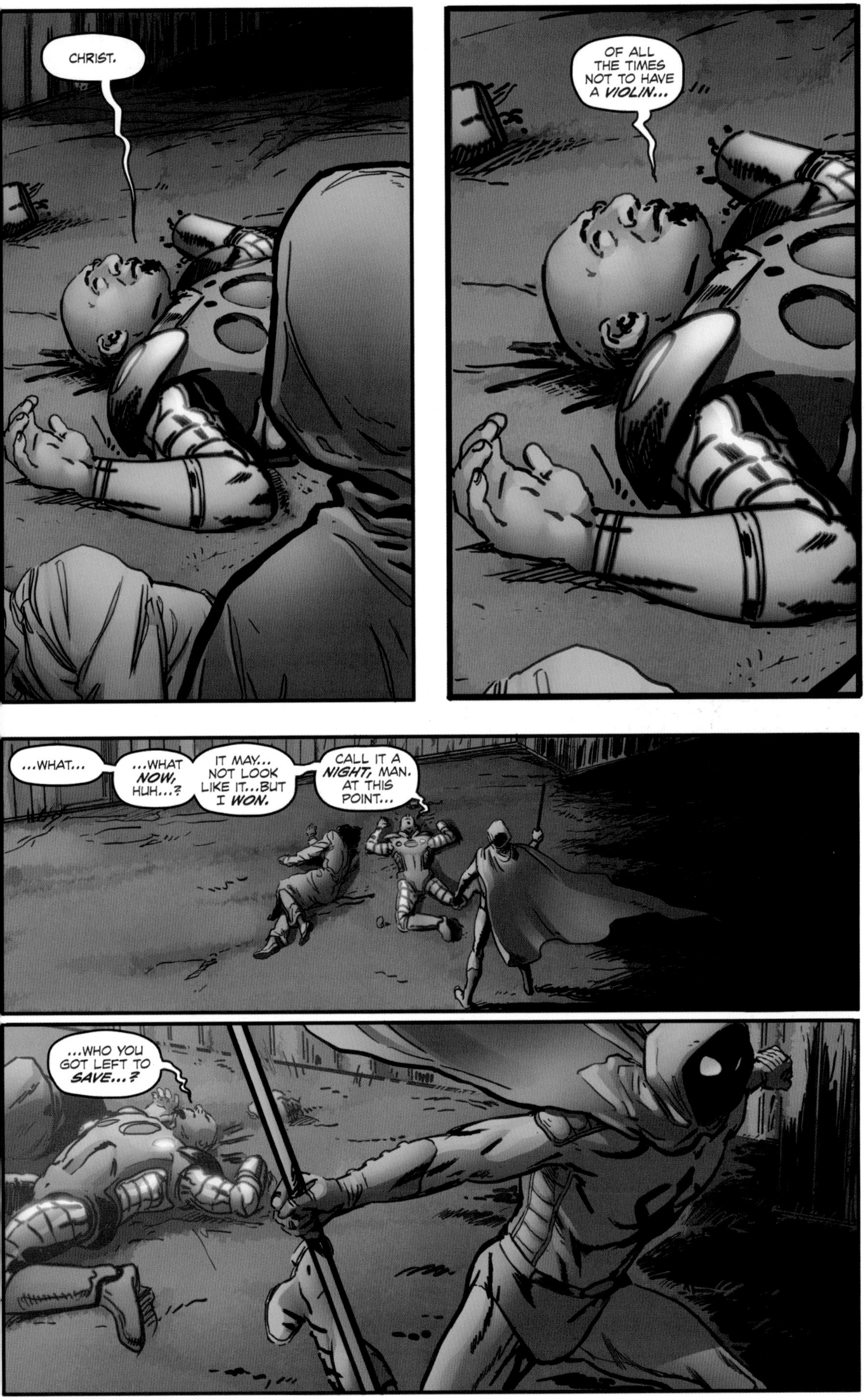
CHRIST.
OF ALL THE TIMES NOT TO HAVE A *VIOLIN*...
...WHAT...
...WHAT *NOW*, HUH...?
IT MAY... NOT LOOK LIKE IT...BUT I *WON*.
CALL IT A *NIGHT*, MAN. AT THIS POINT...
...WHO YOU GOT LEFT TO *SAVE*...?

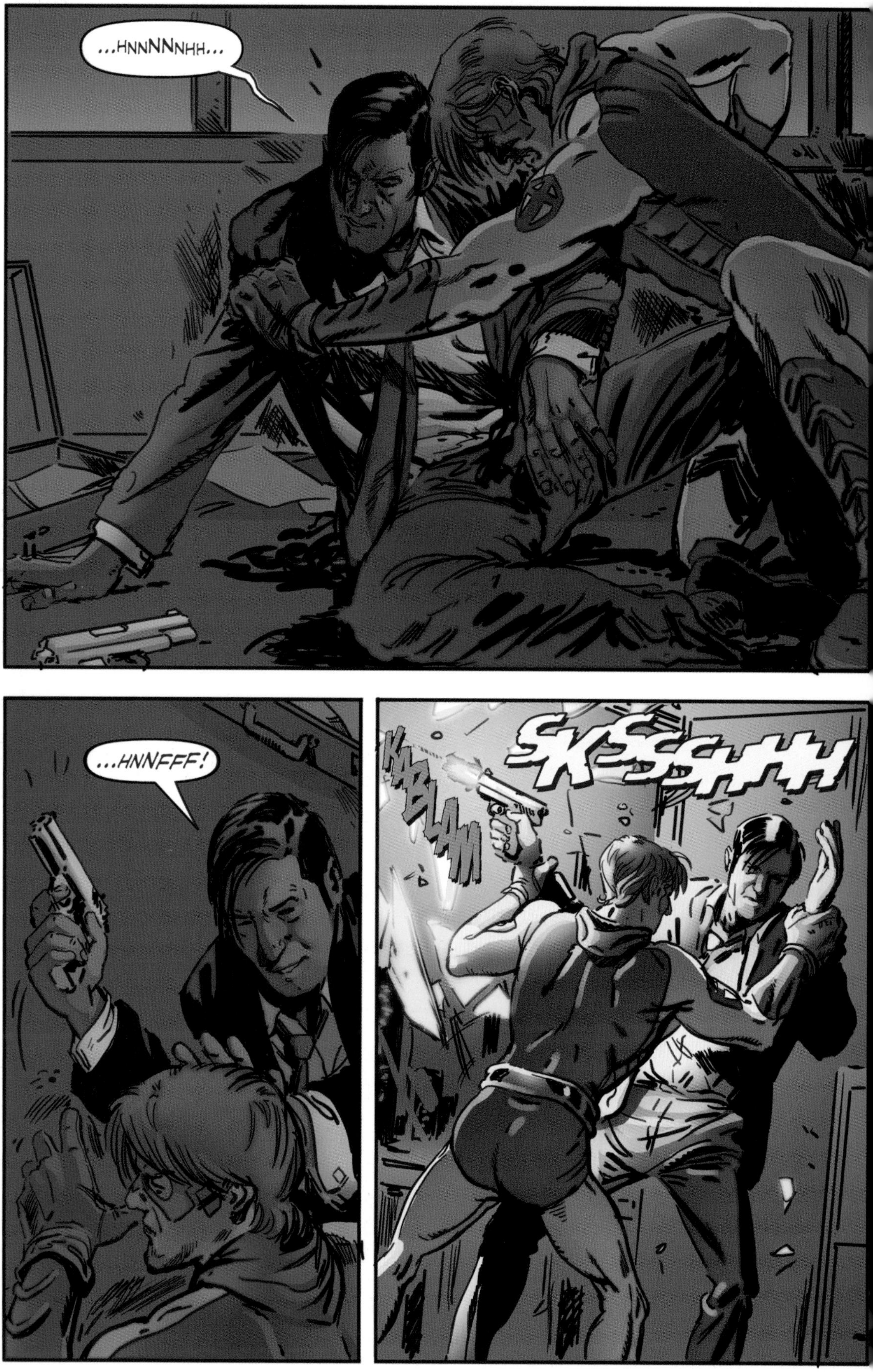
...HNNNNNHH...
...HNNFFF!
KABLAM
SKSSSHHH

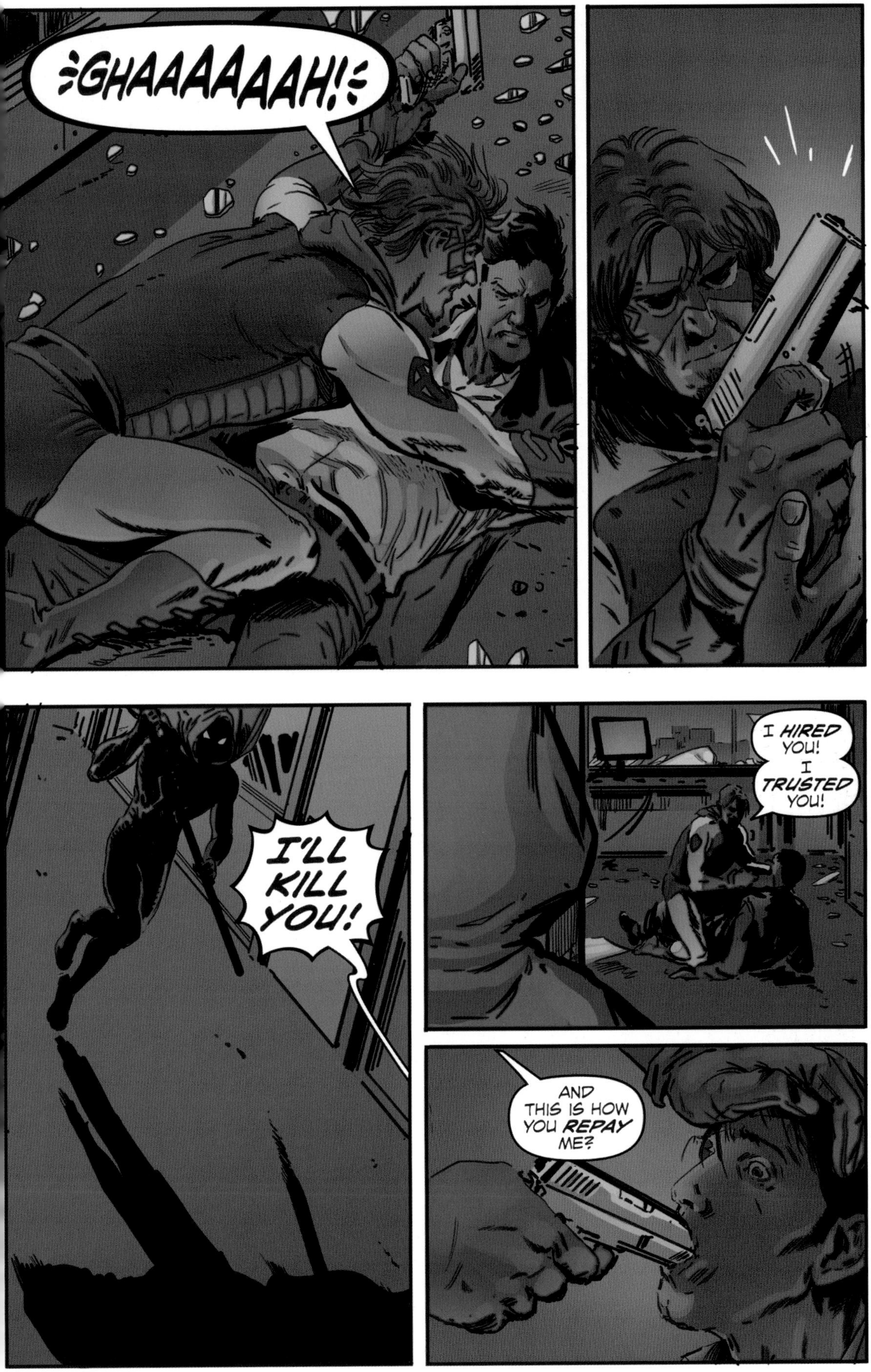
GHAAAAAAH!
I'LL KILL YOU!
I HIRED YOU! I TRUSTED YOU!
AND THIS IS HOW YOU REPAY ME?

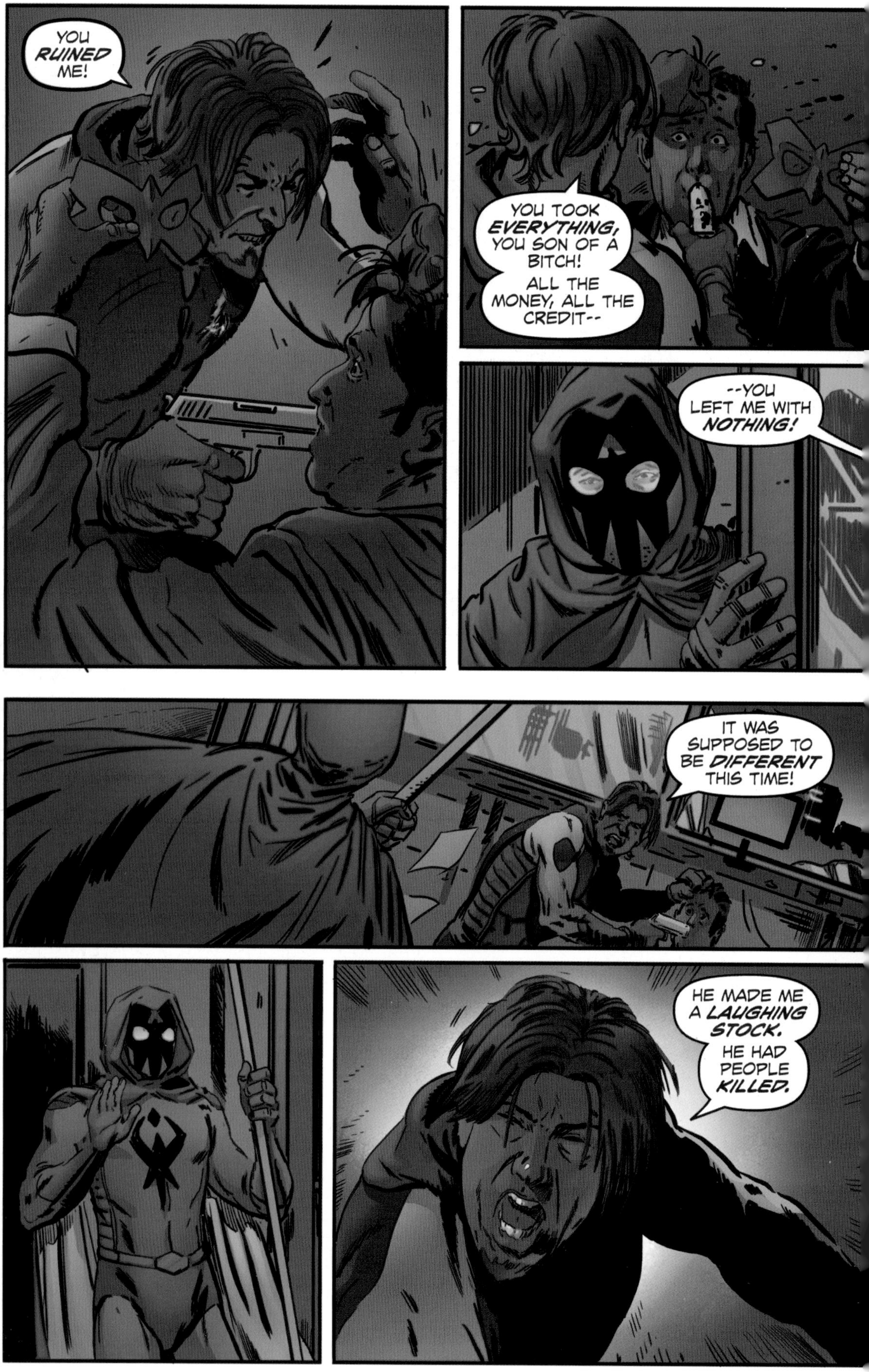
YOU RUINED ME!
YOU TOOK EVERYTHING, YOU SON OF A BITCH!
ALL THE MONEY, ALL THE CREDIT--
--YOU LEFT ME WITH NOTHING!
IT WAS SUPPOSED TO BE DIFFERENT THIS TIME!
HE MADE ME A LAUGHING STOCK.
HE HAD PEOPLE KILLED.

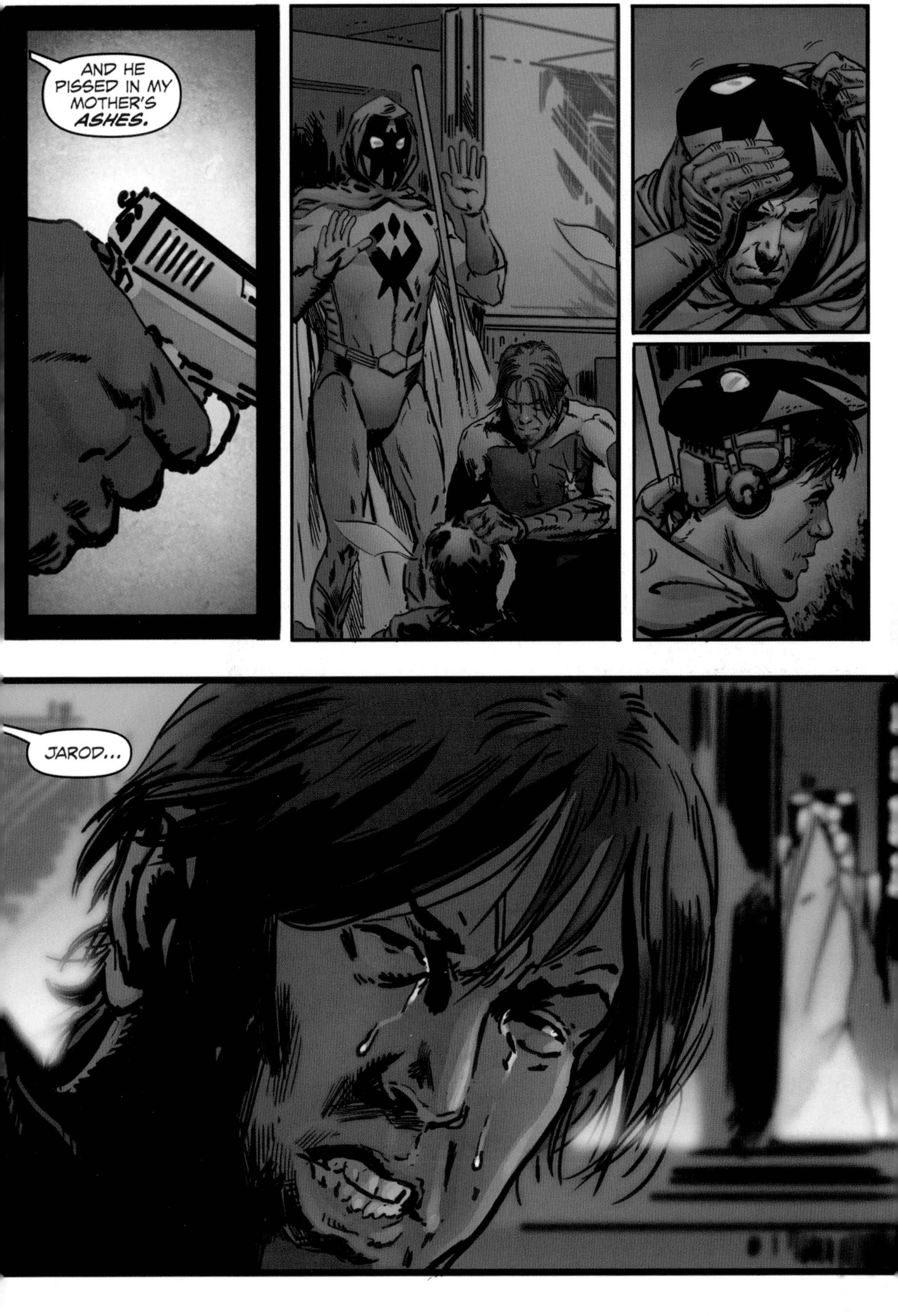
AND HE PISSED IN MY MOTHER'S ASHES.
JAROD...

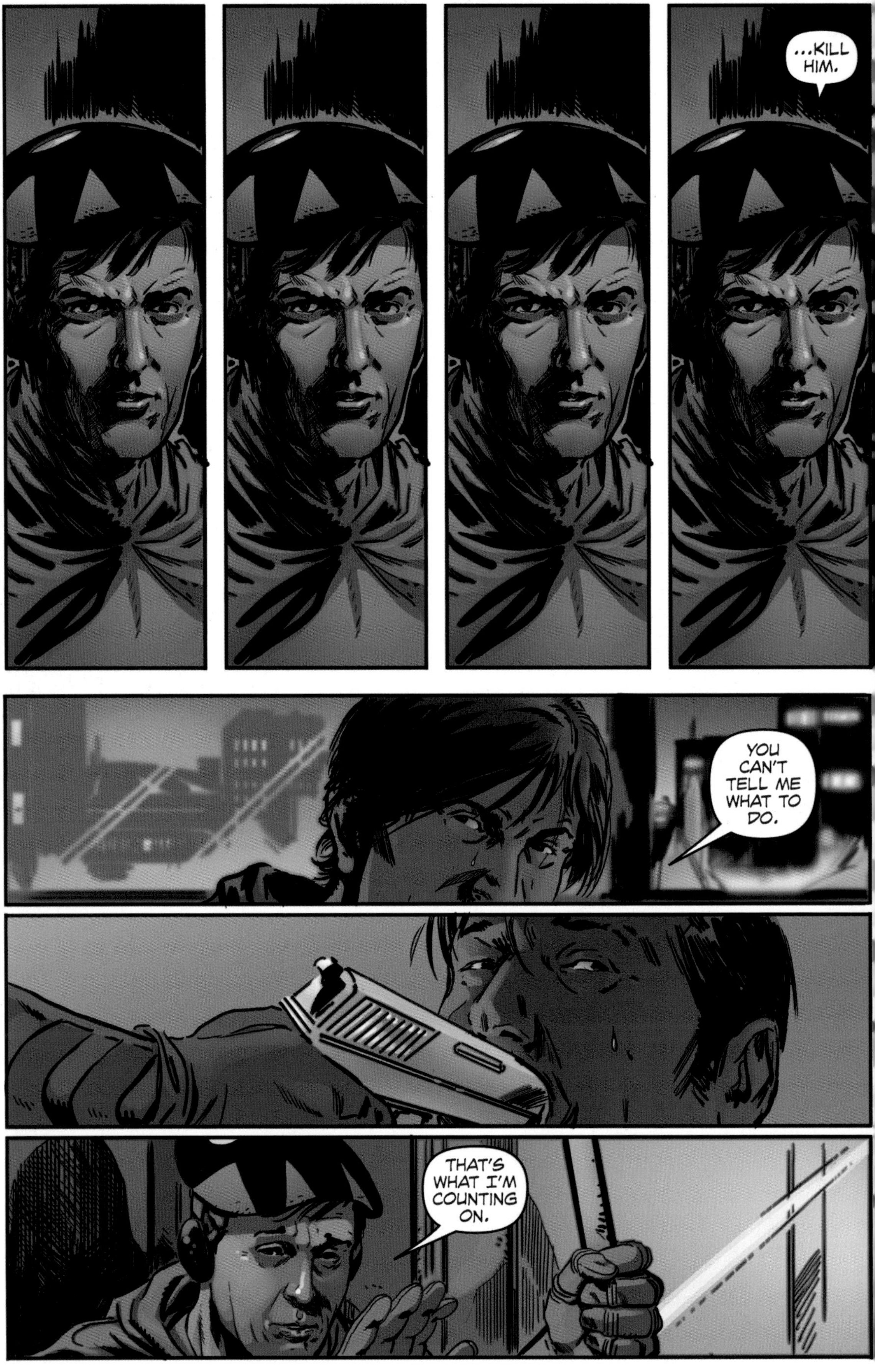
...KILL HIM.
YOU CAN'T TELL ME WHAT TO DO.
THAT'S WHAT I'M COUNTING ON.

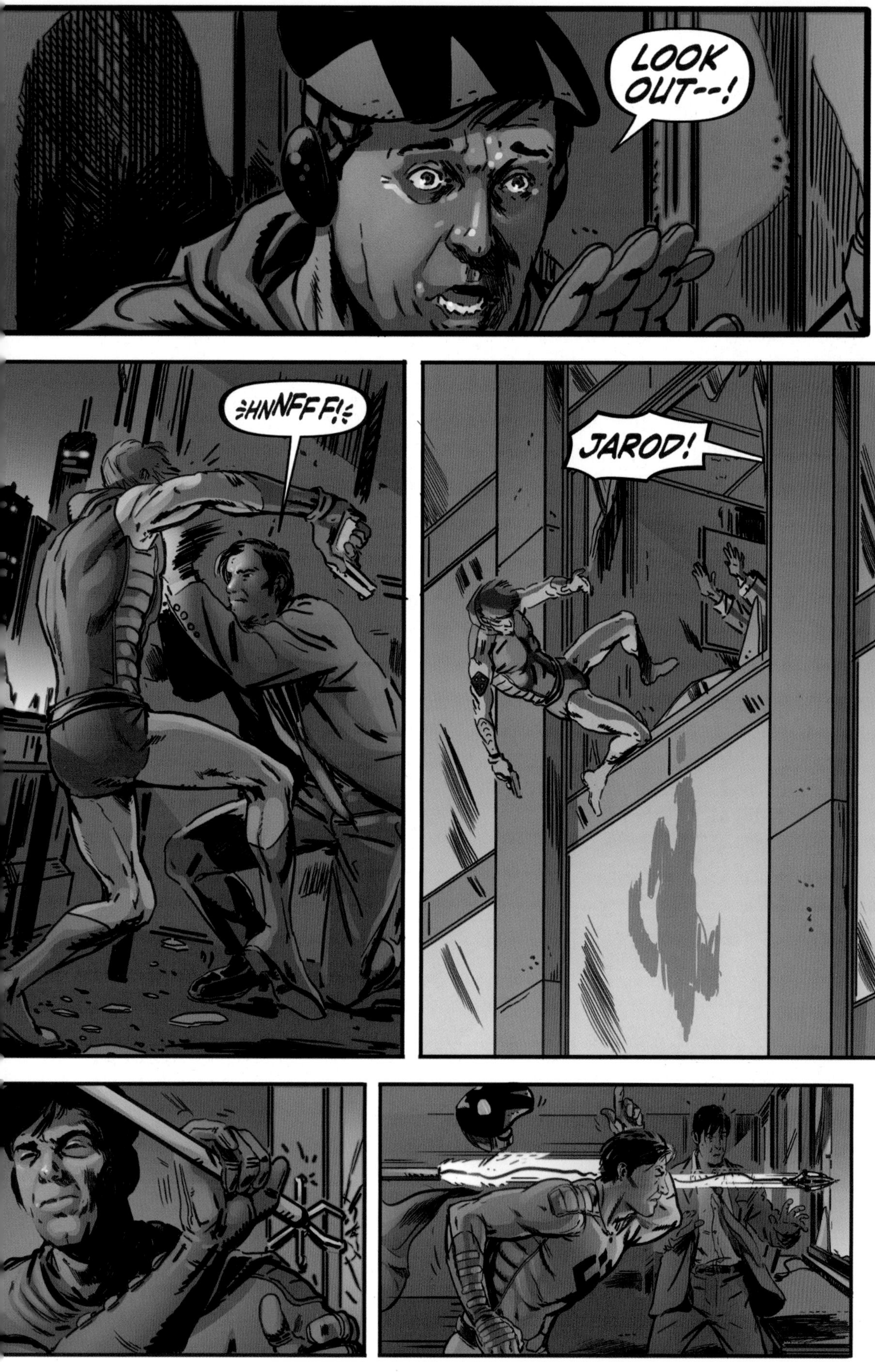
LOOK OUT--!
HNNFFF!
JAROD!

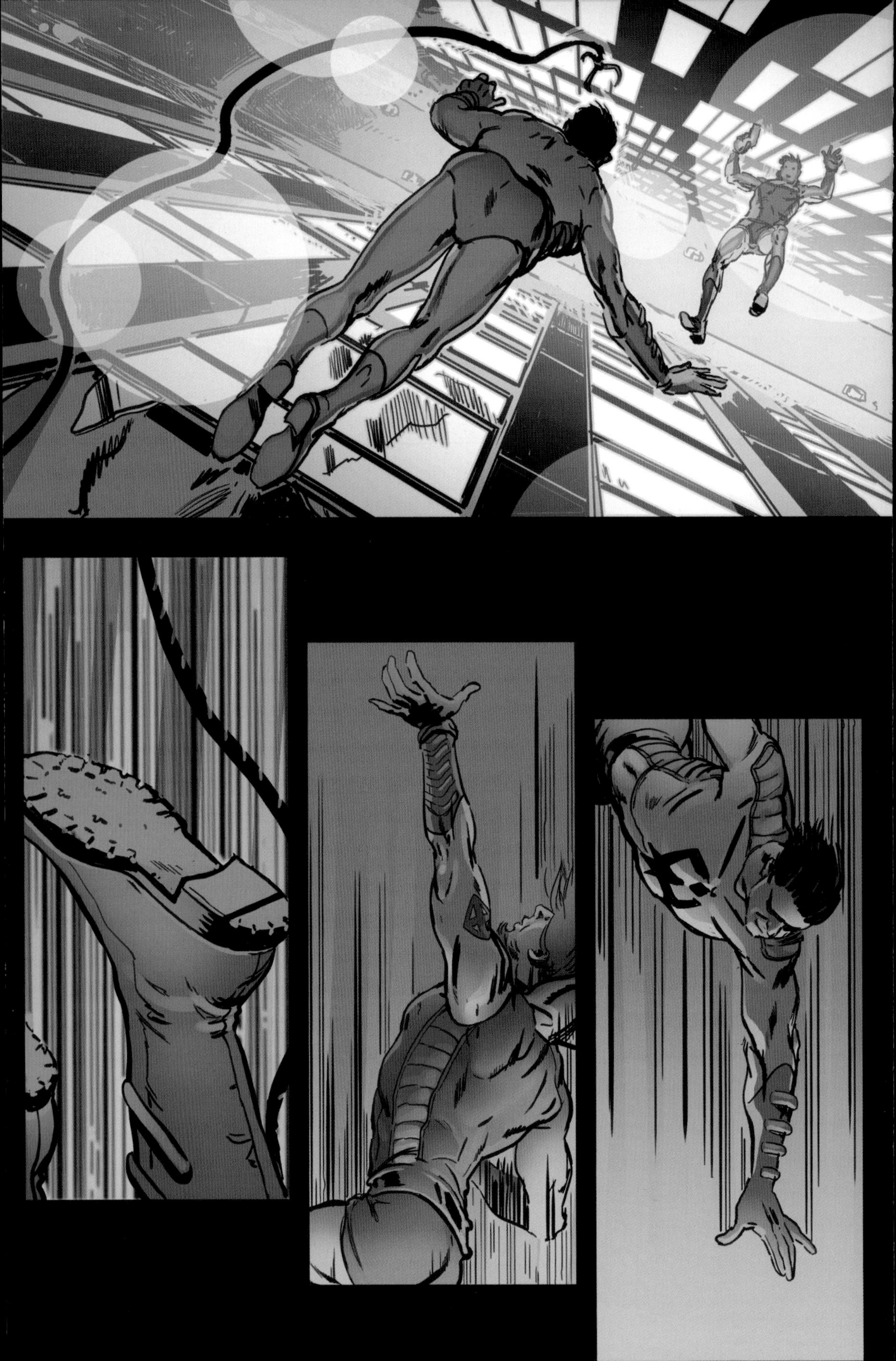

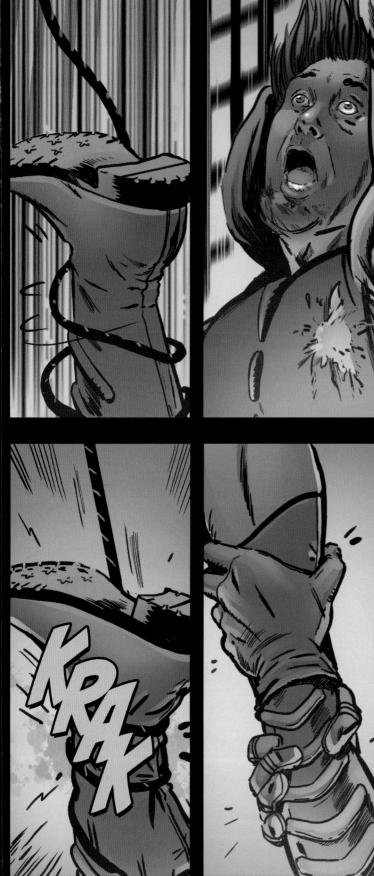
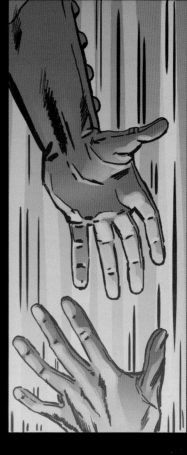

KRAK

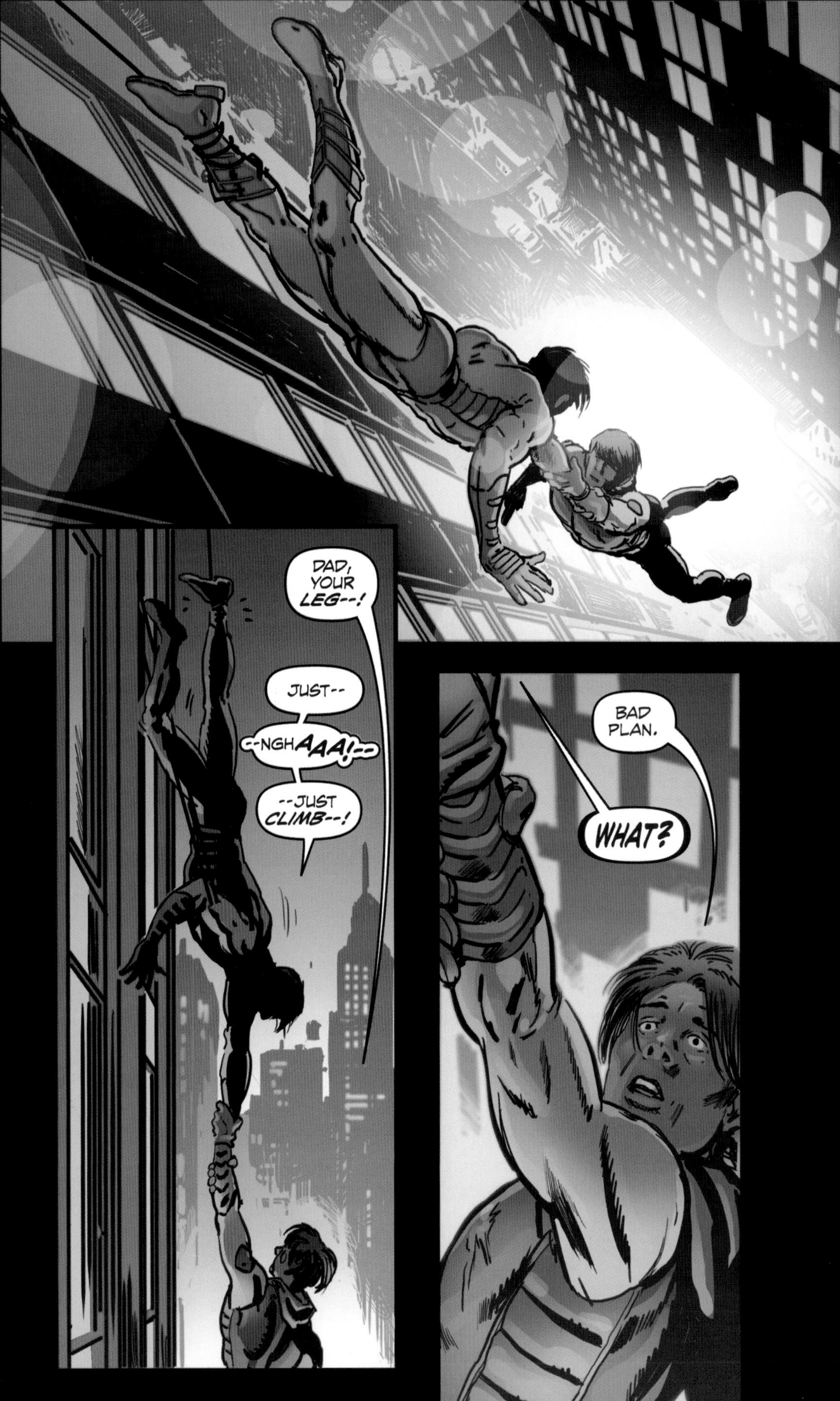
DAD, YOUR LEG--!
JUST--
--NGHAAA!--
--JUST CLIMB--!
BAD PLAN.
WHAT?

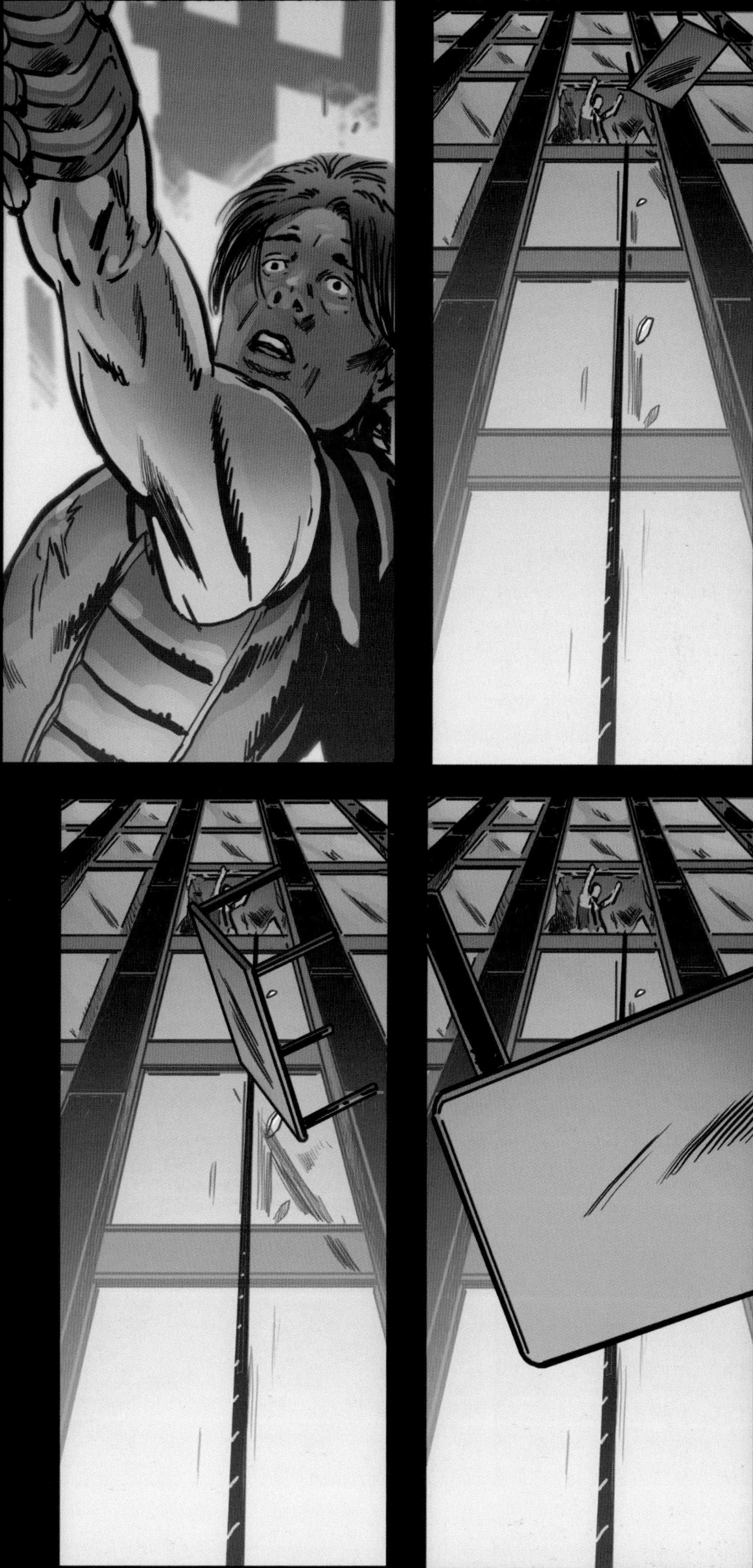

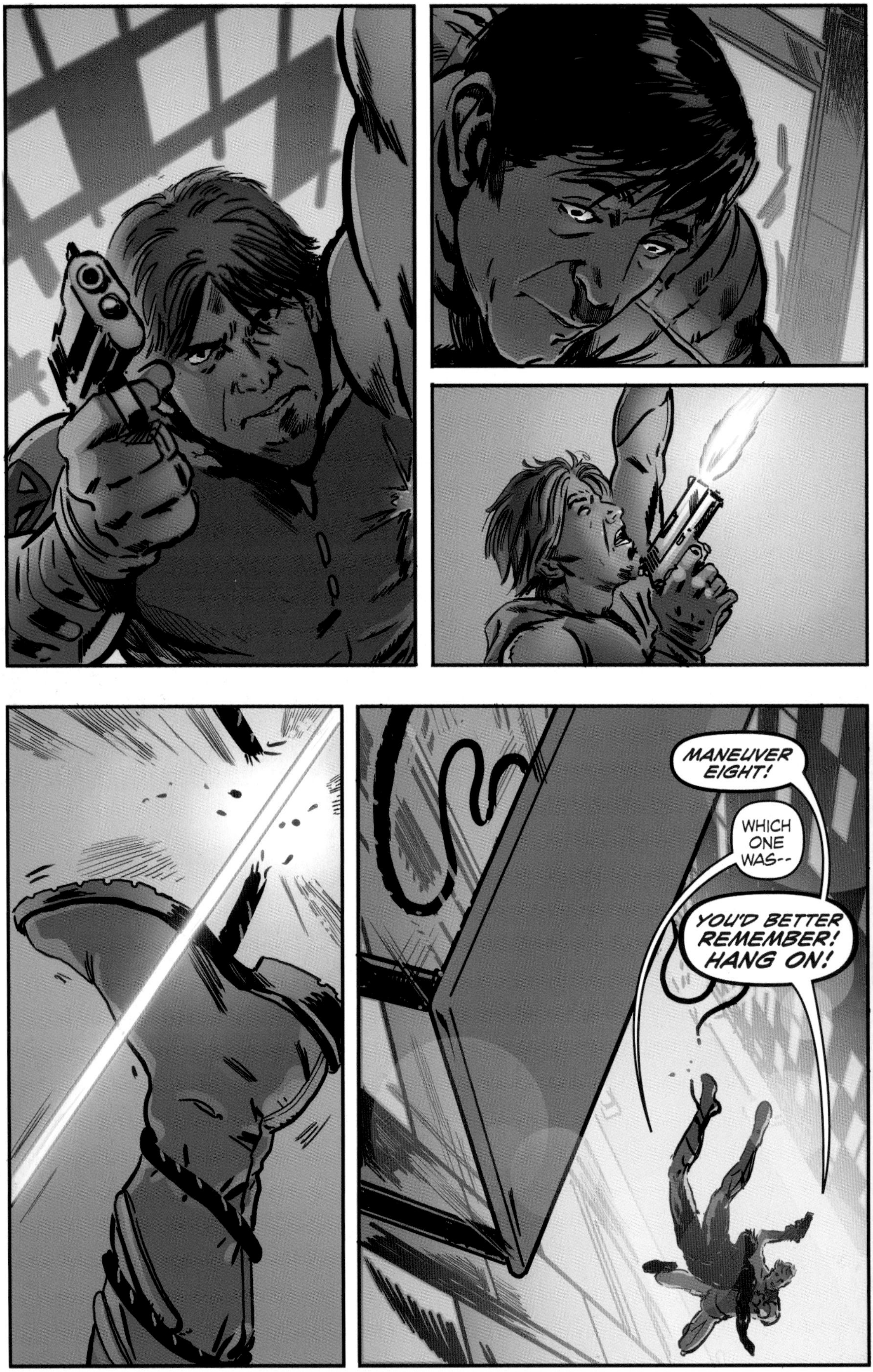
MANEUVER EIGHT!
WHICH ONE WAS--
YOU'D BETTER REMEMBER! HANG ON!

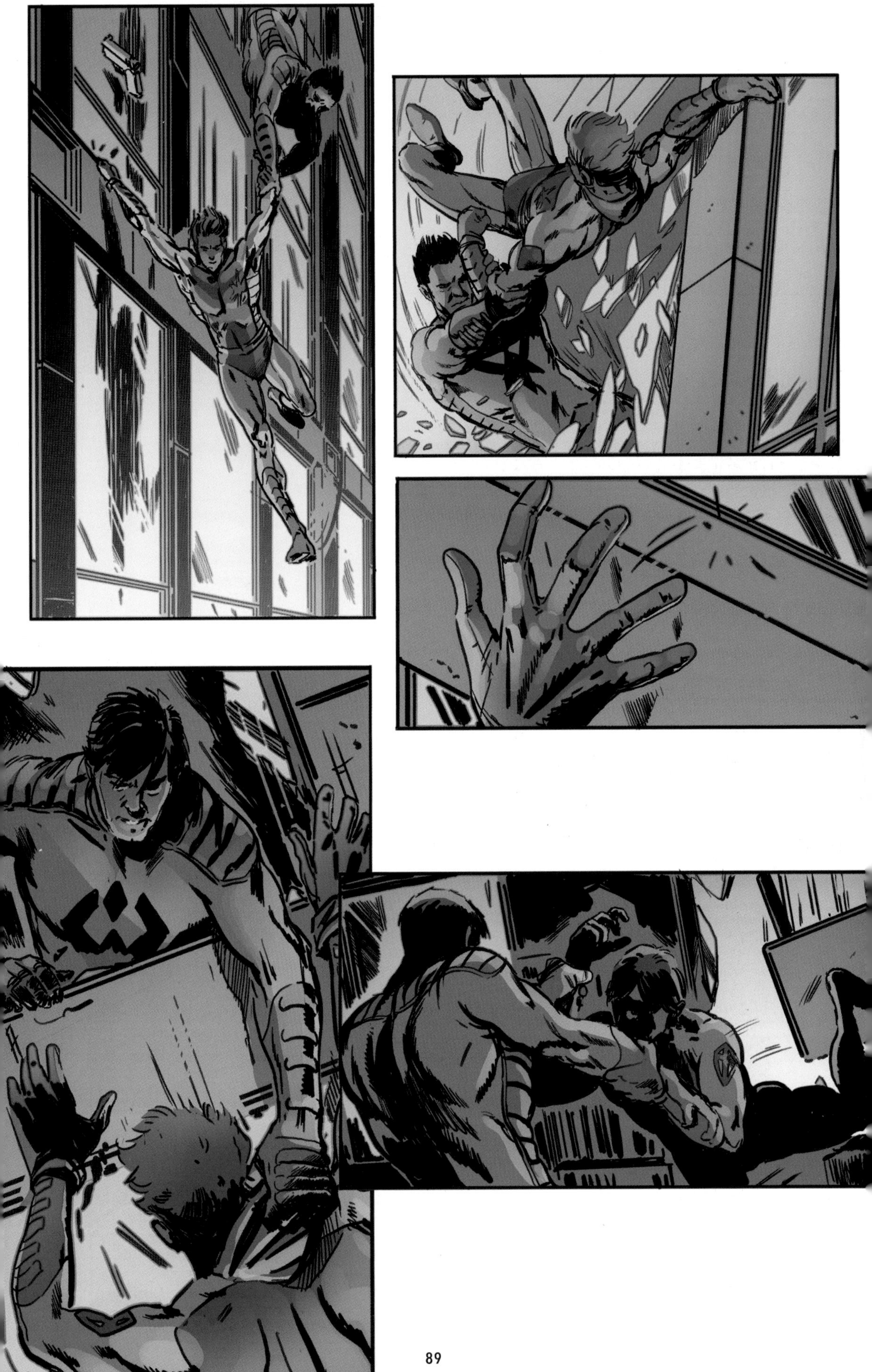

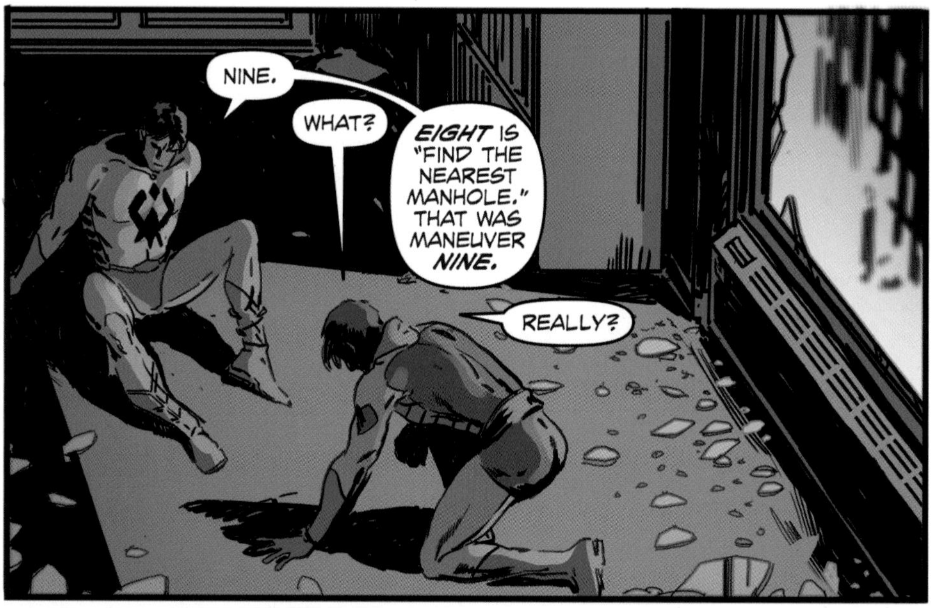
NINE.
WHAT?
EIGHT IS "FIND THE NEAREST MANHOLE." THAT WAS MANEUVER NINE.
REALLY?

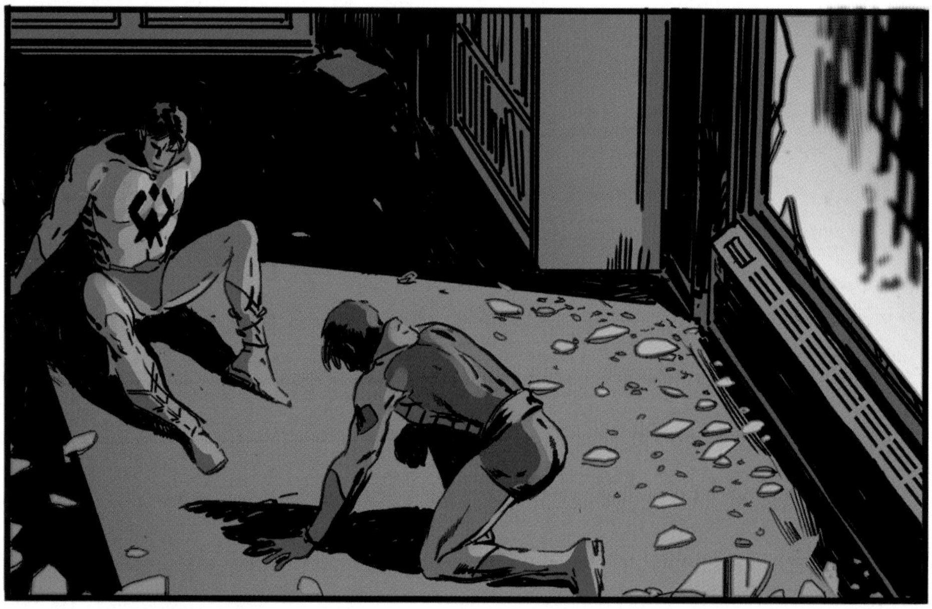

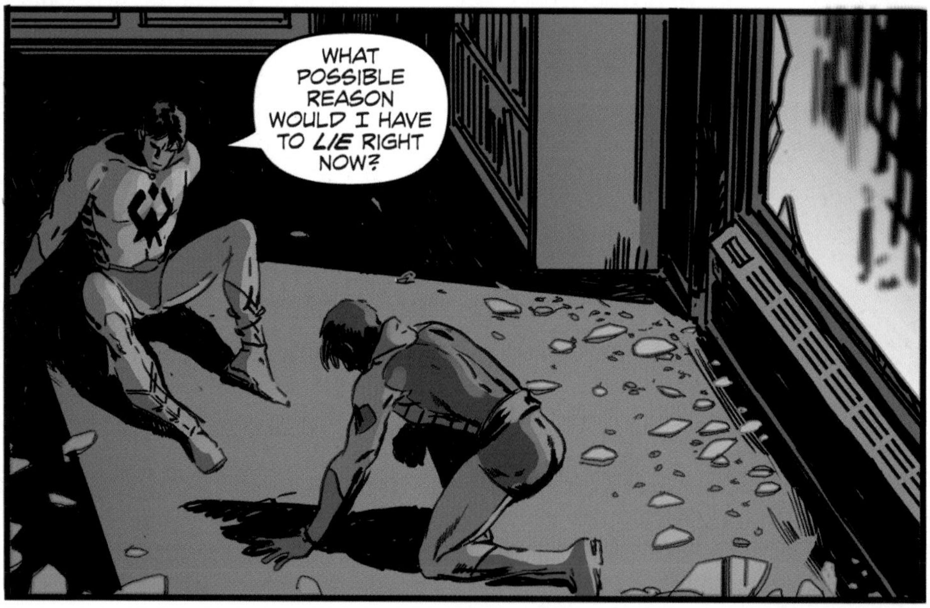
WHAT POSSIBLE REASON WOULD I HAVE TO LIE RIGHT NOW?

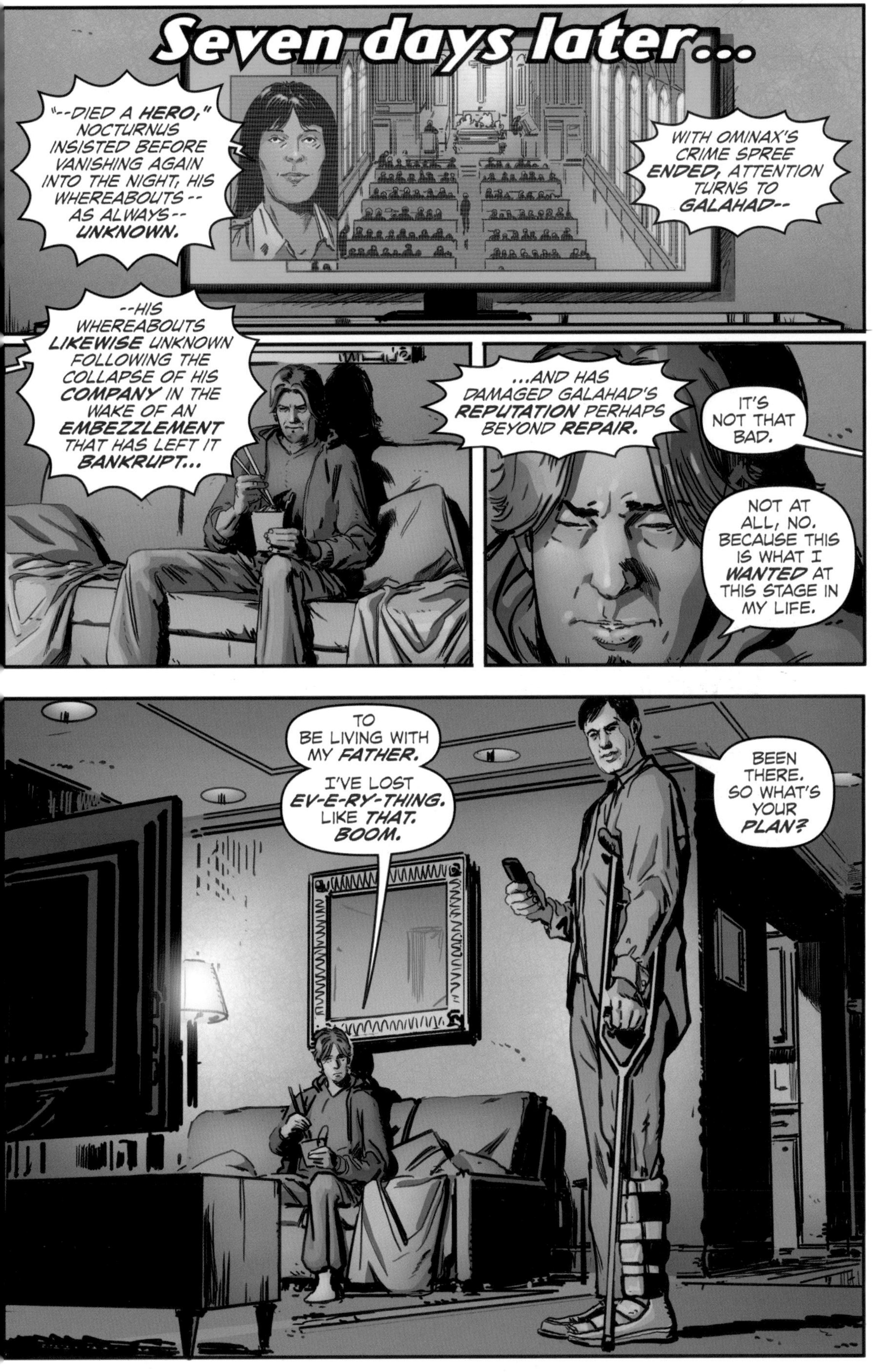

Seven days later...
"--DIED A HERO," NOCTURNUS INSISTED BEFORE VANISHING AGAIN INTO THE NIGHT, HIS WHEREABOUTS -- AS ALWAYS -- UNKNOWN.
WITH OMINAX'S CRIME SPREE ENDED, ATTENTION TURNS TO GALAHAD--
--HIS WHEREABOUTS LIKEWISE UNKNOWN FOLLOWING THE COLLAPSE OF HIS COMPANY IN THE WAKE OF AN EMBEZZLEMENT THAT HAS LEFT IT BANKRUPT...
...AND HAS DAMAGED GALAHAD'S REPUTATION PERHAPS BEYOND REPAIR.
IT'S NOT THAT BAD.
NOT AT ALL, NO. BECAUSE THIS IS WHAT I WANTED AT THIS STAGE IN MY LIFE.
TO BE LIVING WITH MY FATHER.
I'VE LOST EV-E-RY-THING. LIKE THAT. BOOM.
BEEN THERE. SO WHAT'S YOUR PLAN?

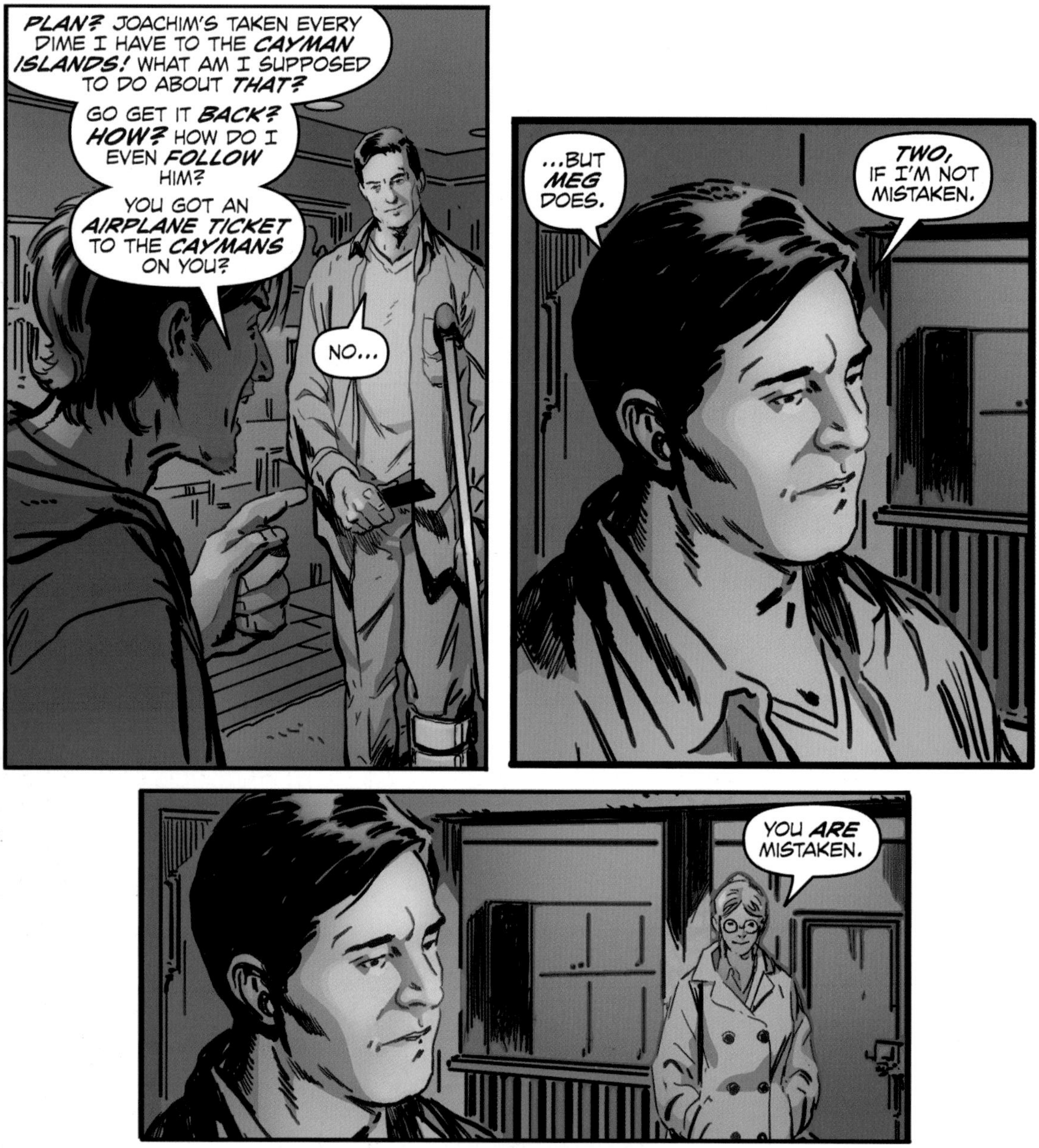
PLAN? JOACHIM'S TAKEN EVERY DIME I HAVE TO THE CAYMAN ISLANDS! WHAT AM I SUPPOSED TO DO ABOUT THAT?
GO GET IT BACK? HOW? HOW DO I EVEN FOLLOW HIM?
YOU GOT AN AIRPLANE TICKET TO THE CAYMANS ON YOU?
NO...
...BUT MEG DOES.
TWO, IF I'M NOT MISTAKEN.
YOU ARE MISTAKEN.

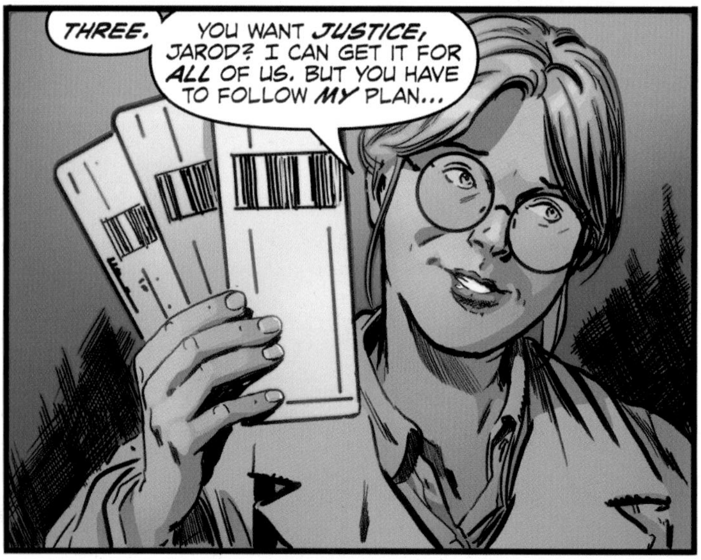
THREE.
YOU WANT JUSTICE, JAROD? I CAN GET IT FOR ALL OF US. BUT YOU HAVE TO FOLLOW MY PLAN...

Our story continues in INSUFFERABLE ON THE ROAD

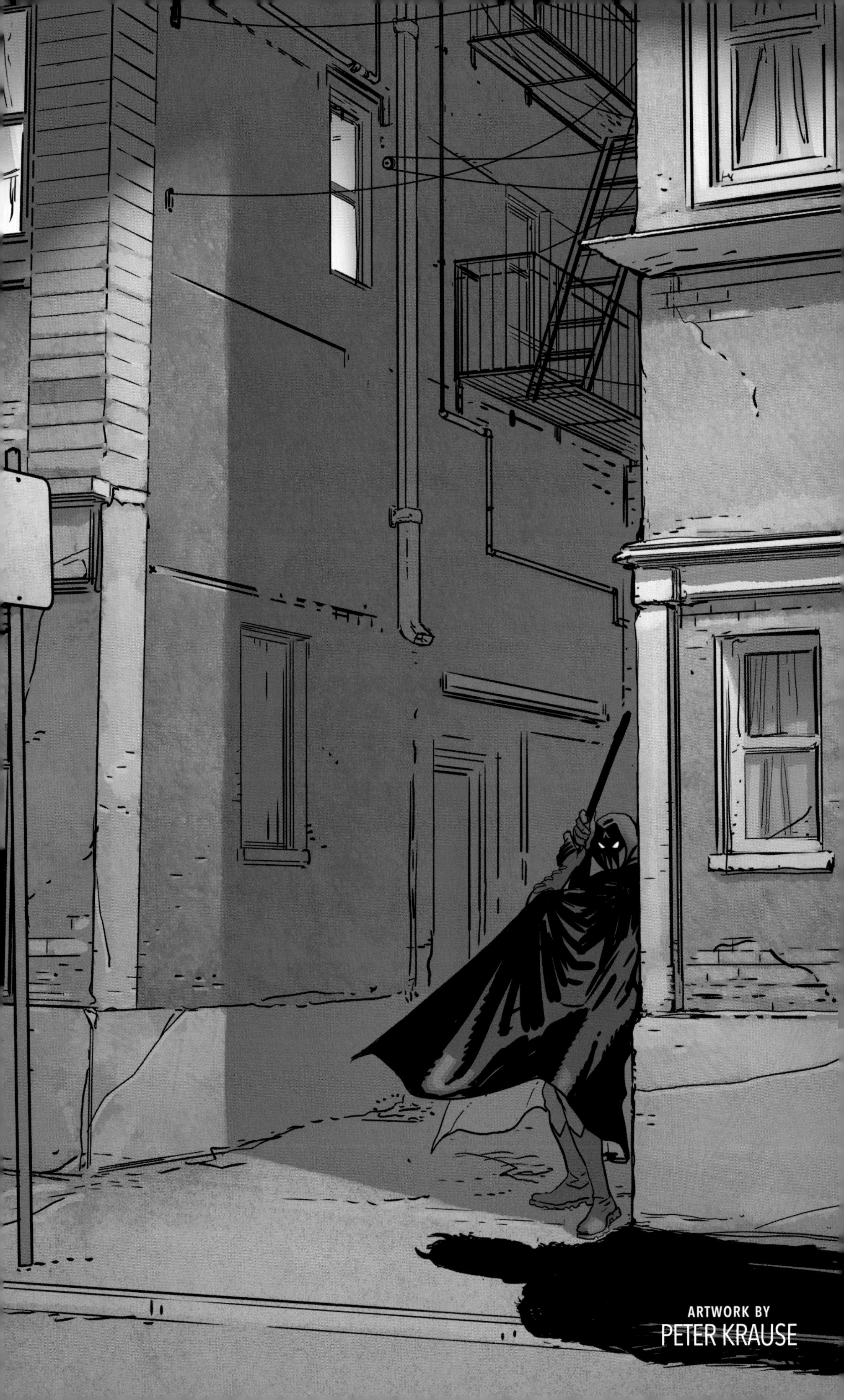
ARTWORK BY
PETER KRAUSE

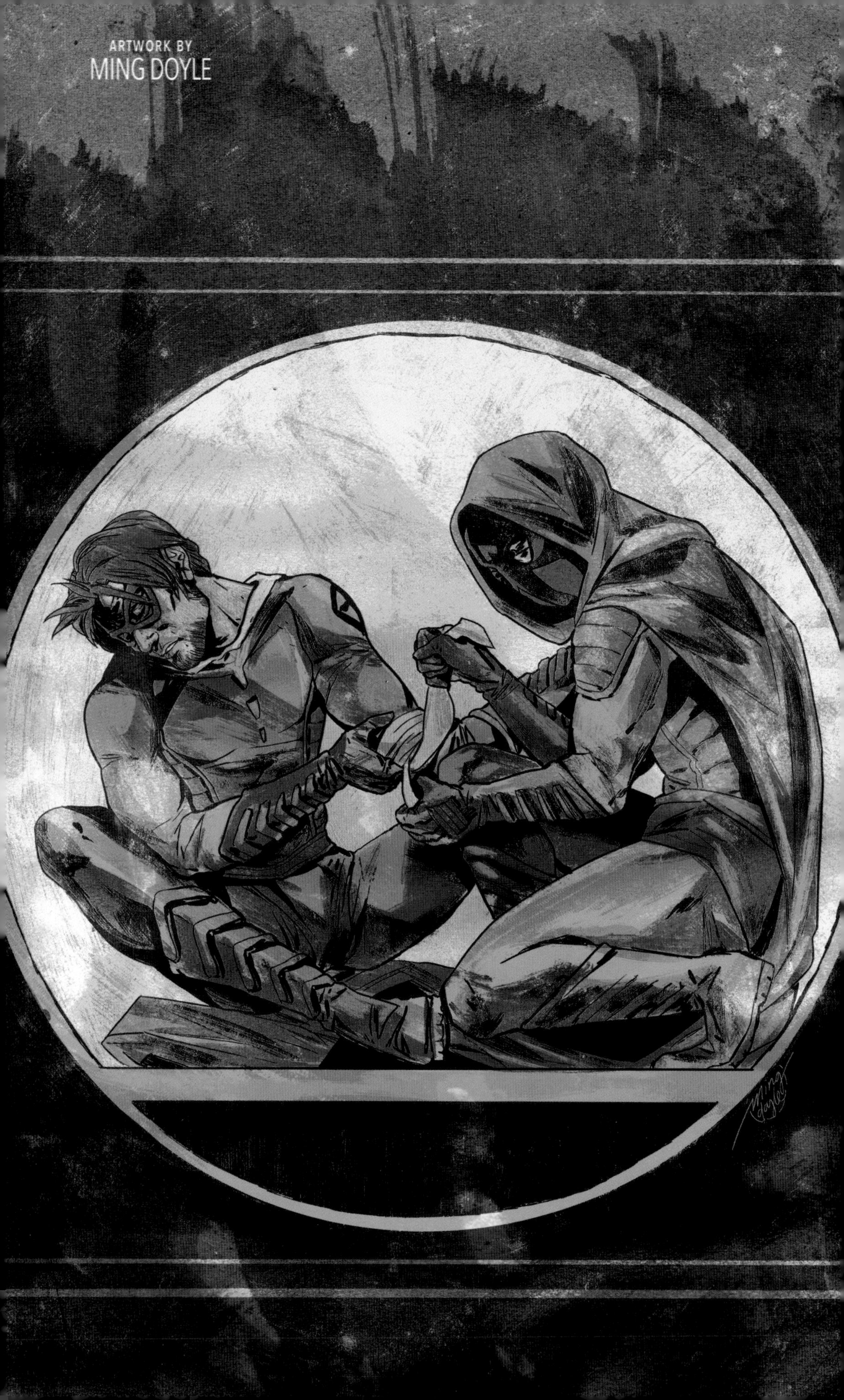
ARTWORK BY
MING DOYLE

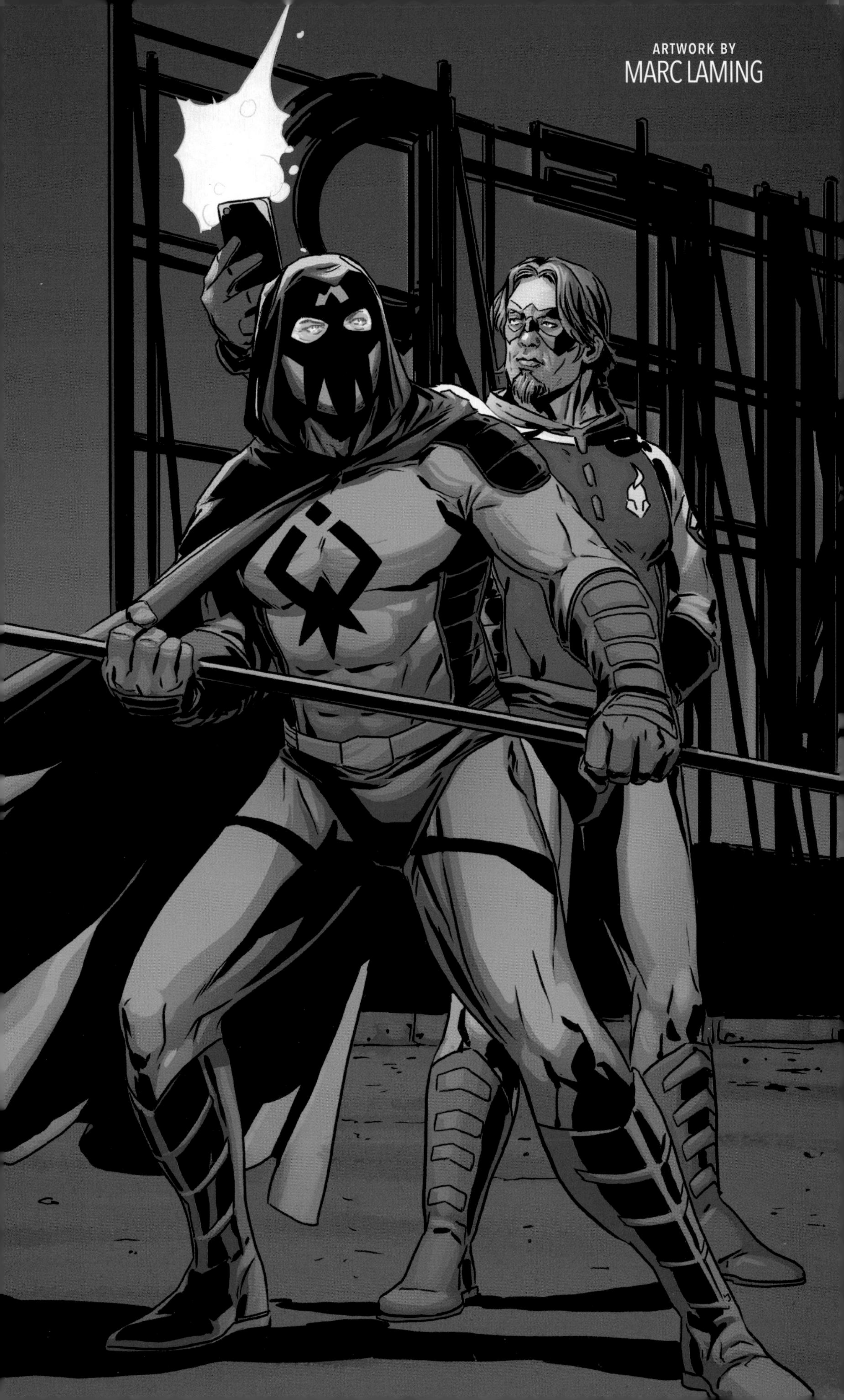

ARTWORK BY
MARC LAMING

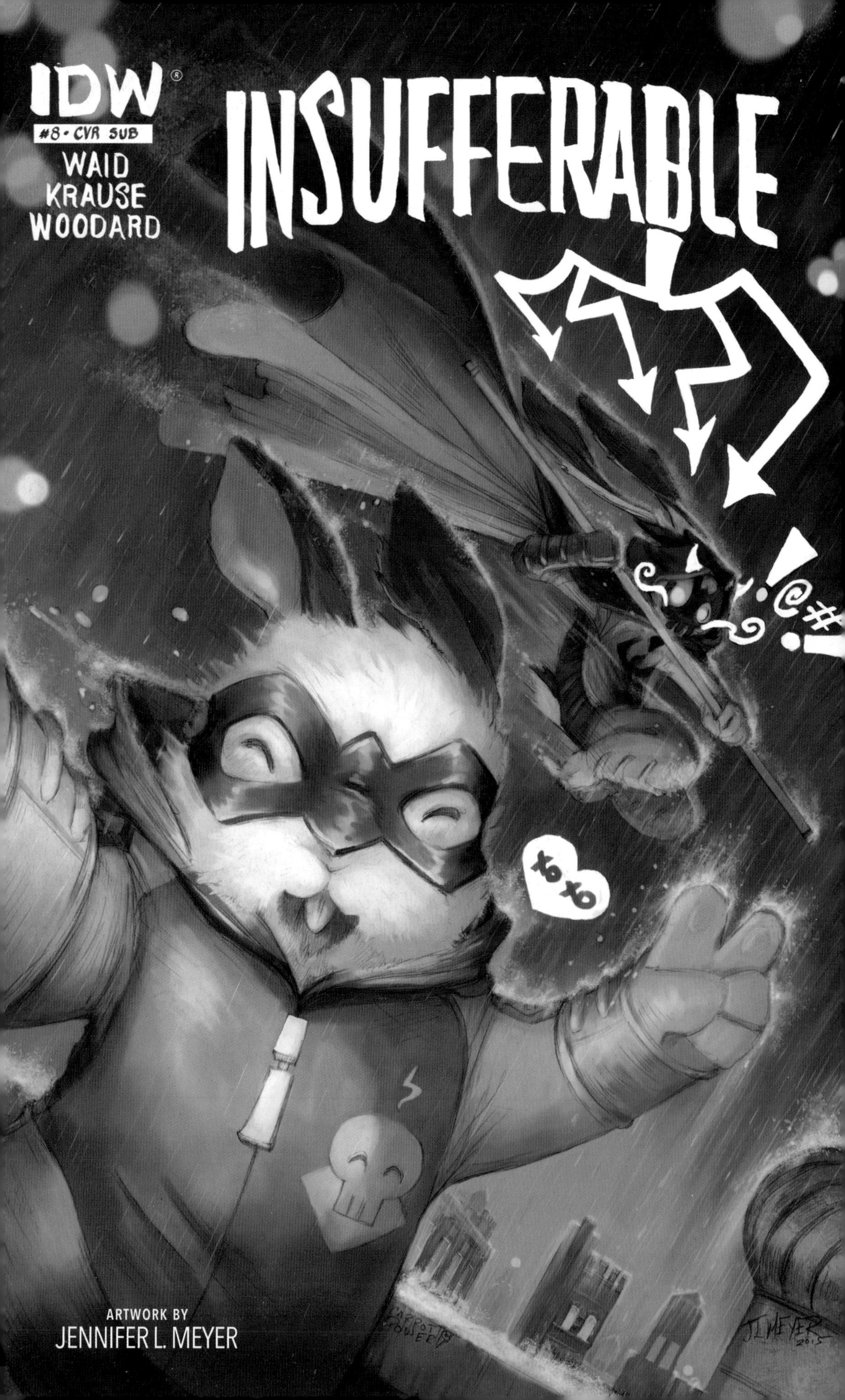

IDW
#8 • CVR SUB
WAID
KRAUSE
WOODARD
INSUFFERABLE
!@#!
XO XO
ARTWORK BY
JENNIFER L. MEYER